THE MUSLIM SOCIAL

Contemporary Issues in the Middle East
Mehran Kamrava, *Series Editor*

For a full list of titles in this series,
visit https://press.syr.edu/supressbook-series
/contemporary-issues-in-the-middle-east/.

THE MUSLIM SOCIAL

SOCIAL

Neoliberalism, Charity,
and Poverty in Turkey

Gizem Zencirci

Syracuse University Press

Copyright © 2024 by Syracuse University Press
Syracuse, New York 13244-5290

All Rights Reserved

First Edition 2024

24 25 26 27 28 29   6 5 4 3 2 1

For a listing of books published and distributed by Syracuse University Press,
visit https://press.syr.edu.

ISBN: 9780815638261 (hardcover)
      9780815638254 (paperback)
      9780815657002 (e-book)

Library of Congress Cataloging in Publication Control Number: 2023039859

The authorized representative in the EU for product
safety and compliance is Mare Nostrum Group B.V.
Mauritskade 21D, 1091 GC Amsterdam, The Netherlands
gpsr@mare-nostrum.co.uk

To Azel Ray and Neza Eren

Contents

Illustrations

Acknowledgments

This book is the product of myriad conversations, encounters, and dis-agreements that occurred over more than a decade of work. The formative years of my intellectual journey began at the Political Science department at Bilkent University. I was fortunate to study with Alev Çınar, Banu Helvacıoğlu, Dilek Cindoğlu, Ümit Cizre, Tahire Erman, Metin Heper, Hootan Shambayati, and Nedim Karakayalı. I also learned a great deal from fellow students in my program: Zeynep İnanç, Elif Çağış, Seçkin Özdamar-Tasan, Özge Çelik Russell, and Erkan Doğan. This book was also shaped by the insightful education I received from scholars at the University of Massachusetts, Amherst where I completed my PhD. I am grateful to Srirupa Roy, Sonia Alvarez, Jillian Schwedler, Barbara Crui-kshank, Nicholas Xenos, Amel Ahmed, Ivan Ascher, and Paula Chakra-varty. I was also fortunate to be part of a graduate school cohort that helped me think through many of the questions that eventually became part of this book. I thank Lauren Handley, Indrani Bhattacharjee, Allison Dale, Anna Curtis, Jeremy Wolf, Dünya Deniz Çakır, Matthew Lepori, Swati Birla, Jen Cohen, Elsa Wiehe, and Yasser Munif for their friendship and support. I am also appreciative of the communal support I received from the Turkish crew at Northampton. I thank Emir Benli, Müjde Yük-sel, Aycan Kapucu, Değer Eryar, Armağan Gezici, Begüm Adalet, Bengi Akbulut, Hasan Tekgüç, İlke Ercan, Ceren Soylu, Suat Küçükgöncü, Bengi Baran, Oyman Başaran, and Serkan Demirkılıç. While completing my PhD in political science, I also received a Certificate in Women, Gen-der, Sexuality Studies at the University of Massachusetts, Amherst, where I had the privilege to study with Banu Subramaniam, Millian Kang, and Ann Ferguson.

The writing of this book benefitted from various kinds of financial support, most specifically the University of Notre Dame's Science of Generosity Dissertation Fellowship, ARNOVA Dissertation Fellowship, and a grant from the Scientific and Technological Research Council of Turkey (TUBITAK). I also thank the School of Arts and Sciences' Faculty Development Fund and the Committee on Aid to Faculty Research at Providence College for their generous financial support.

Over the years, I presented parts of this work at various conferences, workshops, and other venues such as the Middle East Studies Associations' Annual Conferences, North-East Middle East Politics Working Group (NEMEPWG) Meetings, and the Post-Neoliberalism Workshop at the Social Science Research Council's Inter-Asia Conference. Although I benefitted from a variety of conversations, the arguments of this book were greatly improved upon thanks to exchanges with Damla Işık, Emel Akçalı, Zeynep Gambetti, Sarah El-Kazaz, Berna Turam, Bozena Welborne, and Ora Szekely.

I was also fortunate to present my initial thoughts at the POMEPS (Project on Middle East Political Science) Book Proposal Development Workshop where I benefitted greatly from the constructive feedback and sharp criticisms of Sultan Tepe, Marc Lynch, and Lisa Wedeen. The Krakowski family's generous donation to the department of political science at Providence College also made it possible for me to invite Vickie Langohr for a book manuscript workshop, and I am grateful for the valuable comments I received.

A special issue on heritage politics in the *European Journal of Turkish Studies* presented the opportunity to think through some of the preliminary questions that were later incorporated into chapter 2. I developed some of the background ideas for chapter 3 when I wrote an article on sadaqa culture debates in Turkey which was published in the *Asian Journal of Social Science*.

It has been a privilege to work at the department of political science at Providence College. I offer thanks to my colleagues William Hudson, Matthew Guardino, Rick Battistoni, Joe Cammarano, Ruth Ben-Artzi, Tony Affigne, Adam Myers, Susan McCarthy, Doug Blum, Thea Riofrancos, and Mary Bellhouse. Several people read the entire manuscript and

provided clarity and guidance. I thank Paulina Cossette, Rachel Kantro-
witz, and Patrick Shea for their time and attention.

I offer special thanks to a few people: to Alev Çınar for her boundless
love and intellectual reassurance; to Catherine Herrold for her compassionate friendship and tireless encouragement; and to Johanna Ray Vol-
hardt for her willingness to lend a listening ear anytime I encountered
difficulties along the way. I am also indebted to Berta Orellana for her care
and presence.

Finally, I thank my family: Nusret Zencirci, Elçin Balta Zencirci, Sarp
Zencirci, Arven Zencirci, Yener Balta, Patricia-Tarry Stevens, Harold Ste-
vens, and Kenna Stevens; as well as my friends Mine Özcan and Ebru
Akın, who have supported me as if they were family.

I thank Azel Ray and Neza Eren for bringing me endless inspiration,
giggles, and joy; I cannot wait to see what the years will bring. My deepest
gratitude goes to Casey Stevens for his unwavering support and infinite
patience.

Note on Transliteration

For transliteration from Arabic and Turkish, I have used a modified version of the *International Journal of Middle East Studies*' (IJMES) transcription system. All non-English words are italicized, except some Turkish words that refer to names of specific organizations, places, and people. *IJMES* recommends not italicizing the words "waqf" and "zakat," but does not include "sadaqa" in its list of words that exist in common English use. For purposes of clarity and consistency, and since these three words appear repeatedly throughout the book, I have decided not to italicize them.

Abbreviations

AKP	Justice and Development Party (*Adalet ve Kalkınma Partisi*)
CHP	Republican People's Party (*Cumhuriyet Halk Partisi*)
CS	Soulwater (*Cansuyu Yardımlaşma ve Dayanışma Derneği*)
DDB	Department of Associations (*Dernekler Dairesi Başkanlığı*)
DF	Light House (*Deniz Feneri Yardımlaşma ve Dayanışma Derneği*)
DYP	True Path Party (*Doğru Yol Partisi*)
FAKFUKFON	Fund for the Poor and Desolate (Fakir Fukara Fonu)
HDP	People's Democratic Party (*Halkların Demokratik Partisi*)
IHH	Foundation for Human Rights and Humanitarian Relief (*İnsani Yardım Vakfı*)
İŞKUR	Turkish Employment Agency (*İş ve İşci Bulma Kurumu*)
KYM	Is Anyone There? (*Kimse Yok Mu Yardımlaşma ve Dayanışma Derneği*)
MHP	Nationalist Action Party (*Milliyetçi Hareket Partisi*)
MÜSİAD	The Association of Independent Industrialists and Businessmen (*Müstakil Sanayici ve İşadamları Derneği*)
SYDGM	Social Solidarity and Mutual Assistance General Ministry (*Sosyal Yardımlaşma ve Dayanışma Genel Müdürlüğü*)
TDV	Turkish Religious Affairs Foundation (*Türkiye Diyanet Vakfı*)
TEGV	Turkish Education Volunteers Foundation (*Türkiye Eğitim Gönüllüleri Vakfı*)
TEV	Turkish Education Foundation (*Türk Eğitim Vakfı*)
TGTV	Turkish Foundation of Voluntary Organizations (*Türkiye Gönüllü Teşekküller Vakfı*)

TİKA	Turkish Cooperation and Coordination Agency (*Türk İşbirliği ve Koordinasyon Ajansı Başkanlığı*)
TRT	Turkish Radio and Television Institute (*Türk Radyo Televizyon Kurumu*)
VGM	Waqf General Ministry (*Vakıflar Genel Müdürlüğü*)

THE MUSLIM SOCIAL

Introduction

When I met Ibrahim in 2010, he was the forty-five-year-old manager of a small Islamic nongovernmental organization (NGO) in Ankara, Turkey.[1] Ibrahim had been involved in Islamic charity networks since his youth. On this particular day, I was scheduled to meet Ibrahim in his office. When I arrived, I observed that a group of people—mostly young women and their children—were standing outside the entrance. Later, I realized that they were waiting for their names to be called so that they could go inside and collect their aid. Inside, I found Ibrahim with two visitors from the governor's office discussing a new poverty relief program that would be administered jointly with the local government. After his visitors left and we completed our interview, Ibrahim wanted to show me around. The NGO had recently moved into this new building which had been provided by the Justice and Development Party's (Adalet ve Kalkınma Partisi, AKP) municipality for free. Ibrahim apologized for "the mess" and explained that "things were not yet organized." Even so, he introduced me to a number of volunteers who were preparing for the "assistance distribution day." A young man was checking records on a computer, while a young woman was attaching the list of "recipients" to a brown clipboard before stepping outside to let people in. These volunteers worked from an office that had a large wooden desk, new corporate-style furniture, and freshly painted light-blue walls. Five large file cabinets stood against one of the walls, while four chairs were lined up against another one. Ibrahim explained to

---

1. All names and relevant identifying information have been changed. All translations from Turkish are by the author, unless otherwise noted.

1

me that they were in the process of transferring their old files into a new computer database.

After showing me how the electronic database worked, Ibrahim then walked me to the social market—the NGO's largest room where they stored most of the donated goods and other available items. The spatial organization of this warehouse resembled that of a commercial supermarket. As we walked down aisles of nonperishable food, weather-appropriate clothing, and other household items, Ibrahim told me about their "donation management system" which allowed them to account for donated items "as if they were a real business." At one point, he stopped to pick up a pair of red children's shoes and showed me the barcodes affixed to their soles. In an excited voice, he explained:

> You see, every item here has a barcode. This type of work cannot be done with 90% certainty; it must be 100%. We are responsible for the donations that are entrusted to us. We need to be able to account for these items because we will be questioned about our actions in the afterlife. We do not want recipients to feel humiliated; we want them to feel like they are in a real supermarket. It is important that they have a dignified experience.

Ibrahim's account represents a peculiar assemblage that has become normalized in the field of Islamic charity in Turkey. Charitable giving is part of a longstanding religious tradition that ordains Muslims to be generous toward those who are less fortunate. This aspect of the Islamic faith can be seen here in the collection of monetary and in-kind donations which are later redistributed to the poor and the needy. Except Ibrahim's reasoning merged a religious sensibility with a managerial logic: each one of the donated items had to be registered and accounted for. In his mind, such a combination was instrumental for serving the needs of the poor in a dignified—and Islamic—manner. Thus, he cared about the emotional experience of aid recipients as much as he tended to their eternal salvation. This was precisely what he and his coworkers sought to bring about by curating an experience for aid recipients that resembled a visit to a commercial supermarket. Ibrahim was an observant Muslim who prayed in the corner of his office during the workday. He refrained from shaking my hand and avoided making direct eye contact during our conversations. He often invited his female secretary to join us so that we would not be alone in a room. But he also believed that enhancing the emotional well-being of beneficiaries through managerial innovations was an extension of his Islamic devotion. His articulation of faith-based giving through an assemblage of religious, administrative, and emotional concerns is emblematic of a larger shift in the field of social service provision in Turkey.

How does one make sense of Ibrahim's expression of Islamic charity through a vocabulary of managerial practices alongside his concerns about the emotional well-being of aid recipients? What does such a juxtaposition of religious values, managerial rationalities, and affective politics tell us about poverty governance in Turkey? What kind of a welfare regime emerges when private charity is neither excluded nor merely tolerated, but rather actively incorporated into the governmental apparatus?

The Muslim Social suggests that these questions can best be answered by studying the politics of "small things" (Cruikshank 1999, 1)—such as a barcode placed on a donated pair of red children's shoes. These seemingly mundane details, I claim, are technologies of government that arrange and configure social bonds, encounters, and relations. Through an analysis of Islamic neoliberalism as a governmental assemblage, I examine the advent of the "Muslim Social"—an entire apparatus that seeks to govern poverty in accordance with multiple Islamic social projects, and which I argue treats the social as a matter of technical management and affective attachment. As a governmental assemblage, the Muslim Social has parallels with and differs from examples of "social neoliberalism" elsewhere—for example, the "social investment states" of Europe, the "new developmental welfare models" that are prevalent in Latin America, and authoritarian social policy mechanisms introduced by governments in Asia (Dorlach 2015; Duckett 2020; Garay 2016). Moreover, the term *governmental assemblage* underscores the idea that "Islamic neoliberalism" is not a monolithic entity, but a flexible co-articulation of different political trajectories in contingent ways. The Muslim Social emerges as a complex phenomenon, embracing the legitimacy of transparency, new public management, a higher moral value placed on formal social relationships, stricter methods of inspection, and an elaborate system for administering the collection of donations and the distribution of funds. These technologies of managerialism shaped and were shaped by an Islamic language of care, compassion, and charity that cultivated public sentiments among Turkish citizens. The term "Muslim Social," in other words, seeks to capture the governmental assemblages through which a neoliberal welfare regime was produced in Turkey under the AKP's leadership.

This governmental assemblage emerged against the historical backdrop of a state-led developmentalist model. For much of the twentieth century, Turkey followed a secular and pro-Western modernization project that sought to confine religious beliefs to the private lives of its citizens. Turkey's secular-modernist founding ideology, Kemalism, lost its hegemonic power after the market reforms of the 1980s, and has been gradually altered since the AKP came to power in 2002. Along with rapid economic growth, the rise of a Muslim middle and professional class, and enhanced business and trade relations, Islam acquired a new force and meaning for Turkish citizens.

In the midst of these transformations, the AKP introduced a series of legal-institutional reforms that revamped the welfare regime. These administrative reforms were directed not so much at the excess or lack of state power, but rather at the developmentalist welfare regime's "arbitrary, inefficient, and patchwork-like" nature (Buğra and Candaş 2011). Throughout the 2000s, one can thus observe the emergence of a new strategy for governing the social; this concern over the lack of "organization" was shared by public and private actors who argued that the unproductive use of experts, programs, and resources was partly caused by the eradication of Islamic socio-economic customs, practices, and institutions. The primary objectives of welfare reform were twofold: to improve governmental interventions, mechanisms, and programs of social service provision, and to achieve these goals within an "Islamic" framework—combining a nostalgic rendering of the Ottoman imperial past, a selective reading of the Republican state tradition, and a nuanced disavowal of Kemalist ideology. In the process of designing and instituting a neoliberal welfare regime, the AKP and its supporters turned to faith-based notions of care, charity, and compassion. A series of conferences, forums, and workshops were organized during the early 2000s. These venues brought together intellectuals, bureaucrats, and civil society practitioners who debated the role of religion in poverty alleviation, and envisioned multiple Islamic social imaginaries to this end. Consequently, a complex web of interventions, technologies, practices, and rationalities was deployed to find Islamic solutions to modern-day problems. "Government through community" (Rose 1996) gradually became the standard, transforming state–civil society relations and the balance between public welfare and private charity, as well as institutional norms and cultural meanings.

Instead of marking a retreat into traditional belief systems or exemplifying the cooptation of local pristine values by capitalist modernity, the political deployment of "community" in Turkey resembles forms of neoliberal governance elsewhere—such as George W. Bush's "compassionate conservatism" in the United States or David Cameron's "Big Society" program in the United Kingdom (Hackworth 2012; Ware 2011). Yet, emergent modalities of governance in non-Western, Muslim-majority contexts like Turkey are often overlooked in favor of analytical frameworks that perpetuate easy binaries of global Western markets versus local Muslim communities. According to such frameworks of opposition, Islam, due to the innate power of communitarian values, or because of the influence of stagnant religious institutions, is incompatible with capitalism. Frameworks of fusion, by contrast, argue that Muslims are victims of neoliberal globalization. Embedded in this latter argument is the idea that processes of marketization, privatization, and individualization have eroded social bonds, communal relations, and moral values. As a result, Muslims are frequently portrayed either as outsiders or dissenters, and are never considered agents who assemble Islamic practices, traditions, and values with neoliberal elements in creative ways.

In this book, I move beyond these two opposing frameworks of opposition and fusion by adopting assemblage thinking as a theory and methodology.[2] By neoliberalism, I am referring to an assemblage of flexible

2. Assemblage thinking, with its origins in the work of Deleuze and Guattari (1987/2003), is used across a variety of social science disciplines by scholars who want to emphasize fluidity, indeterminacy, and multiplicity (see Anderson et al. 2012; Featherstone 2011; Ong and Collier 2004).

elements that are articulated by local actors in context-specific ways.[3] Such a definition privileges local contexts at the expense of a top-down notion of neoliberalism "as a thing that acts in the world" (Kingfisher and Maskovsky 2008, 118). Assemblage thinking, as a theoretical device, repudiates treating Islam and neoliberalism as uniform entities with deterministic outcomes. Instead, it invites close attention to how each is reproduced, circulated, and lived in practice. In doing so, assemblage thinking makes it possible to highlight not only the malleability of neoliberalism but also the plurality of Islamic piety. Assemblage, thus, is a way of making visible something that is already there: the co-constitution of religious and social experience. Moreover, conceptualizing Islamic neoliberalism as a governmental assemblage intervenes in the assumed dichotomies of global/local, market/community, and universal/particular—binaries that continue to constrain scholarship on religious politics and economic globalization in non-Western contexts. Since Islam is conceptualized as the West's anthropological other, too often it is taken to represent a local sense of pristine "community." But the people whose experiences, ideas, and practices form the focus of this book uphold neoliberal elements, such as commodification, entrepreneurialism, privatization, and individualization, as much as they endorse communitarian values, such as belonging, compassion, and solidarity. A focus on assemblage, therefore, allows acknowledging that community is not external to, but constitutive of, Islamic neoliberalism.

Methodologically, assemblage thinking entails treating contingency, fluidity, and heterogeneity as the norm rather than the exception. I map the ways in which Islamic beliefs and neoliberal elements flow, intersect, and contradict each other, and trace the political effects of these assemblages.

---

3. See Higgins and Larner (2017, 9). Whereas agreement on the precise meaning of neoliberalism does not exist, anthropologists, geographers, and political theorists who emphasize assemblage thinking share several analytical commitments. These include an understanding of neoliberalism more as a context-based practice rather than a top-down ideological imposition; an emphasis on the flexible diffusion of neoliberal elements (accountability, commodification, competitiveness, entrepreneurialism, empowerment, transparency, etc.); and a recognition of the mobile and unexpected ways in which these neoliberal elements merge with local discourses, governmentalities, and subjectivities.

This method is inspired by scholarship that combines an "ethnographic imaginary" with insights from neo-Foucauldian work on neoliberal governmentality (Brady and Lippert 2016; Higgins and Larner 2017; Ong and Collier 2004). These scholars note that assemblages are multidirectional, unexpected, and heterogenous. Hence, their analysis is best conducted, as Nikolas Rose (1990) suggests, through "anatomizing the new relations of power brought into play on this new multiple and fragmented territory of government" (353). For purposes of this book, this perspective makes it possible to unearth the managerial-affective assemblages that constitute the Muslim Social as a governmental apparatus.

Through a multi-sited ethnography of social service provision in Turkey, I examine how actors sought to implement divergent visions of Islamic "community" across various domains, such as the welfare regime, civil society, charitable giving, humanitarian aid, and volunteer programs. Specifically, I demonstrate how four distinct but interrelated Islamic social projects—civilizational revival, populist reform, humanitarian responsibility, and spiritual sanctuary—arranged the field of poverty governance in Turkey, transforming the experience of the poor as well as the subjectivities of those who cared for them. While particular religious traditions constitute a common point of reference for Muslims, the interpretation and reinterpretation of these traditions, contrasting visions of the market, and disagreement over the proper role of faith in a market society all point to a far less homogenous notion of Islamic neoliberalism. A wide range of actors, including activists, bureaucrats, civil servants, experts, intellectuals, politicians, scholars, and practitioners of civil society produced, negotiated, and disseminated these discourses, but most were inspired by Islamic charity. In the process, these actors gave new meanings to faith-based institutions, practices, and traditions of giving, such as *vakıf* ("waqf," endowments), *sadaka* ("sadaqa," voluntary almsgiving), *zekat* ("zakat," compulsory almsgiving), and *infak* ("infaq," individual philanthropy) while redefining who is to be considered as the deserving poor: the *muhtaç* (truly needy), the *mağdur* (unjustly oppressed), and the *mazlum* (innocent victims). Islamic charity operated as a key site of assemblage, serving as a prism for addressing problems of economy and society. But, while actors invoked visions of Islamic charity in order to justify novel technologies of government, the ensuing governmental interventions were much more amorphous, diffuse, and protean than singular and monolithic accounts of "Islamic neoliberalism" would lead us to believe.

The goal of this book is not simply to analyze Islamic charity but to develop our understanding of neoliberalism in general. While the focus here is on how religion was evoked, manipulated, and negotiated by various actors, my broader interest is to understand the diverse ways that human beings actively shape their worlds in our capitalist present, to explore the kind of ethical concerns that animate their visions, and to examine the political implications of their contingent, fluid, and contested interventions.

Islamic Neoliberalism as a Governmental Assemblage

Assemblage thinking makes it possible to move beyond conventional frameworks of opposition and of fusion that dominate the study of Islamic capitalism, and more recently of Islamic neoliberalism.[4] The first view, which I refer to as the *framework of opposition*, argues that Islam inhibits economic growth. Despite a level of disagreement over whether it is exactly Islamic culture, faith, law, or institutions that obstruct capitalism, a large swathe of scholarship affirms this problematic idea. Although this maxim has, by now, largely been discredited, the incompatibility thesis has had far-reaching implications. In a sense, it has operated akin to what Asaf Bayat (2007), in his analysis of the relationship between Islam and democracy, refers to as the "perverse charm of an irrelevant question:" one has to respond to it even when aiming to refute it.

The second view, which I refer to as the *framework of fusion*, makes the opposite claim. Islam and capitalism have always been compatible: instead of hindering economic development, Islam as a religion is inherently

---

4. I do not mean to conflate capitalism with neoliberalism. While capitalism is a system that organizes economic relations according to free-market principles of individual labor, private property, and exchange divorced from social relations, neoliberalism seeks to expand market logics into other areas of social life. Having said that, my point is that debates about the (in)compatibility of Islam and capitalism continue to inform the study of Islamic neoliberalism.

capable of sustaining economic growth.[5] Instead of presenting a trans-historical, static analysis, more recent work in this vein has argued that the blending of Islamic values and markets is a distinctive phenomenon that leads to the assimilation, cooptation, or integration of pious Muslims and Islamist activists into the neoliberal order. Some of these assessments take a celebratory tone, asserting that the rise of Islamic capitalism will defeat Islamic radicalism (Nasr 2009), whereas other scholars, often imbued with a postcolonial sensibility, suggest that the Islamic banking and finance sector remains adept at resisting neoliberal globalization (Hoggarth 2016; Pollard and Samers 2007; Rethel 2011).

These frameworks, despite their opposing views, reinforce an imagined binary between "global capitalism" and "local Islam," often portraying Muslims as outsiders, victims, or dissenters of the world economic order. By contrast, assemblage thinking attends to Islamic neoliberalism's constitutive, dynamic, situated, and heterogenous dimensions. Instead of treating Islamic neoliberalism as a rigid system, or as a hegemonic project, this book illustrates the complexity of Muslims' engagement with capitalism, thereby rejecting frameworks of fusion and opposition. Put differently, *The Muslim Social* focuses on the variegated dynamics of economic imagination and religious interpretation, rather than seeking to uncover the true essence of "Islam," "Islamic economy," or "Islamic neoliberalism."

My approach is similar to recent ethnographic studies of Islamic neoliberalism that have considered the dynamic interaction of religious ethics and market values in various local contexts. Daromir Rudnyckyj's (2010) pioneering study of "spiritual training programs" among factory workers illustrates the emergence of market-oriented interpretations of Islam in Indonesia. In his book, Rudnyckyj eloquently describes how Indonesian Muslims came to understand ethical dispositions, such as hard work and self-discipline, as a constitutive element of their personal faith, thereby highlighting that "religious practice can be conducive to globalization and is not necessarily opposed to it" (19). These insights have been confirmed

---

5. For different explorations of this claim, see Çızakça (2011), El-Gamal (2006), Gran (1979), and Karim (2010).

by others who study the relationship between faith and capitalism in several other Muslim-majority contexts. Sarah Tobin (2016) illustrates the emergence of "neoliberal piety" among middle-class Muslims who are involved in the Islamic finance sector in Jordan; Patricia Sloane-White (2017) describes how Malay Muslims produce "corporate Islam" by reinterpreting Sharia for the modern workplace; and Filippo and Caroline Osella examine how wealthy Muslim entrepreneurs from Kerala, India, understand having a successful business as a path for spreading the cause of Islam (Osella and Osella 2009).

Building on these ethnographic studies, this book adopts a slightly different approach, exploring the ways in which Islamic neoliberalism governs through community, instead of merely analyzing how Muslims react to, participate in, or resist the ascendancy of the market. Underlying my approach is the idea that community is neither external to nor precedes neoliberalism, but rather is constitutive of it. To this end, rather than seeing Turkish Muslims merely as victims or outsiders of neoliberalism, I trace the articulation of Islamic beliefs, ethics, values, and traditions through a series of assemblages that, I argue, resulted in the formation of the Muslim Social as a domain of technical management and affective attachment.

There are several reasons that make Turkey a significant case study for such an analysis. The country's powerful Islamist movement, especially after the AKP came to power in 2002, adopted a pro-market economic outlook, supplanting the movement's earlier anti-capitalist stance with a developmentalist model that sought to combine Islamic values with economic policies that foster trade liberalization, privatization, and competition. The conjunction between neoliberalism and Islamism in the past two decades has been one of the most significant political developments in Turkey, changing the structure of the political economy, patterns of state–civil society relations, and possibilities for social movements.[6] Islamic neoliberalism reinforced the hegemonic power of the AKP, providing the

6. On Islamic neoliberalism in Turkey, see, among others, Acar and Altunok (2013), Atalay (2017), Atasoy (2009), Bozkurt (2013), Karaman (2013), Moudouros (2014), and Patton (2009).

government with political and economic support from various constituencies, such as the Islamic bourgeoisie, faith-based civil society organizations, and conservative-religious business firms.[7] The economic success of the AKP during the 2000s, and the party's initial commitment to democracy, secularism, and improved relations with the West, resulted in the depiction of Turkey as a "model Muslim democracy"—and one that can provide lessons to the larger Muslim world. Yet, this initial enthusiasm waned as the AKP adopted authoritarian state practices, oppressed ethnic and religious minorities, and silenced oppositional voices. Understanding the transformation of Turkish politics under the enduring and problematic leadership of the AKP, with a specific focus on the phenomenon of Islamic neoliberalism, also has implications beyond the Turkish case (some of which I discuss in the book's conclusion).

Neoliberalism and the Social

In addition to advancing a notion of Islamic neoliberalism as a governmental assemblage, this book also provides analytical insight into scholarly discussions about the "social question."[8] In contrast to the presumed opposition between neoliberalism and welfare, the spread of programs such as cash transfers in South Africa, micro-credit projects in India, and poverty relief programs in Mexico illustrates that capitalism in its latest form is preoccupied with different types of social provision (Ferguson 2015; Molyneux 2006; Roy 2010). This concerted "return to social policy" (Razavi 2007) has been interpreted through two oppositional frameworks. Some have argued that these social programs signal the transition away from neoliberalism toward a new politico-economic juncture that is alternately referred to as "post-neoliberalism" (Ruckert, Macdonald,

---

7. For a discussion of neoliberalism and the AKP's political hegemony, see Adaman and Akbulut (2021); Akça, Bekmen, and Özden (2014); and Tuğal (2009). On the formation and transformation of the devout Muslim bourgeoisie in Turkey, see Adaş (2006), Buğra and Savaşkan (2014), Demiralp (2009), Gümüşcü and Sert (2009), and Madi-Şişman (2017).

8. For global analyses of the social question, see Breman et al. (2019) and Leisering (2021).

and Proulx 2017), the "social investment state" (Busemeyer et al. 2018), or "neoliberalism-plus" (Akçalı, Yanık, and Hung 2015). Others have interpreted similar developments with caution, suggesting that neoliberalism operates by coopting, infiltrating, and restructuring domains that were once thought to be separate from market exchange (Bourdieu 2003; Petras 1997; Žižek 2006). Margaret Somers (2008), for instance, argues that concepts like "social capital" illustrate how market-based ways of thinking have infiltrated and privatized the administration of collective goods. In a similar vein, Wendy Brown (2015) suggests that neoliberalism is distinguished by an effort to understand and govern all aspects of human life through a calculative rubric that displaces noneconomic ways of being in the world.

This book moves beyond these frameworks which, at a fundamental level, operate as mirror opposites of each other. While the former framework portrays the "social" as a communitarian impulse that resists or circumvents economization, the latter warns against the growing tendency to think about, and act upon, social problems in market-oriented ways. The case of Turkey shows that pro-poor welfare programs do in fact accompany neoliberal dynamics of liberalization, privatization, and individualization, and that the resultant governmental apparatus cannot be easily analyzed by deploying simplistic dichotomies such as economy versus society, private interest versus public good, or market versus community. Leaving aside its Islamic flavors, the Turkish case is not unique in this regard. In his analysis of the Big Income Grant debates in South Africa, James Ferguson (2015) argues that an unexpected marriage between neoliberalism and the social has been underway since the 1990s. While studying the transformation of the Italian welfare regime, Andrea Muehlebach (2012) indicates that the neoliberal era is marked by an individuated notion of relational care—a form of social solidarity that differs from the metaphysics of national collectivity, but one that nonetheless links citizens to each other. In this point of view, while the state ceases to be the sole agent overseeing collective well-being, and whereas responsibility for addressing social problems becomes diffuse and disjointed, neoliberal modes of governance do not eradicate social bonds, but rather produce new forms of moral belonging and political solidarities, whether it be through instilling an ethos of volunteerism or designing new kinds of public programs.

This analytical frame also converges with Foucauldian scholars who theorize the "social" primarily as a governmental apparatus and study the formation and transformation of this apparatus in relation to shifting analytics of power, knowledge, and governmentality (Collier 2012b; Cruikshank 1999; Ferguson 2015; Foucault 1980, 1991, 2012; Steinmetz 1993). Liberal modernity conceptualized issues such as crime, education, health, poverty, unemployment, and prostitution into social problems in need of governmental attention (Donzelot 1979; Procacci 1991; Rabinow 1989; Steinmetz 1993). Once society was considered to be a natural entity, its problems were henceforth conceived as calculable and governable (Cruikshank 1999, 44). One of the most well-known scholarly analyses of this period is Jacques Donzelot's (1979) examination of the shifting attitudes, customs, and practices of family affairs in eighteenth-century France. The family, or the crisis of the family, Donzelot shows, was the milieu that gave rise to the social through linking a diverse set of problems such as crime, illness, poverty, and unemployment, as well as a wide range of professions, including administrative, developmental, educational, medical, and psychological experts and workers.

In a similar vein, George Steinmetz (1993) suggests that the social is best studied as a domain linked through a variety of regulatory practices, technologies, and discourses. Tracing these "pure little lines of mutation" (Deleuze's "Foreword," in Donzelot 1979, x) illuminates the assemblages that make social life into an "object of and target of a new expertise" (Miller and Rose 1988, 171). Instead of assuming that the "social" is a naturally distinct sphere that exists a priori, a focus on assemblage, in other words, allows tracing articulations and interventions that constitute a new governmental apparatus.

Another key work in this line of scholarly inquiry is Stephen Collier's *Post-Soviet Social* in which he examines how seemingly mundane things like pipes and valves emerged as key sites of governmental intervention. Instead of a "total program of marketization," Collier (2012b) finds that "neoliberal reforms" sought "new ways of programming government through the state that retain the social welfare norms established by Soviet socialism" (3). Like Ferguson (2015) and Muehlebach (2012), Collier also urges us to consider the kinds of social welfare arrangements that emerge in conjunction with neoliberal reforms. I concur with these scholars that our critiques of neoliberalism will not go very far if they reify the neoliberalism versus welfare dichotomy, or see neoliberalism as a universal ideology of marketization that erases local forms of social solidarity. Understanding how practical and political concerns drove actors to envision interventions that creatively combined market logics with communitarian orientations recognizes that these unanticipated assemblages are an acknowledgment of both the power of human agency and the ways in which social bonds are reconfigured instead of erased.

The Muslim Social

The term "Muslim" in *The Muslim Social* refers not to the presumed religiosity of actors that were involved in the provision of social services, but rather to the fact that these myriad social projects shared a vision of constructing a governmental apparatus that addressed problems by reinterpreting and reworking Islamic practices, traditions, and institutions.[9] While tracing the interplay between Islamic values and neoliberal elements in the field of social service provision, I did not, as conventional arguments about neoliberalism would predict, observe the withdrawal of the state, the collapse of the social fabric, or the diffusion of a calculative rubric in all aspects of life.[10] Still, the norms and forms of poverty

9. Conceptually, I use the terms "Muslim" and "Islamic" interchangeably since most actors who were involved in the imagination and implementation of Islamic social projects were pious Muslims, and because they understood charity work as a manifestation of religious identity. But I acknowledge a problem with this usage: it assumes that all Muslims are devout followers of Islam, thereby excluding secular and non-practicing Muslims. For this reason, my use of the term "Muslim" most resembles Jenny White's (2012b) definition of "Muslim nationalism" as the identity of a "pious Muslim Turk whose subjectivity and vision for the future is shaped by an Ottoman imperial past overlaid onto a Republican state framework but divorced from the Kemalist state project" (9). For more information about Muslimism, see Çınar (2005), Çevik (2016), and Yenigün (2017).

10. For an argument similar to the one advanced in this book, see Dorlach (2015).

alleviation that emerged were fundamentally different than the collectivist rationale of the Turkish developmentalist welfare regime. The most significant shift, I argue, was the fact that the new governmental apparatus sought to address poverty by devising technical interventions and curating affective attachments, and that it did so by invoking vocabularies of Islamic charity.

The Muslim Social repackaged political issues and economic disputes—such as inequality, poverty, and unemployment—as primarily matters that can be solved by effective management. As Muslims in Turkey sought Islamic solutions to perceived problems of social governance, they endorsed managerial rationalities that would inform both public service reform and state oversight of civil society organizations. The result was a process akin to what Tania Murray Li (2007) terms "rendering technical": a process through which expert schemes for improvement place certain subjects outside of politics. According to Li, identifying problems and solutions "coemerge[s] within a governmental assemblage in which certain sorts of diagnoses, prescriptions, and techniques are available to the expert" (7) and thus are no longer considered to be political. As James Ferguson's (1994a) groundbreaking study of development in Lesotho and Timothy Mitchell's (2002) work on the construction of the "economy" in Egypt has shown, the process of "rendering technical" operates through multiple channels, changing how problems are conceptualized and acted upon, as well as introducing new methods of bureaucratization, categorization, measurement, and organization. As social problems become sites of technical management, the analytics of power shift and realign. More recent scholarship on the rise of managerialism, likewise, has shown how seemingly neutral administrative practices such as auditing, evaluation, reporting, tracking, monitoring, and planning alter the ways in which political possibilities are imagined and foreclosed (Appe 2016; Eagleton-Pierce 2019; Girei 2016; Hvenmark 2016; Willner 2019).

In addition, the Muslim Social is also defined by a shift toward what Rudnyckyj (2011) terms "governing through affect"—the cultivation, generation, and manipulation of emotional states of being and collective attachments.[11] Islamic neoliberalism taps into and reproduces modes of belonging, feeling, and relating that were already part of the religious experience and social imaginary of Turks, while also creating new modes of attachment that connect audiences with the suffering of distant strangers. In the process, the emotional well-being of those who give and those who receive, as well as the health, strength, and quality of their emotional connections, becomes part of the social relations that must be carefully governed. These affective dimensions also emerge as an object of technical expertise, with the acknowledgment that emotional states cannot be entirely manufactured by governmental interventions. This uneasy folding together of bureaucratic rationalities and emotional sensibilities thus forms the primary subject of this book.

In developing these arguments, I am indebted to scholars who have already examined the transformation of faith-based giving as a way to understand the relationship between Islam and neoliberalism. Mona Atia (2013) shows that the Egyptian charity sector is marked by a fusion between calculative ethics and religious values. Similarly, Cihan Tuğal (2017a) suggests that marketization has transformed the responsibility of caring for the poor into a cold and calculative business in Turkey, and to a lesser extent in Egypt. Like these scholars, I study Islamic neoliberalism through the lens of faith-based giving. I also see faith-based giving as a dynamic site through which Turkish Muslims articulate, discuss, and negotiate the multiple meanings of Islamic "community." Much like a commodity, acts of charity thus epitomize actors' attempts to "fix public meaning" (Douglas and Isherwood 1979, 70). However, there is one key difference. I do not examine whether Islamic charity is becoming more "calculative" or "market-oriented," thereby losing its "communitarian" or "social-justice oriented" composition. Rather, my approach is most similar to Amira Mittermaier's (2013) analysis of the Egyptian charitable sector, which illustrates "the complexity and variety of Muslim attitudes toward charity and unsettled claims about an all-pervasive neoliberalization of

11. For critical work on public emotions and the political economy of neoliberalism, see Analiese and Rudnyckyj (2009), Berlant (2011), D'Aoust (2014), Stewart (2007), and Yang (2014).

everyday life" (275). Mittermaier develops this argument "by approaching Islam as a heteroglossic field in which multiple discourses, logics, and imaginaries converge and undo each other" (276). Hence, I trace the ways in which Islamic-neoliberal assemblages of charity contribute to the formation of the Muslim Social as a technical-affective governmental apparatus. As a meaning-making practice, charity encapsulates how actors draw from Islamic beliefs and neoliberal elements in ways that cannot be categorized merely as economistic or communitarian endeavors.

On Islamism and Social Services

I study the governmental assemblages of Islamic neoliberalism through the lens of Islamic charity—understood as a performative site of meaning-making. Such an analytical framework, although common among anthropologists of Islam and gift-giving, is less widespread among scholars of political Islam and Islamic movements. Examining the effects of neoliberalism, analysts have noted that Islamist movements often benefit from the vacuum created by a state's withdrawal from social service provision (Atia 2013; Gülalp 1999; Herrold 2020). By using frameworks such as "Islam and social policy" or "Islamist social services," scholarship on political Islam focuses either on identifying fundamental religious principles or determining how Islamist movements provide services in exchange for gaining popular support. As a result, Islamic charity is seen either as an outpouring of deep-seated religious values or is treated merely as a political instrument of vote-buying (Brooke 2019; Cammett and Luong 2014; Heynemann 2004; Latief 2013; Szekely 2015; among others). This book, by contrast, examines what charitable giving means for actors involved in social service provision in Turkey—to provide a "thick description" (Geertz 1973) of the ways in which they were drawn to Islamic social projects even though they often disagreed about the role of charity.

As such, this book illustrates the multiplicity of social projects that operate under a contested and plural vision of Islamism. An *Islamic* project, as opposed to an *Islamist* ideology, refers to viewpoints that refer to Islam as a religion and hold that the proper grasp of Islamic beliefs, traditions, and practices is key to addressing modern—public or private, governmental or individual—problems.[12] This distinction allows us to distinguish between "Islamist social services," which refer to aid distributed by Islamist movements for purposes of recruiting followers or harnessing popular support among the masses, and "Islamic social projects," which approach poor relief (somewhat) systematically, and seek to govern poverty according to broader visions of reimagined Islamic social institutions, traditions, and practices that can address the needs of modern Muslim societies.[13] While both are Islam-inspired forms of social service provision, they differ in terms of their ideological commitments and political objectives.

In doing so, *The Muslim Social* reveals a less understood dimension of the "social question" that surfaces through the Islamism–neoliberalism nexus: the fact that most Islam-based political parties seek to design welfare programs that enhance, instead of undermine, programs of economic liberalization. As the Islamic social projects that form the subject matter of this book demonstrate, Muslims deploy neoliberal elements strategically, and do so regardless of whether they portray themselves as embracing Western capitalism or as architects of an Islamic alternative. Yet, perhaps due to the strength of the neoliberalism versus welfare framework, scholarship on Muslim-majority contexts has overlooked the

12. By the term "social project," I am referring to a broad and diffuse way of reimagining social bonds in relation to questions of morality, economy, and piety. This usage echoes Tuğal's (2009) definition of Islamism as "a project that seeks to shape the state, economy and society along Islamic lines" (267). While I agree that Islamism is a project that spans social, economic, cultural, and political domains, throughout the book, I emphasize the multiplicity of social imaginaries that coexist under the contested banner of Islamism, and explore the political and economic ramifications of governmental interventions undertaken in the name of producing the Muslim Social.

13. I borrow the *Islamist* versus *Islamic* distinction from Alev Çınar (2005), who defines Islamists as followers of a political ideology, and uses the term Islamic "to indicate a view, thought, style, or practice that makes reference to Islam as a religion, but is not part of an Islamist ideology" (14). In her study on Hamas as a social institution, Sara Roy (2011) proposes a similar distinction between "Islamic social institutions" and "Islamist social institutions," arguing that not "all who establish, direct, work, participate, support and benefit from Islamic institutions . . . are politically motivated Islamist activists" (9).

emergence of novel discourses, technologies, rationalities, and interventions that seek to provide relief to disadvantaged populations while simultaneously committing to nationwide programs of economic liberalization. Yet, this was precisely what happened in Turkey as the AKP, with the support of a cross-class coalition forged between the Muslim bourgeoisie and the urban poor, emerged as the dominant political party promising material well-being while favoring Islamic-conservative lifestyles. The dawn of the Muslim Social occurred at a historical juncture when pious Muslims rushed to enact their visions of Islamic community in ways that supplemented the AKP's ongoing welfare reforms.

Neoliberalism in Turkey: Economy, Assemblage, Governmentality?

While political economy-based and structurally oriented perspectives have dominated the study of neoliberalism in Turkey, there are also scholars who instead rely on three interrelated schools of thought that resonate with the theoretical commitments of this book: Foucauldian governmentality frameworks, the urban assemblage literature, and anthropological perspectives. While these lines of inquiry converge by their refusal to treat neoliberalism as an overarching ideological force, they differ in terms of how much significance they attribute to the on-the-ground articulation of neoliberal practices, rationalities, and technologies.

Neo-Foucauldian governmentality scholars' main contribution is their focus on the production of neoliberal subjectivities, which allows them to move beyond state-centric or class-centric explanatory frameworks. Özbay et al.'s (2016) edited volume, for instance, focuses on "the micro, capillary sites of everyday politics" (4) of marketization, privatization, and individualization observed in domains such as migration flows, agricultural policy, environmental activism, and women's healthcare. A number of other studies, likewise, highlight that seemingly mundane and unrelated phenomena such as yoga studios, financial literacy campaigns, ministerial public spots, and urban renewal projects operate as sites for the production of competitive, entrepreneurial, responsibilized neoliberal subjectivities (Akçalı and Korkut 2015; Ayhan 2019; Erkmen 2021; Güvenç-Salgırlı and Aykan 2018). However illuminating these works may be, they fall short of exploring how Turkish people themselves construct, negotiate, and reimagine these modes of subjectivity instead of merely being at the receiving end. This neglect is partly due to the use of a governmentality framework without an attention to on-the-ground practices of meaning as well as a preference for analyzing subject formation at the expense of unintended consequences.

A second line of inquiry is advanced by scholars who use the "urban assemblages" (Farías and Bender 2012; McFarlane 2011b) framework to study the neoliberal transformation of Turkish cities, often with an explicit attention to Istanbul. The papers in a 2011 special feature of the journal *City*, aptly titled as "Assembling Istanbul," focus on ethnic identity, urban renewal projects, disaster management, and religious sites in order to demonstrate how "universalizing formations—of the global, the neoliberal, the urban—are themselves constituted out of particular situated assemblages" (Angell, Hammond, and van Dobben Schoon 2011, 645). More recently, Yetişkul and Demirel (2018) extended insights of this special issue to understand gentrification in Istanbul's Cihangir neighborhood through the lens of urban assemblage theory. Although I agree that assemblage theory is helpful to understand the role that urban experiences play in relation to processes of dispossession, resistance, and claiming place in Istanbul (Mills 2014), I also believe it is imperative to extend this analytical framework to explore other aspects of the Turkish neoliberal experience.

Several other Turkish scholars have referred to "Islamic-neoliberal assemblages" in their ethnographic and interpretive analyses of shifting gender discourses, religious self-help books, and the reorganization of state–civil society relations in Turkey (albeit with varying degrees of emphasis; Acar and Altunok 2013; Atalay 2017; Işık 2014; Sayan-Cengiz 2020). This scholarship provides valuable information about the malleability of neoliberal elements and their blending with Islamic vocabularies, but pays less attention to the transformative effects of these assemblages that go beyond a critique of authoritarianism, marketization, or Islamization. This is partially because Islamic neoliberalism in Turkey unfolds not in the context of a liberal democratic system, but rather in a political regime marked by democratic decline. But it is still necessary to examine the impact of Islamic neoliberalism beyond frameworks of authoritarianism, Islamism, and capitalism.

Nevertheless, there are also scholars who have attempted to conduct more in-depth analyses of Turkey via assemblage thinking. One is Ebru Kayaalp's (2014) *Remaking Politics, Markets, and Citizens in Turkey: Governing through Smoke,* in which she conducts an actor–network analysis of shifting ideas and interventions surrounding tobacco policy. Her analysis is similar to mine in terms of our mutual emphasis on indeterminacy, multiplicity, and practice, even though Islam plays a more minor role in the story she tells. Much like actor–network theory-inspired urban assemblage theorists, Kayaalp acknowledges the agency and transformative power of tobacco and examines how this crop "shows an assemblage of both humans (policy makers, experts, bureaucrats, farmers, merchants) and nonhumans (machines, technical reports, formulas, cigarettes)" (8). While I am less interested in the agency of donated goods, I similarly seek to demonstrate how Islamic charity is governed through an assemblage of religious vocabularies (devotion, faith, prayer), technical measures (audits, documents, filing systems, datasets), and emotional registrars (compassion, love, pity, solidarity). Another valuable study that deploys assemblage thinking is Timur Hammond's (2014) work on Istanbul's Eyüp district—a popular site of religious pilgrimage. Hammond suggests that assemblage "enables one way of reconceptualizing the 'religious' as a heterogenous bundle of materialities, practices, and meanings that nevertheless coheres" (682). In this refreshing work that thinks about religion without assuming uniformity, Hammond highlights not only the diversity of Islamic interpretations but also the interlinked nature of spiritual and material concerns as individuals try to make sense of their world. The present book, likewise, examines the co-constitution of affective, religious, and technical registrars in the field of social service provision but does so by using a much looser spatial framework in order to demonstrate similarities across disparate urban sites.

On Neoliberalism as Assemblage

Since the 2000s, different strands of scholarship have criticized assemblage theory for overextending the use of the term "neoliberalism," neglecting the primacy of the global economic order, and overlooking the detrimental impact of neoliberal forms of governance (Anderson et al. 2012; Brenner, Madden, and Wachsmuth 2011; Collier 2012b; Hilgers 2013; McFarlane 2011a; Peck 2013; Wacquant 2012). The dispute between assemblage and governmentality-inspired versus political economy-based approaches—or nonstructural versus structural frameworks—to neoliberalism is too complicated to analyze within the scope of this chapter. Nevertheless, two points are worth discussing further as they may help situate the theoretical commitments that inform this book: first, about how we might understand the relationship between fragments and structures, and second, concerning the issue of whether to draw boundaries between neoliberal and non-neoliberal forms.

First, assemblage thinking is often criticized for attending to the local/particular at the expense of the global/universal. According to Brenner, Madden, and Wachsmuth (2011), the ontological assumptions of assemblage theory fail to consider the "context of context" or the "political-economic structures and institutions" that result in "specific forms of inequality and deprivation" (233–34). While this line of inquiry welcomes the study of cross-national differences, even advocating for a focus on "variegated neoliberalization," the authors still consider neoliberalism as an overarching structure that shapes local context more than being shaped by it (Brenner, Peck, and Theodore 2010). The implication is that, in their "rush" to provide a corrective to the shortcomings of previous scholarship on the issue, assemblage theorists have swayed to the other end of the analytical spectrum by excessively focusing on fragments, thereby neglecting the issue of how diverse segments relate to the whole.

Contrary to these claims, assemblage thinking does not call for a study of the "local" in a manner that is divorced from global processes. Rather, it invites us to consider the local production of neoliberal discourses, elements, practices, rationalities, and technologies without attributing a hegemonic essence to neoliberalism. In this respect, *The Muslim Social* follows assemblage theorists who, in response to criticisms, explain that studying neoliberalism as a form of assemblage does not entail a disregard of international forces, macroeconomic dynamics, or capitalist categories, such as commodity, labor, or value. According to Colin McFarlane (2011a), it is possible to see "political economies and structures . . . as relational products assembled through multiple routes, actors, histories, contingencies, resources, socio-materialities and power relations" (37). Thus, a study of Islamic-neoliberal assemblages such as this one can illuminate how universal phenomena like the "hybrid welfare-mix" emerge out of nostalgic sentiments toward a glorified Ottoman past, concerns about the effectiveness of public service provision, and a political desire to modernize the role of faith-based giving. In the words of Anna Tsing (2005), it is imperative to study universals as partial and practical projects that are only "effective within particular historical conjectures that give them content and force" (8). The layered complexity of charitable acts, practices, and ideals that compose the Muslim Social preclude any other approach.

What makes assemblage thinking valuable is that it allows privileging a perspective of the world as individuals see it. What do actors on the ground consider to be the main problem? What do they propose as a solution? How do they go about articulating and addressing these perceived issues, with what kind of justifications, and to what ends? When Ibrahim praises the numerical barcode taped under a pair of shoes, he is simultaneously concerned with religious piety *and* bureaucratic rationality. Or when Turkish actors involved in social service provision talk about the benefits of a collaborative state–civil society relationship, for instance, their reference point is not just the "neoliberal doctrine" of public–private partnerships, but the presumed efficiency of Ottoman-Islamic waqfs in addressing poverty (chapter 2). Only an interpretive use of assemblage thinking allows us to understand the power of these "precarious yet creative world-making" (Biehl and McKay 2012, 1222) claims. After all, Turkish Muslims' admiration for neoliberal technologies of government are neither instances of false consciousness nor examples of cooptation, but rather the contingent outcome of shifting governmental assemblages formed and transformed on the ground.

The second set of issues I want to briefly consider relates to the question of neoliberalism's limits. The governmental assemblage framework is often accused of defining a whole range of disparate discourses, practices, rationalities, and technologies as "neoliberal" in a manner that lacks precision. According to Loïc Wacquant (2012), "it is unclear what makes a technology of conduct neoliberal: certainly, such bureaucratic techniques as the audit, performance indicators and benchmarks . . . can be used to bolster or foster other logics" (71). Andrew Kipnis (2007) suggests that the only way to ameliorate this problem is to make clear analytical distinctions between neoliberal, un-liberal, and anti-liberal forms of governance, even if they often exist side by side. Others, by contrast, are troubled with the lack of a clear boundary between pro-market and communitarian dispositions. On this point, Tuğal (2017b), for instance, suggests that studying "community" only as a neoliberal technology "culminates in a story of inevitability which reinforces depoliticization under neoliberalism by exaggerating the latter's omnipotence" (460). Accordingly, in his analysis of the liberalization of Islamic charity, Tuğal advocates that there remains a key difference between marketized and communitarian forms of giving.

These are significant concerns, but ultimately they stem more from a desire to locate axes of resistance and less from an acknowledgment of coexisting, multiple, and flexible configurations (Collier 2012a, 192). In general, Marxist, Gramscian, and even Bordieuan perspectives find it impossible to imagine an alternative to neoliberalism unless we can keep the revolutionary potential of community in sight. I do not mean to suggest that all progressive impulses of communitarianism in Turkey have already been folded within neoliberal technologies of government (Zencirci 2020). Rather, I posit that viewing the "politics of the social" through this dichotomy obscures noticing other kinds of shifts in governmentality, such as the emergent technical-affective registrars that form the subject of this book. As Andrea Muehlebach (2009) argues, studying neoliberalism as "politically malleable" allows for an "exploration of neoliberalism that pays attention to the simultaneity and mutual dependency of forms and forces that scholars frequently think in oppositional terms" (498). In a similar vein, Ferguson (2007) demonstrates that neoliberal governance often has a pro-poor orientation, and invites us to find new ways of studying politics that acknowledge the peculiarities of "social neoliberalism." Leftist critique is still possible if we abandon the search for the limits of neoliberalism, and instead excavate the political possibilities that exist within its layers. This option requires, first and foremost, acknowledging how seemingly oppositional forces are often assembled through a dynamic process of mutual constitution.

The Muslim Social demonstrates that as bureaucrats, citizens, donors, managers, and volunteers seek to govern according to an Islamic imaginary, they also adopt, negotiate, and reproduce neoliberal elements, practices, and technologies. Assemblage theory allows us to understand these unexpected combinations, as new charitable arrangements become imbued with multiple meanings such as communitarian values, technical solutions, religious traditions, and emotional connections all at once. Once the messiness of the social world is acknowledged instead of being rejected, new avenues for analyzing the peculiar workings of neoliberal power open up.

Islamic Charity and Religious Civil Society Turkey

Charity is a key part of the Muslim religious imaginary and orders understandings of social relationships as well as moral responsibilities. Like other religious traditions, Islam, broadly defined, stipulates that Muslims must give away a certain amount of their wealth for the well-being of society.[14] While some forms of almsgiving are directly ordained by the Qur'an, others are advised by the Prophet Muhammad. The most prominent Islamic charitable traditions include waqf, zakat, and sadaqa.

According to Islamic law, when a property is declared a waqf, it means that the owner has relinquished their right of ownership. Once founded, a waqf becomes an immovable piece of property and can neither be destroyed nor altered. Waqfs have fulfilled a variety of economic, social, and political functions in Muslim-majority societies, such as sustaining family life, maintaining public order, providing infrastructure to newly conquered lands, legitimizing imperial rule, and establishing ownership of land and estate (Doumani 2017; Hoexter 1998; Singer 2012). Zakat is one of the five main pillars of the Islamic faith and orders Muslims to give away 2.5% of their wealth to the poor and the needy. The Surat al-Tawba (9:60) defines eight categories of people as eligible to receive zakat.

---

14. On Islamic charity, see Benthall (1999), Kochuyt (2009), Sabra (2000) and Singer (2008). For more recent work, see Derbal (2022), Mittermaier (2019), and Moumtaz (2021).

These include the poor, the destitute, civil servants tasked with collecting zakat, slaves and people in bondage, debtors, travelers, recent or potential converts to Islam, and those who are on the path of Allah. In contrast to zakat, sadaqa is entirely voluntary. Giving sadaqa is advised by the Prophet Mohammed, and the Qur'an includes many references to the value of giving sadaqa without specifying the amount, the frequency, or the suitable recipients of this gift. In ordinary language, sadaqa might also be used by street beggars or with reference to an act of generosity that is done without any worldly expectation.

While these faith-based forms of giving have persisted throughout modern Turkish history (Singer 2011), like most Muslim-majority countries, there exists a gap between a longstanding history of Islamic charity and a more recent story of religious civil society in Turkey (Herrold 2020, 27; Kuzmanovic 2012, 11). According to the conventional narrative, religious civil society "flourished" during the 1990s as a result of economic and political liberalization that followed a long era of state domination. Much of the literature on Turkish civil society, in fact, highlights the limited nature of civil society development, examines the impact of the Europeanization process, and speculates about how NGOs may contribute to democratic politics (Kadıoğlu 2005; Keyman and İçduygu 2003; Şimşek 2004; Yılmaz 2005; Zihnioğlu 2013). Nilüfer Göle (1994), for example, argued that the 1990s were marked by an "autonomization of civil society" and the rise of a self-directed social sphere that was, for the first time in Turkish history, capable of opposing state power (213). Göle, like most scholars of this issue, treats state and civil society as mutually exclusive domains. Yet, as Yael Navaro-Yashin (1998) has argued, such a dichotomous perspective overlooks how the discourse of civil society was used by various constituencies, such as the Islamists, secularists, and the Turkish state, to enhance their political legitimacy. A similar argument is put forth by Jeremy Walton (2017) in his analysis of how Muslim NGOs in Turkey use the discourse of religious freedom. Walton (2017, 4–5) introduces the "civil society effect" as a corollary to Timothy Mitchell's (1991) concept of the "state effect" in order to capture how the distinction between state and civil society is constructed, negotiated, and put into practice. Instead of seeing state and civil society as distinct entities that have (or should have) clear boundaries, this perspective focuses on the ways in which the illusion of distinction between state and civil society is manufactured (also see Zencirci and Herrold 2022).

Approached in this manner, the main question involves unpacking the ways in which the "state" and "civil society" are positioned, constructed, and imagined vis-à-vis one another. One of the main goals of this book is to demonstrate the ways in which the boundaries between state and civil society are reconfigured through unique social imaginaries that see Islamic civil society as an extension of the state apparatus. While each chapter examines a different articulation of Islamic charity as expressed through social projects of civilizational revival, populist reform, humanitarian responsibility, and spiritual sanctuary, these aspirations, claims, and goals also include proclamations about the proper relationship between state and civil society under the governmental regime of the Muslim Social.

Methodology

This book combines analytics of governmentality with a multi-sited ethnography (Brady 2014). By analytics of governmentality, I am referring to the Foucauldian study of power/knowledge understood as the "conduct of conduct"; it is a framework that focuses more on flows, currents, and networks, rather than an understanding of authority through a dichotomy of freedom versus oppression. In terms of the study of neoliberalism, an analytics of governmentality invites studying political sovereignty beyond the confines of the state (Burchell, Gordon, and Miller 1991; Cruikshank 1999; Rose 1996). Like other scholars who rely on this methodology to understand shifts in governmental reason, I analyze the ways in which employees, managers, and volunteers involved with Islamic NGOs and public SYD waqfs (*sosyal yardımlaşma ve dayanışma vakıfları*, social aid and mutual assistance endowments) began to use budgets, documents, forms, statistics, and plans to articulate problems, categorize populations, and formulate solutions.

While the method of governmentality illuminates the aspirational plans and unintended consequences of Islamic social projects, it does not necessarily involve a focus on experiences, subjectivities, and solidarities that might transcend the intentions of planners and visionaries.[15] An ethnographic focus, simply put, allows recognizing agency in ways that escape the power of neoliberalism as well as Islamism. Specifically, an ethnographic imaginary "involves reflecting upon the particular geographic and temporal contexts within which practices or technologies of government unfold" (Brady and Lippert 2016, 4). Such a framework differs from conventional anthropological approaches that focus on a singular site or group, instead privileging a multitude of actors and institutions that are nevertheless connected through diverse governmental assemblages. At the same time, an ethnographic focus on meaning-making implies that Islam, neoliberalism, *and* Islamic neoliberalism should be seen as an amalgamation of contingent and fluid cultural practices instead of being seen as fixed and monolithic entities. In this sense, an ethnographic imaginary bears an affinity to the style of inquiry that is commonly referred to as interpretive methods in political science (Bevir and Rhodes 2010; Wedeen 2002; Yanow and Schwartz-Shea 2006). Interpretivists argue that culture, understood as a shared set of "semiotic practices," is crucial for political inquiry (Wedeen 2002, 723). Following these insights, I unpack the ways that Muslims articulate the meaning of charity; conceptualize relations between need, poverty, and welfare; and formulate ideas concerning the distribution of social responsibility between public and private institutions. These varied opinions, I assert, are sites of meaning-making where Islamic-neoliberal assemblages are articulated, contested, and negotiated.

Fieldwork

This book brings together a host of different actors and institutions, all of which I encountered during fourteen months of fieldwork in Turkey from July 2009 to August 2010. This initial fieldwork was followed up by additional short trips in 2013, 2015, and 2019. During these periods, I was based in Ankara and traveled to Istanbul, Izmir, and Gaziantep to meet with

15. In the *Anti-Politics Machine*, James Ferguson (1994b) argues that the real effects of a discourse can be discerned by investigating "not the intentions guiding the actions or one or more of its animating subjects, but in the systematic nature of the social reality which results from those actions" (18).

managers and volunteers of Islamic NGOs, as well as bureaucrats and civil servants working at public SYD waqfs. I conducted a total of seventy-two in-depth interviews with a range of informants such as bureaucrats, civil servants, experts, intellectuals, NGO personnel, donors, volunteers, and practitioners in Turkish civil society. Interviews were semi-structured, often taking place in one- to two-hour meetings; at other times, they occurred whenever I was able to hold a conversation with my interlocutors—during a tea break at a conference, while riding a bus to a nearby village to "expand the horizons" of poor children, or as we folded donated clothing in NGO warehouses. I also spoke, less officially, with countless other Turkish citizens on subjects such as almsgiving, poor relief, and the AKP's social programs.

At the beginning of my fieldwork, I was interested in talking to civil society organizations across the secular–Islamic divide that had begun to rely on private donations to finance their operations. Over time, I shifted my focus to Islamic NGOs and public SYD waqfs which, I had come to realize, were operating as the main institutional pillars of the Muslim Social. In addition to reaching out to people who were affiliated with nationwide Islamic NGOs such as Deniz Feneri (Light House Social Solidarity and Mutual Assistance Organization, DF), Kimse Yok mu (Is Anyone There Social Solidarity and Mutual Assistance Organization, KYM), Cansuyu (Soulwater Social Solidarity and Mutual Assistance Organization), and Insani Yardım Vakfı (Foundation for Human Rights and Humanitarian Relief, IHH), I also interviewed employees and volunteers of citywide Islamic NGOs, which often had only one office and thus operated at a smaller scale.[16] To protect their privacy, and given the fact that some of these organizations—such as the Kimse Yok mu NGO (affiliated with the Fethullah Gülen movement)—were later shut down by the AKP, I decided against providing location-specific details of my interviewees. To further protect their anonymity, I also opted not to specify the names of smaller Islamic NGOs.

16. Most analysts of Turkish civil society consider these four Islamic NGOs as having played a prominent role in the expansion of social service provision under the AKP regime, even if their political relations with the AKP regime waxed and waned over time (see Göçmen 2014, 2018; Morvaridi 2013).

The organizations included in this study, however, share several defining characteristics. Regardless of their legal status, they operate across the state–civil society divide, often partnering with other NGOs, municipal governments, and public SYD waqfs. Their primary mission is to help poor and disadvantaged groups. Complicating distinctions between charity, humanitarianism, philanthropy, and welfare, both Islamic NGOs and public SYD waqfs finance their operations through a combination of public funds and private donations.

Most of the people I interviewed were educated, middle-class, urban individuals. They identified as pious (*dindar*) and conservative (*muhafazakar*) Muslims and practiced Islam in their everyday life. Some came from Islamist activist circles, whereas others grew up in moderately pious households. Most, but not all, of the women I interviewed wore a headscarf, and most, but not all, of the men refrained from shaking my hand. Although they were drawn to the premises and promises of political Islam, they were not necessarily the AKP's enthusiastic supporters. Even so, they believed that the AKP shared their religious sensibilities, and often identified with the AKP more than they did with other political parties.

I also interviewed social service providers and practitioners of civil society that did not consider themselves to be a part of the Muslim Social. These included Republican People's Party (Cumhuriyet Halk Partisi, CHP) municipal governments' poverty relief departments, mosque-based mutual aid organizations, and leftist solidarity associations, as well as secularist-Kemalist NGOs. These conversations were instrumental in helping me understand others' perceptions of this governmental apparatus. Opinions varied: conservative Muslims found the modernization of Islamic charity problematic, secularists argued that the AKP's social programs fostered a culture of dependency among the Turkish poor, while leftists imagined themselves to be engaged in an alternate form of solidarity that fostered vertical relationships instead of reinforcing power differences. While I was not able to include these criticisms and debates in this book, they nevertheless provided crucial information about the Muslim Social.

In addition to semi-structured interviews and informal conversations, I participated in volunteer meetings, fundraising events, and assistance distribution days held by Islamic NGOs; met with bureaucrats working at state welfare institutions; observed and participated in everyday practices of Islamic giving; and attended conferences about Islam and social policy. Since they often needed additional hands, some of these organizations saw me as an eager volunteer who could be put to work. Others invited me to the "package-preparation events" in order to show me their innovative approach to volunteer management, or to "aid distribution days" because they wanted me to gain a firsthand experience of their respectful approach to aid distribution. I also attended social gatherings, such as banquets and picnics, and simply spent time hanging out and drinking tea with donors, managers, and volunteers. While participating in these events, I met with aid recipients and talked to them about their experiences. Despite the efforts of well-intended civil servants, managers, and volunteers, I learned that the poor did not always have pleasant encounters. I discuss some of these dimensions in the concluding chapter.

Lastly, the arguments of this book are substantiated by three sets of written texts. I collected and examined articles, magazines, brochures, and other promotional materials published by Islamic NGOs, the SYDGM (Sosyal Yardımlaşma ve Dayanışma Genel Müdürlüğü, the General Ministry of Social Assistance and Mutual Solidarity), and other government institutions; conducted archival research on the topic of Islamic charity and social welfare in Turkey by relying on newspaper articles, scholarly works, and governmental publications (going back to the 1930s)[17]; and analyzed the works of Muslim intellectuals who wrote on topics such as the relationship between Islam and capitalism, the government of poverty, management of charitable funds, and the responsibility of the state for ensuring the welfare of Turkish citizens.[18]

17. Archival research was conducted at the library of the Waqf General Ministry of Turkey, the National Library of Turkey, the Library of the Centre for Islamic Studies (ISAM), the Library of the Vehbi Koç and Ankara Research Center (VEKAM), and the Republican Archives of the Office of the Turkish Prime Ministry.

18. This database is the product of a multi-year project on the Islamic intellectual field in Turkey which involved identifying, collecting, archiving, and analyzing more than a hundred journals, magazines, and other periodicals that have been published and circulated since the 1990s. The initial project is titled "The Production, Dynamics

The Book

I center the study of Islamic neoliberalism in Turkey in the post-2002 period, when religious languages of care, charity, and community proliferated across the public–private divide. Each chapter of this book thus examines a distinctive Islamic social project; demonstrates how pious Muslims understood and negotiated the meaning of faith, economy, and social responsibility; and traces the governmental assemblages that accompanied these multiple visions. These include the project of civilizational revival, which nostalgically reimagines Ottoman institutions in order to revitalize good governance (chapter 2); that of populist reform, which seeks to enhance the freedom of poor people by creating a dignified aid experience (chapter 3); humanitarian responsibility that orbits around a renewed sense of transnational Islamic solidarity (chapter 4); and the idea that Islam provides a spiritual sanctuary that cultivates volunteer Muslim subjectivities (chapter 5). Each chapter also illustrates how Islamic traditions of charity—waqf, infak, sadaqa, and zakat—acquired new meanings as they were expressed through neoliberalism. Together, these governmental assemblages provide insight into the symbolic discourses and material practices that constitute the Muslim Social.

The book begins with a historical account of the social domain in Turkey. Instead of adopting a policy-centric framework, chapter 1 maps the coevolution of the public (secular) welfare regime and private (religious) charitable practice throughout Republican history. Such an analysis illustrates that perceptions of social problems, and the governmental interventions envisioned to address those problems, fluctuated over time. During the early Republican period (1923–45), the Turkish state's primary focus was socially engineering a modern, secular, urban citizenry. Starting in

and Key Concepts of Current Islamic Political Thought in Turkey: Civilization, Justice, and Order," and was generously funded by TUBITAK's (the Scientific and Technological Research Council of Turkey) 1001 Grant Program (project number: 115K283, principal investigator: Alev Çınar). This project was followed by another one titled "The Islamic Intellectual Field and Political Theorizing in Turkey," funded by EU Horizon 2020 Marie Sklodowska Curie Action Fellowship Grant to project coordinator Alev Çınar). See https://islampolthoughtinturkey.com/ for more information. Also see Zencirci (2021).

the 1950s and 1960s, social politics came to be understood as a way to govern business–labor relations and regulate workers' movements. Poverty alleviation gained currency only after the onset of economic liberalization in the 1980s. Despite these conceptual shifts and institutional changes, the Turkish state played an indirect role in welfare provision and often relied on charitable funds for financing public goods. After mapping these historical continuities, legacies, and ruptures, the chapter turns to the AKP's welfare reforms in the 2000s.

While chapter 1 provides a broad overview of the legal-institutional changes that were instigated by the AKP in the name of welfare reform, the remaining chapters each capture a different governmental assemblage of Islamic neoliberalism. Chapter 2 lays out the production and dissemination of the waqf civilization rhetoric and examines how this rhetoric played a key role in the reconfiguration of the Turkish welfare regime. The AKP's project of civilizational revival argues that Ottoman-Islamic institutions provide an authentic template for good governance that must be restored. By marking Ottoman-Islamic waqfs as fundamental institutions of the Muslim Social, civilizational revival promotes the idea that managerialism equals good governance. Such an articulation, in turn, relegates social problems to the technical domain. As an assemblage of Islamic neoliberalism, the project of civilizational revival glorifies the imperial past while simultaneously justifying rules of collaboration, administration, and accountability among Islamic NGOs and public SYD waqfs.

Chapter 3 turns to the expansion of social assistance programs under the AKP regime. I read debates surrounding these social assistance programs through the lens of populist reform—a social project that portrayed new technologies of aid as an example of a "pro-people" approach. I show how Islamic notions of sadaqa and an obscure Ottoman practice of almsgiving (sadaqa stones) were deployed in the reimagination of respectful and freedom-enhancing technologies of aid, namely, the package system, the social market, and the social card. Paradoxically, I also show that these attempts to improve the aid experience of the Turkish poor occurred while SYD waqfs and Islamic NGOs were adopting intrusive technologies of information: documents, house visits, and datafication procedures. This governmental assemblage thus treated the poor as an object of power/knowledge and did so in the name of serving the people.

Chapter 4 probes Islamic humanitarianism under the AKP regime and argues that the construct of a transnational Islamic community was central to the project of humanitarian responsibility. This governmental assemblage not only mobilized religious values for transnational efforts of giving but also repurposed Islamic notions of the deserving poor in order to generate a sense of obligation toward Muslims residing in far-away places such as Ethiopia, Niger, Sudan, and Pakistan. By analyzing the languages of solidarity promulgated by Islamic NGOs with a specific focus on the visual representation of the Muslim poor, I demonstrate how humanitarian responsibility operated as a form of distant, yet intimate, attachment between Turkish "saviors" and their disadvantaged others. But, while working to strengthen bonds between individuals, communities, and countries, I also show that the social project of humanitarian responsibility overlooked cultural, economic, and geographical differences among Muslims.

Chapter 5 analyzes the Islamic project of providing a spiritual sanctuary to Muslim individuals. Through a study of formal volunteer programs that have been initiated by various state institutions and Islamic NGOs, I contend that this project portrayed Islam both as a way of asserting individual autonomy as well as a guard against excessive individualism. I develop this argument by examining how the protection of Turkish Muslims from the ailments of capitalism, such as loneliness, individualism, and the loss of close-knit groups, were linked to an idealized image of Islam as a sanctuary. After turning to the personal narratives of three volunteers, the chapter concludes by discussing how pious Muslims experienced formal volunteer programs through a variety of divergent cultural rubrics, which further complicates monolithic depictions of Islamic neoliberalism.

In the conclusion, I discuss what kind of political implications the Muslim Social has—as a sphere of technical management and affective attachment—for understanding politics in Turkey, the larger Muslim world, and for the relationship between capitalism and governance in our contemporary present. In the midst of alarming political developments, such as Turkey's "authoritarian reversal," the deep-seated clash between the AKP and the Gülen Movement, the heightened military conflict between the Turkish state and Kurdish groups, as well as an impending economic crisis, this book shows how a concern for society's well-being can coexist with political oppression, authoritarian state practices, and the widespread violation of human rights. To probe this dissonance between social governance and political democracy, I conclude the book by discussing this paradox of how the political will to govern the social is predicated upon the exclusion of certain segments of the population that are deemed ungovernable. I have also added an epilogue to briefly discuss how the Muslim Social operated in the aftermath of the devastating February 2023 earthquake in Turkey-Syria.

I

From the Modernist Social to the Muslim Social

In March 2020, with the onset of the COVID-19 pandemic, the Turkish state announced a nationwide fundraising campaign titled "We are enough for each other, Turkey!" (*Biz Bize Yeteriz Türkiyem*), organized in response to mayors from the opposition party—especially Ekrem İmamoğlu—who had started their own philanthropic campaigns. The AKP instead asked Turkish citizens to channel their generosity toward state-sponsored programs. By matching private donations with public funds, the government promised to create a "shield of social protection" for families that had been negatively impacted by the pandemic's economic fallout. In a symbolic act of self-sacrifice, President Erdoğan even donated seven months of his salary to the campaign and encouraged Turks to give whatever they could, even if they could afford only a miniscule amount.[1]

The COVID-19 solidarity campaign exemplifies a venerable tradition of Turkish politics: the state partially financing public social programs with the help of private donations. On the one hand, the state is portrayed as an object of affection, in need of peoples' care and attention. On the other hand, the state remains omnipotent by representing itself as the only institution capable of delivering charitable funds to deserving populations. As a result, Turkish citizens experience a state-mediated form of social solidarity.

The existence of this governmental practice illustrates that a "split-screen approach" (Goodlad 2001, 592) that distinguishes between public

---

1. For more information on this campaign, see Kaptan (2020).

welfare and private charity is not suitable for understanding the parameters of social governance in Turkey. Rather, a study focusing on the history of the social question needs to attend to shifts in the public welfare regime, fluctuations in the meaning and form of private charity, and the transformation of the relationship between public welfare and private charity without assuming that these two domains are mutually exclusive. This reframing is even more crucial given the conventional assumption which locates public welfare within a secular framework and equates it with a rights-based notion of citizenship, while associating private charity with a faith-based notion that privileges immediate relief.

Instead of seeing the history of the Turkish welfare regime through these binary oppositions, such as public welfare versus private charity, secular citizenship rights versus religious relief, the following historical account thus presents a more nuanced perspective that reveals two overarching themes. First, while universal welfare programs were rare throughout modern Turkish history, the state still played a key role in the provision of social assistance, but mainly through a combination of indirect means and ad hoc mechanisms. Second, private charitable practices, symbols, and traditions were never tangential to the Turkish welfare regime. Depending on the political atmosphere, governmental authorities relied on a pastiche of religious, secular-Kemalist, humanitarian, and patriotic discourses to foster national solidarity, often in partnership with a wide range of civil society organizations with varying degrees of autonomy.

Despite the persistence of these themes, the structure and rationale of governmental interventions about the social have been in flux, acquiring several meanings and functions throughout modern Turkish history. What follows, then, is not a linear transition, where traditional concepts, practices, and interventions are replaced with modern ones. Rather, this chapter depicts a complex historical trajectory, where shifting ideas about state, market, and civil society; fluid attitudes about the effectiveness of public welfare versus private aid; fluctuating interpretations of Islamic charity; and changing developmental discourses have each played a key role in the evolution of the social question in Turkey. In the late modern Ottoman Empire, concerns about social modernity were related to demographic changes brought on by the large-scale movement of people to urban centers. During the early Republican period (1923–45), the Kemalist regime focused on the construction of a modern Turkish citizenry through social engineering. Beginning in the 1950s, under the influence of the Cold War, bureaucrats, intellectuals, and politicians began to approach social policy as a matter pertaining to business–labor relations and the management of collective workers' rights. And after the 1980s, governmental authorities reframed the social question as one that primarily pertained to the provision of in-kind and material assistance to disadvantaged populations.

Late Ottoman Era and the Advent of the Social Question

Until the eighteenth century, poverty relief was not on the imperial agenda, and it remained a sporadic, decentralized, and informal effort (Bonner, Ener, and Singer 2003; Ener 2005; Ginio 2003). From the late eighteenth century onward, political authorities introduced poor-relief institutions, such as the Poor House of Istanbul (Istanbul Darülacaze Müessesi), the Imperial Hospital for Children (Hamidiye Etfal Hastanesi), and the Ottoman Red Crescent Society (Osmanlı Hilal-i Ahmer Cemiyeti). These imperial institutions were supported by voluntary societies, thereby starting the tradition of partnerships between political authorities and charitable organizations (Özbek 1999, 7). Ottoman imperial authorities' growing interest in assisting and controlling such categories of people stemmed from the emergence of new ideas about idleness, work, and productivity (Özbek 2009, 784). In addition to these institutions, which served larger segments of the urban population, charitable societies began to provide relief to the poor in Istanbul (Exertzoglou 2010). Philanthropic activities were partly a response to the demographic changes faced by the Ottoman population. These efforts rearranged relationships between different groups, developed novel techniques of power and institutional structures, and redefined the meaning of specific activities.

Additionally, various categories of people, such as abandoned children, beggars, criminals, prostitutes, orphans, vagrants, and veterans, came to be seen as "social" problems in need of governmental intervention

(Başaran 2014; Ergut 2002; Hafez 2021; N. Özbek 2009; M. Özbek 2010). The emergence of bureaucratized forms of poor relief and the advent of new forms of charitable giving coincided with the increasing public visibility of the "undeserving" poor in urban centers such as Istanbul and Cairo (Ener 2005; Maksudyan 2014). On the one hand, the social category of the "deserving" poor gradually became intertwined with questions of modernity, state building, and the political economy of urban change. On the other hand, the provision of social services served a variety of functions, such as enabling the formation of a middle-class identity among philanthropists, acting as a social control mechanism of "unwieldy" populations, as well as legitimizing the power of imperial authorities through displays of public generosity (Özbek 1999, 2003, 2009).

While efforts to govern the social became gradually more prominent during the late Ottoman period, Islamic charitable institutions remained tangential to these efforts. During most of Ottoman rule, zakat was collected as part of the imperial system of taxation, whereas sadaqa took place within the physical space of waqf complexes, which included buildings such as bath houses, mosques, hospitals, soup kitchens, public fountains, and schools (Peri 1992; Shefer 2003; Singer 2006). Although these buildings provided a variety of social services, the poor were not their primary focus. In fact, during most of the Ottoman era, waqfs functioned largely as a medium of property transference, allowing successful individuals— aristocrats, bureaucrats, and governors—to pass their temporary ownership of land and estate to their kin without defying imperial authorities. Much like the impact of European colonialism in other Muslim-majority contexts (Oberauer 2008; Pianciola and Sartori 2007; Powers 1989), this system of property rights came under attack when, beginning in the eighteenth century, Ottoman leaders, under the influence of European powers, began to perceive waqfs as problematic institutions in need of administrative and legal reform (Çizakça 2000; Kuran 2001; Singer 2011). Ottoman modernization efforts began with the founding of the Evkaf-i Hümayun Nezareti (Ministry of Evkaf) by Sultan Mahmud II in 1826. In the name of preventing corruption, the ministry liquidated waqf assets and properties to the imperial budget. While some of these funds were put toward philanthropic efforts, a direct link between Islamic charitable institutions and the social question was not yet forged.

Kemalism and the Modernist Social

With the establishment of the Turkish Republic in 1923, the question of the social, as has been the case in other countries in the Middle East, became inseparable from the nation-state-building project (Aybars and Tsarouhas 2010; Jawad 2009; Karshenas and Moghadam 2009). Turkey's founding leader, Mustafa Kemal Atatürk, and his political cadre focused on constructing a unified national identity while striving toward secular modernity. Within such an ideological context, the social was redefined as a site that served the construction of a secular, modern, and ethnically Turkish understanding of citizenship. While the state did not set out to create a public welfare regime, it encouraged and oversaw the provision of social services by voluntary organizations which were tasked with supplanting religious charity with its patriotic counterparts.

The founding ideology of the Turkish Republic—Kemalism, expressed by Atatürk and disseminated by the CHP—believed in the supremacy of the European civilization, seeking to emulate its cultural norms, political institutions, and techniques of governance while simultaneously distancing itself from the Ottoman past (Bozdoğan and Kasaba 1997; Çınar 2005). A series of comprehensive reforms were undertaken as part of the modernization project. The Kemalist regime made one crucial assumption: religious beliefs and practices belonged to the private sphere and were thus to be excluded from the public–political realm. To this end, the new regime abolished the Islamic caliphate (1924), closed religious convents and communities (1925), and encouraged the adoption of a Western lifestyle among Turkish citizens. In terms of national culture, Turkishness was defined as a homogenous identity that superseded ethnic or religious differences (Kadıoğlu 1998; Yeğen 1996; Yılmaz 2013). At the same time, religious practices, traditions, and organizations—some of which provided poverty relief—were deemphasized.

In contrast to other Muslim-majority countries with an Islamic constitution, such as Pakistan, Malaysia, and Saudi Arabia, where the collection of zakat funds and other charitable donations were organized under the auspices of the government, the Turkish Republic considered Islamic charity a private matter while systematically seeking to utilize assets, funds, and properties in the service of the nation-state-building project.

For example, while Kemalist ideology portrayed waqfs as "backward" Ottoman-Islamic institutions that had prevented Turkey's cultural and economic progress toward European civilization, it had no problem using these assets and properties for building state infrastructure (Özaral 2012; Zencirci 2015a). To this end, the Kemalist modernization project banned the management of waqfs by religious brotherhoods in 1925, the duties of the Evkaf Ministry were taken over by the newly established Vakıflar Genel Müdürlüğü (Waqf General Ministry, VGM) in 1935, and the government created a special committee for the abolishment of waqfs in 1937. Despite resistance from numerous social groups who were concerned about the erosion of property rights, the Kemalist regime was able to eradicate, demolish, or repurpose most waqf assets and properties by the 1950s.

In other instances, the Kemalist regime regulated the collection of Islamic donations but did so by using the language of patriotic philanthropy as opposed to the familiar vocabulary of Islamic charity (Buğra 2007, 37). It was during the 1928 Ramadan holiday celebrations that the government distributed envelopes to each district in Ankara, encouraging citizens to donate their zakat, including zakat *al-fitr* (*fitre ve zekat*) to government-adjacent philanthropic organizations, thereby redefining Islamic charity as a duty of patriotic citizens (Adak Turan 2004, 83–86). The Kemalist regime also mandated citizens to donate the skins of sacrificial Qurban animals to the Turkish Aeronautical Association, claiming that this resource was best used to improve the country's aviation industry. Instead of a total ban of Islamic charitable giving, the regime thus sought to channel religious impulses toward nationalist sentiments.

On the economic front, after a brief experiment with laissez-faire economics, Turkey adopted etatism, a state-led model of economic development. This protectionist ideology emphasized industrial growth, limited international trade, and subsidized major industries such as agriculture, electricity, and textiles (Birtek 1985; Pamuk 2000). Poverty was considered a result of industrial backwardness instead of being attributed to economic inequality or the implementation of uneven developmental strategies. Instead of class, ethnic, or religious cleavages, the Kemalist government conceptualized social stratification through an urban versus rural dichotomy (Karaömerlioğlu 1998).

Despite the pronounced etatism of the period, public welfare programs were considered a "luxury" that could not be afforded by a "backward" and "poor" country like Turkey (Buğra 2008, 98–100). While universal welfare programs were mostly nonexistent, the Kemalist regime interfered in social problems and oversaw public services in several ways. For example, to solve the urban poverty problem, the state encouraged wealthy citizens to channel their social generosity to organizations such as the Red Crescent (Kızılay), Philanthropy Lovers Association (Yardım Sevenler Derneği), and the Children's Protection Society (Çocuk Esirgeme Kurumu; Buğra 2008; Libal 2000). The Kemalist regime promoted the creation of an "active society" that would voluntarily support the "notion of a strong state, secularist developmentalism and the modernist project" (Keyman and İçduygu 2013, 26). In addition, during this period, bureaucrats, doctors, and philanthropists sought to improve the culture and health of the Turkish population through a series of educational, medical, and charitable interventions (Alemdaroğlu 2005; Evered and Evered 2012; Evered and Evered 2013; Güvenç-Salgırlı 2011; Kezer 2009; Lüküslü and Dinçşahin 2013; Navaro-Yashin 2000). Motivated by a sense of modern scientific management, these actors came to see issues as diverse as education, exercise, homemaking, malaria, and prostitution as social issues in need of attention and intervention.

Several other organizations, such as the People's Houses and state economic enterprises, also played a role in the provision of social services. People's Houses were established during the 1930s and 1940s in provincial towns across Turkey. By combining nationalist indoctrination with a ruralist discourse that glorified the Anatolian masses, People's Houses acted as a bridge between the political elite and local populations (Karaömerlioğlu 1998; Karpat 1963). These ideological agents of the Kemalist regime were also tasked with addressing social problems in their vicinity (Lamprou 2015). Muhittin Celal Duru, the author of a CHP guidebook titled "Social Assistance: Its Principles and Practices," provided the following recommendations to People's Houses which were asked to accelerate their outreach efforts after Atatürk's death in 1938:

> The real job of social assistance committees is to identify those who are helpless in their community, such as women, children, or those who are disabled, sick, and old, to generate loving and philanthropic sentiments among members of that society, and to ensure that these emotions are brought to the highest degree by using their powers of criticism and persuasion. In addition, committees should support charity groups, assist sick individuals in getting to the hospital, find accommodation for farmers and families that travel from villages, locate jobs for the unemployed, provide in-kind and material assistance, if necessary, procure resources to finance these operations, and organize trips, put on shows and ceremonies for fundraising purposes. (Duru 1939, 140–41)

These instructions illustrate not only that the Kemalist regime considered social problems such as illness, poverty, and unemployment as one of its governmental responsibilities, but also that social care was to be provided through cultivating religious charitable sentiments and mobilizing local communities. This example also shows that the Turkish regime's habit of relying on local offices for raising funds and distributing social assistance is not a recent phenomenon, even if it was not yet expressed through an Islamic vocabulary.

In addition to People's Houses, state economic enterprises, another early Republican institution, provided a variety of social services. Starting in the 1930s, state-run factories and mines created social work departments. The primary goal was to prevent absenteeism among workers and increase the retention of labor forces. Through these units, state economic enterprises offered free or subsidized meals, constructed housing units, provided housing assistance, and distributed work clothes and in-kind payments. State-run facilities also offered access to free health care and dispensed medicine to industrial workers (Arnold 2012; Gürboğa 2009; Makal 1999; Nacar 2009).

The provision of social services through these multiple channels served the twin goals of nation-building and state-led economic development. Although workers and villagers often resisted attempts to engineer a modern, urban, and secular citizenry, these ad-hoc social benefits still forged a connection between the Turkish state and the ordinary people, even if they did so sporadically and unevenly. More importantly, the legacy of the state encouraging, supporting, and overseeing auxiliary organizations' provision of social services, and the Kemalist regime's strategic use of Islamic charity, remained an influential aspect of welfare governance in subsequent decades.

The Cold War Period and the Social as Collective Rights

After two decades of a CHP-led single-party regime, Turkey transitioned into a multi-party democracy in 1945. The main political opposition, the Democrat Party (Demokrat Parti), won the 1950 national elections and governed until 1960, when its leader, Adnan Menderes, was deposed and later executed in a military coup. Presenting himself as the guardian of the agricultural masses, Adnan Menderes—one of Erdoğan's political heroes (Danforth 2015)—articulated a language of rural populism, increased public funds for agrarian development, encouraged public expressions of Islam, and, most significantly, reversed the Kemalist ban on Arabic Ezan (Adhan) prayers. While the Menderes era was not necessarily defined by an expansion of welfare programs, US-backed agricultural reforms had positive effects on the country's distributional dynamics (Boratav and Özuğurlu 2006). Moreover, it was during the 1950s that Turkey adopted import-substitution industrialization (ISI) as the country's new economic model, allowing large landowners and big merchants to shift their capital to textile production and food processing (Pamuk 1981).

In terms of social governance, this period witnessed the redefinition of the social as a matter pertaining to collective rights. First, there was a concerted effort toward enhancing the capacity of developmentalist welfare programs.[2] In addition to health insurance programs and retirement benefits, the Menderes government also introduced agricultural support policies in order to sustain the rural populace and manage migration to

2. These new programs include the Workers Insurance Programs (1945) and the Retirement Chest (1949), which were introduced before Menderes came to power.

urban centers (Gürel 2011). In 1964, these diverse programs were combined under the umbrella of the Social Security Institution (Sosyal Sig-
ortalar Kurumu, SSK). A separate insurance program for self-employed
and agricultural workers (Bağ-Kur) was established in 1971. These programs aimed at providing health insurance and old-age benefits to public
employees and others who were part of the formal economy, as well as to
their immediate family members (Özbek 2006, 189). Although those who
worked in the formal employment sector received benefits (such as pensions and insurance), individuals who were not part of the formal employment sector were left to be cared for through traditional networks, such as
extended families or rural-to-urban migrant communities.[3]

A slightly different understanding of the social, one that was concerned
more about class-based conflict and less about rural-to-urban migration,
was also present. After the liberal 1961 Constitution allowed the formation of class-based parties and eased restrictions on associational activity, the 1960s and 1970s witnessed a period of politicization during which
cycles of protest, street politics, and violence between militant groups were
a common occurrence (Doğan 2010; Mello 2010). Much that was written
about social policy at the time, such as the groundbreaking work of Cahit
Talas (Gülmez 2007), predictably understood the social question as one
that pertained to the management of business–labor relations and class-
based conflict. There was also an attempt at reframing philanthropy's
main goal as the creation of a skilled labor force through contributions
to "health, education, and cultural arts" (Singer 2011, 564). A number of
legal-institutional changes, most prominently the 1967 Waqf Law, paved
the way for private foundations to lend philanthropic support to the state
in areas such as health and education. For the first time in Turkish history,
philanthropic organizations were granted tax exemptions in exchange for
their efforts to create a skilled labor force and supervise the Turkish youth.

However, neither public social programs nor philanthropic initiatives were able to stabilize the violent confrontations between left-wing

3. Buğra and Keyder (2006) refer to this aspect of the Turkish welfare regime as
"inegalitarian corporatism" (211).

and right-wing groups that plagued Turkey throughout the 1970s (Bal and Laçiner 2001; Gunter 1989; Sayarı 2010). By the end of the decade, predicaments of the ISI model, including a shortage in consumer goods, hyperinflation, labor unrest, and rising unemployment levels, eventually culminated in the foreign debt crisis of 1979 (Arıcanlı and Rodrik 1990; Bayar 1996; Önder 1998).

Economic Liberalization and the Social as a Safety Net

On September 12, 1980, high-ranking generals from the Turkish Armed Forces overthrew the government, blaming elected officials for the political violence and economic instability of the 1970s. Between 1980 and 1983, Turkey was ruled by a military authoritarian regime which declared a nationwide emergency, banned politicians, jailed leftist dissidents, and restructured the constitutional regime (Cizre-Sakallıoğlu 1997; Tachau and Heper 1983). Despite this oppressive atmosphere, the return to civilian politics after 1983 also expanded avenues for political participation, permitted certain kinds of associational activity, and encouraged artistic and cultural production (Gürbilek 1992). Thus, the 1980s were a paradoxical period that witnessed both the expansion and restriction of political expression: whereas class-based activism was discouraged, the cultural atmosphere of the decade made it possible for numerous groups—such as pious Muslims, liberal women, and ethnic Kurds—to criticize the secular, modernist, and homogenous construction of Turkish national identity (Bozdoğan and Kasaba 1997).

During this decade, the developmental model of ISI was abandoned in exchange for the massive financial support received from the International Monetary Fund (IMF) and the World Bank. Turgut Özal, first as the economic advisor to the military government (1980–83), and later as the leader of the center-right Motherland Party (Anavatan Partisi, ANAP) and prime minister of Turkey (1983–89), oversaw the implementation of the structural adjustment program. Like his contemporaries Ronald Reagan and Margaret Thatcher, Özal was a neoliberal leader who combined fiscal austerity with moral conservatism. Under his leadership, the Turkish state gradually relinquished control over economic planning, privatized state-owned industries, and incentivized the business community so that domestic firms could become competitive players in the international marketplace (Kalaycıoğlu 2002; Öniş 2004). Further, Özal played a key role in the dissemination of the Turkish-Islamic synthesis—a new understanding of national identity that allowed, and at times encouraged, religious beliefs to occupy a larger role in political and social life (Çetinsaya 1999).

These large-scale changes were accompanied by a new notion of the social question as primarily a matter of poverty alleviation. A significant development was the introduction of the Social Fund (Sosyal Yardımlaşma ve Dayanışma Fonu, SYDF) in 1986. Often referred to as FAKFUKFON,[4] the goal of this fund was to provide a social safety net and protect the poor from the destructive effects of structural adjustment. Despite the fact that similar funds, at the urging of the IMF and the World Bank, had been introduced in a number of countries in the Global South, such as Mexico, Egypt, and Brazil, during the 1980s, Özal described this new initiative as a "restoration" of Turkish-Islamic solidarity, which was deemed superior to the "mechanical understanding of social solidarity found in the West" because assisting the poor, it was argued, came naturally to Turks who were "motivated by family values and a love for community" ("Özal: Sosyal Dayanışma Bizde Batıdan Farklı" 1986). When "economic measures support the social values that give life to Turkish society," then "social justice, social security, and social harmony will be ensured," an ANAP brochure explained ("Anavatan İktidarının Yüzakı İcraatlerinden Biri" 1987, 5). The government promptly created 750 public SYD waqfs across the country. Although FAKFUKFON was mostly financed by the public budget, the main purpose was to—once again—convince private citizens to channel their philanthropic contributions to public SYD waqfs located in their neighborhood, thereby generating "a steady flow of income from the rich towards the poor" ("Fakirlere Müjde" 1986). At the local level, the board of trustees (*mütevelli heyeti*) had to include philanthropic citizens, representatives from civil society organizations, and state officials

---

4. FAKFUKFON is the abbreviated form of *Fakir Fukara Fonu*, which is best translated as the "the fund for the poor and the destitute."

(Yıldırım 2010, 13). In addition to making decisions about the use of their allocated budget, the board of trustees was also tasked with cultivating a philanthropic spirit and collecting donations from their immediate community.

Even though most public SYD waqfs failed to attract large sums of voluntary donations, the idea that citizens should assist the state through faith-based giving was significant because it folded Islamic charity within the early Republican discourse of patriotic philanthropy, while reframing the distinction between private charity and public welfare. The hybrid public–private structure of the Social Fund was criticized across the political spectrum. Some politicians claimed that SYD waqfs undermined the secular principles of the Turkish welfare regime and reversed Turkey's modernization by bringing back "archaic" ways of helping the poor (Zencirci 2015a, 545). Others, by contrast, were troubled by the fact that SYD waqfs were created by the state, instead of being initiated by wealthy individuals as ordained by Islam (Öktem and Erdoğan 2019, 211). Despite their divergent views, both sets of criticisms were troubled by the explicit incorporation of Islamic charity into the public welfare regime.

Political Islam and the Grassroots Provision of Social Services

Through the late 1980s and 1990s, the budget and role of SYD waqfs increased steadily, but these offices did not become a key node of the Turkish welfare regime. While the Social Fund merely tasked public SYD waqfs with providing sporadic aid to a small group of needy individuals located within their vicinity, ad hoc social benefits were estimated to have reached more than nine million people by 2001 (Buğra and Keyder 2006, 223). At the same time, successive economic crises, changes in the structure of the labor market, and erosion of extended family ties created a form of "new poverty"[5] in Turkey. The existing social insurance and health care systems were unable to address the changing needs of the population (Buğra 2003). In addition to the Social Fund, several additional programs, such as

---

5. On new poverty in Turkey, see Adaman and Ardıç (2008), Erdoğan (2007), and Romano and Penpecioğlu (2009).

the health-care-focused 1992 Green Card (Yeşil Kart), were introduced to provide support to the disenfranchised urban masses, but none was able to provide a comprehensive safety net (Kısa and Younis 2006).

Like other Muslim-majority countries, declining state budgets and cutbacks in social spending contributed to the rise of the Islamist movement in Turkey (Bayat 2002). Beginning in the 1980s, a variety of Islamist groups with informal networks and grassroots orientations became politically active in metropolitan centers such as Ankara and Istanbul. Although they had fragmented interests and diverse political goals, these Islamist groups were unique in terms of their emphasis on a religious politics of identity and a critique of the Kemalist establishment (Gülalp 2001; Narlı 1999; Yavuz 1997; White 2002). Some of these Islamist movements founded waqfs to formalize their operations, while others organized through other means.[6] Regardless of their institutional form or legal category, all Islamist groups saw themselves as part of a grassroots movement that opposed secularist Kemalism. In their understanding, Islamic groups represented a "democratic civil society" that was in tune with the needs of the "people," while the Kemalist elite signified top-down authoritarianism (Navaro-Yashin 1998; 2002). The fact that Islamist associational and philanthropic networks were amateurish, informal, and fragmented was brought up to justify their grassroots orientation and democratic power, thereby legitimizing the Islamist movement vis-à-vis the secularist-military establishment.

During this period, Islamists provided a variety of social services to the urban poor through a combination of formal organizations and informal grassroots networks. The rising Islamist movement, led by the Welfare Party (Refah Partisi, RP) and Necmettin Erbakan, gained political power through a combination of grassroots electoral mobilization, effective use of a populist-Islamic rhetoric, and a shared perception of its

6. In addition to the religious connotations of waqfs, there was another reason for Islamist groups' gravitation toward waqfs. To curb the power of leftist political movements, the military government had introduced the No. 2908 Law of Associations (1983), which made it cumbersome to organize under other legal categorizations, such as associations (see Zevkliler 1995, 144).

ideological distinctiveness (Kamrava 1998; White 2002, 2012a). The party received votes not only from the urban poor, but also from the Muslim bourgeoisie who had benefited from the economic reforms of the 1980s (Narlı 1999; Gülalp 1999; Öniş 1997). In 1994, candidates from the RP, including Erdoğan, were elected as the municipal governors of a number of urban neighborhoods in Ankara and Istanbul. In the following years, these municipalities showed their administrative skills by solving three major problems that had troubled urban life: garbage, potholes, and mud (Akıncı 1999). The effective provision of social services by municipal governments played a central role in Refah's electoral success in the 1995 national elections (White 1997; Yavuz 1997). In 1996, the RP formed a coalition government with the center-right True Path Party (Doğru Yol Partisi, DYP). The Refah-Yol coalition marked a significant point in Turkish politics because, for the first time, Islamists were allowed to share power as a dominant political partner (Öniş 2001). But the rise of the Islamist movement was interrupted with the February 28, 1997, "postmodern" coup, when military officers indirectly ousted the democratically elected government (Lombardi 1997). From the perspective of the Turkish Armed Forces, RP's political success represented a threat to Kemalist principles of secularism (Cizre-Sakallıoğlu and Çınar 2003). In the aftermath of the February 28 process, Islamist networks were disillusioned and demobilized, later regrouping under the leadership of the AKP but with new ideological commitments (Tuğal 2009, 147–91).

The AKP's Reforms and the Reconfiguration of the Turkish Welfare Regime

When the AKP was founded in 2001, the party's leadership emphasized that their ideological stance resembled the Christian Democrats of Europe (Hale 2005; Özbudun 2006). Now a shining example of moderate Islam, the AKP promised to merge a conservative-religious sensibility with a commitment to capitalism, democracy, secularism, and human rights. During the months leading up to the 2002 national elections, the AKP toned down its religious rhetoric, instead campaigning on the promise of economic prosperity and a national identity based on a vision of Muslimhood. While Islamist themes were still prominent in the AKP's political rhetoric, there was a concerted effort to demonstrate that the movement's anti-systemic tendencies had been tamed. While the AKP's commitments to democracy and human rights have fluctuated over time, the political concerns and economic conjuncture of the early 2000s set the stage for the formation of the Muslim Social as a governmental apparatus.

Once elected, the AKP implemented the economic liberalization program that was recommended by the IMF and the European Union. At the same time, the AKP's commitment to free markets had to protect the cross-class coalition between the Muslim bourgeoisie and the urban poor (İnsel 2003). Economic liberalization, in other words, had to be carried out in a manner that would not disadvantage these groups. According to Marcie Patton (2009), these ideological shifts and political considerations led the AKP to pursue a "synergy between neoliberalism and communitarianism," including an emphasis on "the ethics of community combined with the dynamics of the free market" (440). In terms of the welfare regime, this synergy brought a paradoxical outcome. The state withdrew from some aspects of social governance (such as health care, insurance, and pensions), while expanding its role and reach in other areas, such as relief programs (Eder 2010). The AKP revamped the administration of numerous public welfare programs, eradicating some and combining others. The Social Security Reform Package (2006) tried to centralize the Turkish welfare regime under one rubric (Buğra and Candaş 2011). Some of the key changes included modifications to the formal employment benefit system and the introduction of market-based incentives so that private companies could sell health services and insurance programs (Çoşar and Yeğenoğlu 2009; Elveren 2008). The partial marketization of social benefits was accompanied by an expansion in health coverage and improved access to services (Ağartan 2012).

At the same time, the state began to play a larger role in the provision of social services. The initial impetus for the expansion of social assistance programs was the World Bank's 2001 Social Risk Mitigation Project which established a conditional cash transfer program in Turkey (Yükseker 2009, 272). Strengthening the bureaucratic capacity of public SYD waqfs was one of the conditions for the disbursement of funds (Öktem and Erdoğan, 2019). In 2004, the Social Fund was transformed into a new welfare directorate (Sosyal Yardımlaşma ve Dayanışma Genel Müdürlüğü, SYDGM).[7] In addition to the World Bank's conditional cash transfers, this directorate was tasked with monitoring, streamlining, and overseeing the variety of social programs administered by public SYD waqfs that had initially been created by Turgut Özal in 1986. In contrast to their negligible role in social welfare provision during the 1990s, from the 2000s onward, SYD waqfs became central nodes of the Turkish welfare regime (Dodurka 2014, 2). The new social assistance programs that were administered by SYD waqfs were fundamentally different from the comprehensive logic of welfare developmentalism. The key idea behind developmentalist welfare programs had been universal eligibility (as long as certain conditions were met). Agricultural subsidies, for instance, were provided as a component of citizenship, the process of application was straightforward, and benefits were not timebound. By contrast, new social assistance programs targeted a subgroup of the population, were often limited to a specific kind of need or purpose, and were generally given for a set amount of time. These programs are also distinctive due to their primary focus on the needs of disadvantaged urban families.[8] For instance, in 2018, the SYDGM website listed six clusters of aid:

1. Family Assistance: food, housing repair, public housing assistance, heating assistance, cash transfers to soldiers' families in need, assistance to orphans, and monetary payments to new mothers.

2. Educational Assistance: school supplies; conditional cash transfers; free school meals, textbooks, transportation services; and the construction of dormitories.

3. Disability Assistance: programs for seniors, for people with certain kinds of terminal illnesses, and for relatives who provide at-home care for disabled family members.

---

7. In 2011, this ministry was combined with several other social programs and institutions. The newly expanded ministry was renamed the Family and Social Policy Ministry (Aile ve Sosyal Politikalar Bakanlığı). As of 2021, this ministry is called the Family, Work, and Social Services Ministry (Aile, Çalışma ve Sosyal Hizmetler Bakanlığı).

8. On the AKP's family-centric political ideology, see Akkan (2018) and Kılıç (2008).

4. Special Assistance: soup kitchens, disaster and emergency aid, and assistance for individuals who accrued damages due to terrorist activity.

5. Health Assistance: support for disabled individuals, reimbursement of general health care premiums, and conditional cash transfers.

6. Assistance for Foreigners: social harmony support and conditional cash transfers ("Social Assistance Programs").

In addition to these programs, which combined cash provision, in-kind support, and material assistance, other programs focused on transforming the poor into independent and self-sufficient individuals. The "Income-Generation Projects" (Gelir Getirici Projeler) of the SYDGM, for example, sought to integrate the poor into the labor market. Like similar programs elsewhere, these social projects gave small financial loans to foster entrepreneurship among the poor. These projects taught the poor how to become active economic entrepreneurs—now that they knew "how to fish," there was no longer a need to "give them fish." Beginning in 2016, some social programs required applicants to register with the Turkish Employment Agency (İŞKUR, İş ve İşçi Bulma Kurumu) before they could be eligible for aid (Bolat 2016). Although microfinance and work-fare types of poverty relief programs were also introduced, they were not as widespread as social assistance programs that provided direct and immediate relief to low-income families or unemployed individuals.

These diverse welfare programs called for an expansion of financial means. While the budget allocated to relief programs had previously been a miniscule percentage of the gross domestic product (GDP), after 2002, the budget—both in terms of the absolute amount and the relative percentage—gradually increased as a variety of direct cash and in-kind programs were introduced. Between 2001 and 2004, the budget allocated to SYDGM and VGM tripled (Buğra and Adar 2007, 47). Social assistance-related spending increased tenfold between 2002 and 2018 ("Sosyal Koruma ve Gelir Dağılımı Göstergeleri" 2021). During the past two decades, the number of public SYD waqfs went from 750 in 1986 to 975 by 2013 and to 1003 by 2020 ("Sosyal Yardımlaşma ve Dayanışma Vakıfları" 2020).

Further, as a political party that originated from the Islamist movement, the AKP had to find a way to respond to the needs of grassroots networks and relief organizations, many of which had been negatively impacted by the repressive political environment of the post-1997 period. To this end, the AKP encouraged Islam-based networks of the 1990s to legalize their operations by registering as formal NGOs. Now connected to the SYDGM ministry, some of these organizations were retitled as social solidarity and mutual assistance associations (*sosyal yardımlaşma ve dayanışma dernekleri*) and were encouraged to focus on poverty relief (Göçmen 2014; Morvaridi 2013). Leading organizations in this new category included the Light House (Deniz Feneri), Anyone There? (Kimse Yok Mu), the Soulwater (Cansuyu) organizations, and the IHH. In addition to these more established national organizations, there are also various organizations that provide social services in Anatolian cities such as Kayseri and Konya.

In exchange for granting formal legitimacy, the AKP increased its oversight of Islamic charitable giving and incorporated these Islamic NGOs more directly into the governmental apparatus. The "NGOization" (Alvarez 1998; Choudry and Kapoor 2013) of Islamic charity had multiple ramifications.[9] Islam-based associational, civic, and philanthropic networks gradually abandoned their focus on "community-based voluntary relations," instead adopting organizational configurations that emphasized professional management and bureaucratic expertise (Sunar 2018, 15). While during the 1990s Islamist groups saw themselves as part of a network of grassroots activists, in contrast, Islamic NGOs established after the 2000s became willing to collaborate with the state (Zencirci 2014; Zihnioğlu 2018). These shifts were accompanied by intellectual transformations in Turkish Islamism, particularly the replacement of a pluralist, democratic conception of civil society with a state-centric one (Köseoğlu 2019).

---

9. For a similar take on the NGOization of Islamic charity, albeit in a different national context, see Borchgrevink (2020).

These Islamic NGOs are a specific breed. On the one hand, they diverge from earlier Islam-based associational, civic, and philanthropic networks in several ways: they specialize in poverty alleviation, provide humanitarian and emergency aid, operate at a national or international scale, raise funds through media advertisements and TV programs, and embrace bureaucratic forms of legitimacy, such as accountability, transparency, and professionalism (Göçmen 2018; Sunar 2018). On the other hand, they differ from their secular counterparts by using a divine vocabulary of faith-based giving, structuring their activities around the religious calendar, emphasizing the sacred obligation to give by including sections from the Qur'an and hadiths in their advertisements, and organizing special charity campaigns during prominent Islamic seasons, such as the month of Ramadan, the Five Islamic Holy Nights (Kandil), or the Holy Birth Week (Kutlu Doğum Haftası). As a result, these faith-based organizations attract donors, members, and volunteers who share a religious sensibility and come from conservative backgrounds. Funds are used for a wide range of charitable causes, such as the distribution of food packages, provision of free coal and cleaning materials, delivery of school supplies and winter clothes to poor children, administration of soup kitchens, and even the provision of temporary housing to people whose relatives are in the hospital.

In the eyes of the AKP, public SYD waqfs and Islamic NGOs were comparable organizations even if they fell on the opposite sides of the state–civil society distinction. Both sets of organizations served to "enact" Islamic visions of civilizational revival and populist reform by reviving Ottoman-Islamic cultures, practices, and traditions of social generosity, such as waqfs and sadaqa (chapters 2 and 3).

In addition to public SYD waqfs and Islamic NGOs, during the AKP era, municipal governments began to play a more central role in the distribution of aid (Bayraktar and Tansung 2016). Drawing from the legacy of 1990s Islamic municipal activism, the AKP encouraged municipal governments to ramp up their poverty alleviation efforts. Over the years, AKP municipal governments expanded and improved their social programs: they set up foodbanks, built donation boxes, and provided cash, food, and heating assistance through programs for the elderly, widowed, and ill individuals in their jurisdiction. The mantle of "social municipalism" (*sosyal belediyecilik*) was taken up by CHP municipal governments, and similar programs were implemented by HDP municipalities and were operative until the AKP's crackdown on Kurdish politicians after the June 2015 national elections. In the AKP's municipal districts, social service provision is often a collaborative effort, bringing together civil society practitioners, party bureaucrats, and local businesspeople (Buğra and Keyder 2006, 184; Eder 2010, 178). Cooperation and competition go hand in hand as they seek contacts, resources, and prestige. In fact, each one of these organizations—public, private, municipal—operates as one node of a broader political patronage network.

Several new laws and regulations facilitated the circulation of money between state institutions, business firms, Islamic NGOs, and public SYD waqfs. Changes to Charity Law No. 2860 in 2004 eased restrictions on fundraising. Some organizations immediately received a special "public interest" status, which meant that they could collect donations without getting permission from the government for each campaign (5871 Sayılı Yardım Toplama Kanunu 1983). Moreover, in contrast to previous laws which considered only private foundations to be eligible for tax exemptions, new regulations such as the Tax Law of 2004 enabled business firms to receive tax credits in exchange for donations. Another governmental shift came with the introduction of food banking in 2004 with Law No. 5179. By categorizing foodbanks as nonprofit organizations, this law made it possible for public SYD waqfs and Islamic NGOs to collect non-monetary donations, such as food and clothing items, and redistribute them to the poor (Görmüş 2018; Koç 2014). Further, the 2005 Municipal Law No. 5393 authorized municipal governments to solicit contributions and disburse social assistance as if they were voluntary organizations (Göçmen 2014, 99). At the same time, conservative politicians and state bureaucrats began to appear at various charity events and explicitly encouraged Islamic banks, corporations, and business firms to engage in philanthropy (Apaydın 2015). These firms were openly encouraged to donate food and clothing items as well as household goods in exchange for tax benefits.

The AKP also endorsed an Islamic language that extolled the virtues of charitable giving and encouraged volunteerism (Kaya 2015). For example, in 2012, the Family and Social Politics Ministry introduced the "Ambassadors of Love" project (Gönül Elçileri Projesi) in order to "create awareness about the concept of volunteerism, contribute to the expansion of volunteer work, and strengthen the human capital that can contribute to social development" ("Gönül Elçileri" 2018). This umbrella program included several subprojects that focused on children, women's empowerment, eldercare, intergenerational harmony, disabled individuals, and poverty. A similar scheme, this time targeting young adults, was introduced by the Sports and Youth Ministry in 2015. The "Young Volunteers" program aimed to "create opportunities for young people to serve Turkish society" by matching potential volunteers with various national and international projects ("Genç Gönüllüler: Bir Gençlik Projesi" 2018). Furthermore, the Ministry of Social Affairs and the Turkish Higher Education Council signed a protocol and introduced the "Community Service and Social Responsibility" projects. These state-sponsored programs were inspired by a new genre of social responsibility initiatives that were implemented across Turkey's private universities. Although these endeavors initially emerged as a result of university students' aspiration to help others, their success had a wide-ranging effect: as civic engagement became part of the curriculum, these voluntary activities lost their activist spirit, rather becoming a venue for university students to improve their employment chances.[10] This governmental emphasis on a culture of volunteerism, moreover, altered how Muslim individuals understood the goals of their volunteer work, creating a conjuncture where religious concerns mixed with liberal, humanitarian, and political motivations (chapter 5).

Lastly, the Muslim Social is distinctive due to its transnational foci. After coming to power, the AKP pioneered several initiatives to expand Turkey's regional economic power. For example, in 2003, the Turkish state introduced the "Strategy to Enhance Economic Relations with African

10. For an insightful critique of social responsibility projects organized by private universities in Turkey, see Shamir (2008).

Countries" (Afrika Ülkeleri ile Ekonomik İlişkilerin Geliştirilmesi Strate-jisi) and declared 2005 the "Year of Africa." Initiatives like these com-bined economic interests with philanthropic goodwill. In fact, after the AKP entered office, economic and humanitarian aid increased exponen-tially, amounting to millions of dollars by 2013, with Turkic nations usu-ally receiving more developmental aid, and Muslim-majority countries largely receiving more humanitarian aid (Kavaklı 2018, 617). Transna-tional humanitarian efforts were carried out through multiple channels, including state institutions, semi-governmental bodies, and NGOs such as the Turkish Cooperation and Coordination Agency (Türk İşbirliği ve Koordinasyon Ajansı Başkanlığı, TİKA), Disaster and Emergency Man-agement Authority (Afet ve Acil Yardım Yönetimi Başkanlığı, AFAD), Turkish Airlines, and Doctors Worldwide (Yeryüzü Doktorları Derneği; Dülger 2017). In addition, a variety of Islamic NGOs, including IHH, DF, and KYM, were encouraged to extend the scope of their developmental and humanitarian activities. Many of these NGOs operate "parallel" to the AKP's foreign policy and are supported by the state in several ways, such as providing technical and diplomatic support for their overseas operations and covering certain kinds of expenses, including the airplane tickets of volunteer doctors (Çomak 2011; Aras and Akpınar 2015; Çelik and İşeri 2016). The geopolitical expansion of the Islamic humanitarian imaginary also altered perceptions of religious duties and brought forth new constructions of the Muslim poor (chapter 4).

This historical account of shifting notions of the "social" question in Turkey illustrates that governmental interventions have had different goals in different times, ranging from the control of urban populations to the construction of modern citizenship, and from the management of business–labor relations to the provision of poverty aid. Although these interpretations were prominent in different historical periods, they have largely coexisted, supplanting instead of replacing previous ideas and practices. Despite these fluctuations, two aspects of the social question have remained the same: first, the fact that the Turkish state has always emphasized private charitable giving within its citizenship practices, eco-nomic paradigms, and political ideologies; and second, that the state's role in public welfare provision has neither increased nor decreased over time but has rather shifted its procedures and foci.

Against this historical background, I suggest that what distinguishes the AKP era is neither a shift toward a relief-based understanding of poverty alleviation nor a retrenchment of the welfare state, but rather a concerted effort to expand the welfare regime in accordance with reimagined practices, traditions, and institutions of Islamic charity. Nevertheless, as the next four chapters illustrate, the Muslim Social was not the product of a carefully laid out grand plan, but rather an apparatus borne out of multiple social projects, with complementary, yet distinct, aspirations.

2

Civilizational Revival, Neo-Ottomanism, and Good Governance

In July 2009, I met with one of the upper-level administrators of the Waqf General Ministry. I explained that I was interested in Turkish civil society and mentioned my recent archival research on the 1967 Waqf Law—which had been instrumental in introducing American-style philanthropic foundations in Turkey. In response, he told me that the 1967 Waqf Law had nothing to do with authentic waqfs. If I wanted to truly understand the origins of civil society in Turkey, I had to look elsewhere. Handing me a hefty book on Islamic law, he explained: "Take this, it is from my personal library; let it be my gift to you. Study it carefully so that you get the correct information about waqfs in our civilization." Taken aback, I asked him what he meant by the "correct information." He explained:

> Waqfs are the first examples of civil initiatives in Turkish history. Let me tell you. Once we were invited to a conference about foundations, so we went to Europe. We gave presentations, listened to talks, met with people, that kind of thing. I forgot most of those talks, but I still remember a conversation I had with a German guy. At one of these workshops, he turned to me and asked: "Why are you even here? There is nothing for you to learn from us. After all, it was the Ottomans who first came up with these benevolent institutions. We should be coming to your country so that we can learn from you."

He continued, "Many young people in Turkey today think that they must learn the fundamentals of good governance from Europe." However, there was no need to copy the West: "We do not need Europeans to teach us how to be compassionate, or how to be prosperous in the economic realm."

For him, the restoration of Ottoman-Islamic institutions was a necessary step for solving the governmental problems of Turkey. By giving this
account, he wished to impress upon me a sense of civilizational awareness.
He quickly moved between themes of Europe, philanthropic practices in
Islam, and civic culture to a discussion about Turkey's place in the world
order, its economic potential, and its culture of social generosity.

The conjunction of such referents presents a textbook example of the
conflation of global, Western, and neoliberal elements with local, traditional, and Ottoman-Islamic motifs. Like this administrator, many of
my interlocutors believed that waqfs provided a blueprint for an effective
model of governing poverty.[1] During myriad encounters, I was treated
as a recipient of indigenous knowledge, someone that had to be educated
about our "civilizational" past—a history that had been hidden from me.[2]
In fact, beginning in the 2000s, the AKP proclaimed itself as the agent
of Turkey's civilizational revival, supposedly leading the resuscitation of
Ottoman conventions, methods, and procedures of good governance. The
best way to govern Turkey, it was argued, was not by mimicking European
institutions, but by reviving local, native, indigenous-Islamic ones. Far
from being an official discourse mobilized by the ruling party, high-level
bureaucrats, or Muslim intellectuals, the Ottoman-Islamic model of good
governance was debated, negotiated, and practiced by various actors on
the ground.

In this chapter, I examine how the neo-Ottoman imaginary of civilizational revival promoted waqfs as model institutions for governing

1. According to Islamic law, when a piece of property is declared a waqf, it means that
the owner has promised to use assets and resources in the service of society. While the
literature on waqfs is vast and well beyond the scope of this book, my approach aligns well
with anthropological and historical perspectives that emphasize the flexibility of waqfs,
and that analyze waqf-making in relation to broader questions of cultural life, economic
practice, and political power (see Singer 2018). For two insightful overviews of the scope
of waqf studies, written twenty years apart, see Hoexter (1998) and Moumtaz (2018).

2. My interactions were similar to Patricia Sloane-White's (2017) encounters with
the Malay Muslim Sharia elite, where she felt like she was treated "no longer as a source of
knowledge, but a recipient of theirs" (25).

the Muslim Social.[3] This novel understanding of waqfs diverged from Kemalist notions that defined waqfs as relics of the Ottoman past—an era of ineffectual governance and economic backwardness.[4] The Ottoman Empire, according to official Turkish state ideology, had lagged behind Europe due to the refusal of religious leaders to embrace modernization. Their shortsighted readings of Islam, in turn, restricted imperial authorities' capacity and willingness to instigate a comprehensive transformation of cultural, economic, and political life. By contrast, the Islamic project of civilizational revival portrays waqfs as Ottoman-Islamic institutions of good governance.

Although the restoration of Ottoman-Islamic heritage is often presented as a guard against the harmful effects of Western capitalism, this heritage is produced in ways that reinforce neoliberal elements, reforms, and subjectivities. Chien Yang Erdem (2017), for instance, proposes the term "Ottomentality" to capture the "convergence of neoliberalism and neo-Ottomanism" (720). Likewise, when my interlocutors talked about good governance, they were referring to a form of power that was intrinsic to Ottoman lands—a "pure" and "timeless" set of institutional practices that set Muslim-majority polities apart from their Western counterparts. However, actors who glorified waqfs as institutions of good governance also came to understand elements of neoliberal state–civil society relations—that is, public–private partnerships, professionalization, institutionalization, financial transparency, and public accountability—as manifestations of civilizational revival. Through this governmental assemblage, neoliberal rationalities of good governance acquired new meanings.

3. By civilizational revival, I am referring to a conviction widely shared by AKP supporters that perceives the AKP era as one that seeks—and, according to some, has accomplished—the renewal of the Ottoman-Islamic civilization. I am not a party to debates concerning Turkey's civilizational "location," nor do I assess whether AKP has accomplished its civilizational ideals. Instead, I study civilizational revival as a multifaceted discourse and seek to uncover its claims, contradictions, and implications.

4. Statements about cultural heritage are a product of contemporary political concerns, even if they seem to focus primarily on the distant past. For a brief discussion, see McLean (2006).

Good governance—objective, scientific, and bureaucratic—was not associated with Western notions of technical expertise but understood as a key element of Ottoman-Islamic heritage. The interplay between languages of care and practices of management, in turn, transformed the Muslim Social into a technical problem. Put differently, civilizational revival not only produced a glorified vision of the imperial past, but also provided a conceptual framework for understanding and enacting neoliberal rationalities of collaboration, administration, and accountability among both Islamic NGOs and public SYD waqfs.

In the following pages, I analyze the interplay of Ottoman themes, Islamic motifs, and neoliberal elements, and map the civilizational discourse on waqf revival in Turkey.[5] By providing a selective reading of the Ottoman past, I show that the Islamic project of civilizational revival reimagined waqfs as models of good governance in order to solve perceived problems of the contemporary Turkish welfare regime. Before going into detail about how Islamic-neoliberal assemblages reconfigured state–civil society relations in Turkey, I briefly discuss the relationship between neoliberalism and good governance.[6]

Neoliberalism and Good Governance

The idea of good governance was promoted by the World Bank and the IMF alongside the introduction of structural adjustment programs (Grindle 2012; Nanda 2006; Woods 2000). For these reforms to work properly, the argument went, developing countries had to improve their administrative apparatus in ways that upheld and enhanced bureaucratic norms and practices associated with accountability, budgeting systems, effectiveness, transparency, expertise, and professionalism. Public-sector reform was thus a crucial aspect of aid conditionality (Gisselquist 2012; Mkandawire 2005). The European Union also promoted good governance, requiring candidate countries to undergo public administration reforms as part of the harmonization process (Börzel, Pamuk, and Stahn 2008; Hout 2012).

---

5. On the politics of waqf revival in Egypt, see Pioppi (2004).

6. For overviews of governance debates, see Dellepiane-Avellaneda (2010) and Walters (2004).

Developmental and foreign aid agencies, likewise, began to require NGOs in the Global South to adopt various managerial techniques in exchange for funding. Expectations about good governance thus became an integral element of civil society promotion and international development (Alvarez 2017; Brinkerhoff and Goldsmith 2005; Frewer 2013).

For its advocates, good governance is meant to eliminate "problematic" features of public administration, such as bribery, corruption, and patron-clientelism, thereby ensuring the provision of social services in an effective, measurable, and sustainable fashion (Gans-Morse et al. 2018; Mungiu-Pippidi 2015). When the managerial capacities of public institutions and civil society organizations improve, the argument goes, political democracy and economic development will become more likely outcomes for countries in the Global South.

In contrast, several studies have postulated that the good governance agenda sustains neoliberalism. Marxist and Gramscian accounts often see good governance as a political tool used by the IMF and World Bank to bolster the interests of private capital (Kiely 1998; Taylor 2004). Others argue that good governance reforms are problematic because they seek to restructure state institutions and civil society organizations in accordance with criteria and language drawn from the private sector (Knafo 2020; Lapsley 2009). Another line of criticism argues that good governance, due to its depoliticizing effect, is detrimental to democratic participation and rights-based claims-making (Davies 2007; Gledhill 2018; Kiely 1998; Mkandawire 2005; Swynegedouw 2005).

Scholars with a postcolonial sensibility further argue that the "good governance agenda" is based on Eurocentric understandings of state–civil society relations, which neglects the historical role of the state in developmental contexts (Andrews 2008; Brinkerhoff and Goldsmith 2005; Grindle 2012; Jones 2013; Kiely 1998; Nanda 2006). In their view, the good governance framework erroneously relies on a Weberian dichotomy and sets up a dichotomy between Western (i.e., rational, technical, and formal) bureaucracies and non-Western (i.e., personal, patronage-based, and informal) ones, thereby suggesting that local institutions often govern well even without adopting mechanisms of "good governance."

While much has been gained from both sets of criticisms, both over-look the fact that good governance is as much a local phenomenon as it is a global one. By considering good governance merely a part of the global/Western agenda, these studies reduce local actors who adopt, negotiate, and reinvent languages, mechanisms, and practices of good governance to victims, instead of acknowledging their creative agency.

In contrast, ethnographic studies highlight that "good governance" is often received, performed, and contested in specific localities in divergent ways; they demonstrate that these assemblages may result in unanticipated political and economic effects (Anders 2009; Eggen 2012; Frewer 2013). In addition to highlighting the centrality of the local context, such a frame-work also has implications for understanding the relationship between good governance and corruption. Since the 2000s, a series of corruption scandals—such as the 2009 Deniz Feneri (DF) case and the 2013 "Shoe Box" incidents—have occurred in Turkey, each bringing into question the nexus of political and economic connections between the state, Islamic NGOs, public SYD waqfs, and the Muslim bourgeoisie (Bedirhanoğlu 2021; Gürbüz 2014; Işık 2012; Kimya 2019). While it is possible to study the civilizational discourse of good governance and the adoption of manage-rial techniques, such as standardization, reporting, and tracking, merely as anti-corruption efforts, by contrast, I read these recent corruption scan-dals and the "culture of suspicion" (Bornstein 2012, 65) surrounding them as a productive moment for exploring the formation of Islamic-neoliberal assemblages around administrative norms of accountability, credibility, and legitimacy. My approach is thus similar to that of scholars who study corruption not as a problem to be solved but as a problematization to be unpacked (Harrison 2006). Seen in this way, the rise of public concern over NGO corruption reveals the widespread internalization of a certain set of expectations, beliefs, and norms about good governance, rather than their refusal (Parry 2000).

Neo-Ottomanism and Civilizational Revival

Nostalgia toward Ottoman waqfs fits squarely within the rising trend of neo-Ottomanism—one of the key features of contemporary Turkish public life since the 1980s.[7] The production, dissemination, and contestation of Ottoman-Islamic heritage has unfolded in conjunction with neoliberal economic reforms and the rise of political Islam. Departing from Kemalism's official history thesis, which portrayed Central Asia as the ancestral land of a pre-Islamic, Turkish civilization, Turgut Özal introduced neo-Ottomanism in the 1980s when he adopted the "Turkish-Islamic synthesis" as a guiding compass for the restoration of cultural heritage and national identity (Yavuz 2020, 107–26). During the 1990s, the Islamic-conservative Refah Party used neo-Ottomanist themes in its party programs and communicated a unique strand of imperial nostalgia to its supporters (Yavuz 2020, 127). For example, after the 1994 municipal elections, Refah mayors planned a series of cultural events focusing on Ottoman arts and textiles, organized large-scale commemorations of the 1453 Ottoman conquest of Istanbul, and sponsored the construction of Ottoman-themed tea gardens and restaurants (Çınar 2001; Çolak 2006; Houston 2001). Today, Ottoman nostalgia works on and across a variety of additional scales: reconfiguring the spatial parameters of urban life, altering the temporal logic of national commemorations, shaping the thematic universe of tourist attractions, and expanding the transnational reach of television dramas.[8] At the same time, contested narratives of Ottoman heritage abound, with different understandings of the Ottoman empire

7. Existing literature understands neo-Ottomanism as a foreign policy orientation, an assertion of national identity, a form of cultural heritagization, and a kind of spatial politics. Although my analysis resonates with these interrelated frameworks, I am more intrigued by the Islamic-neoliberal governmental assemblages that accompany neo-Ottomanism, rather than the intentions of those who adhere to it. On AKP's uses of neo-Ottomanism as a foreign policy framework, see Yanık (2016). For considerations of neo-Ottomanism as an articulation of Turkish national identity, see Çınar (2001), Yavuz (2020), and White (2012b, 9). On the question of how Ottoman nostalgia operates as a process of heritagization, see Zencirci (2014, 19). On neo-Ottomanism and the reconfiguration of urban space, see Walton (2010), Yavuz (2016), Mills (2011), and Öncü (2010).

8. On neo-Ottomanism in museums and television programs, see Aykaç (2019), Bozoğlu (2019), Carney (2014), Kraidy and Al-Ghazzi (2013), and Tunç and Tunç (2021).

playing a key role in the construction of the Turkish national identity and orientations toward modernity.[9]

While Ottoman nostalgia has diverse origins and multiple manifestations, its political power became more pronounced after the AKP came to power in 2002. The AKP's political vision marks the spatial borders of the Ottoman-Islamic civilization as the lands ruled by the Ottoman Empire during the height of its power (i.e., the sixteenth and seventeenth centuries), encompassing present-day Turkey, the Balkans, the Middle East, and North Africa. Civilizational revival calls for a restoration of imperial arrangements, connections, and identifications that were presumably shared across time and space. Turkey, seen as the heir of the Ottoman-Islamic civilization, is tasked with both protecting and reviving this cultural and political heritage. Such a nostalgic portrayal frames Turkey's troubles as a consequence of the mismatch between the country's cultural "essence" and its leading institutions. This argument is shared by some Muslim intellectuals who often use "civilization" as an analytical tool in their efforts to find authentically Islamic solutions to modern-day problems (Çınar 2019). By harnessing both the nostalgic appeal and the intellectual significance of the civilizational imaginary, the AKP presents itself as the agent of civilizational revival; blames the Kemalist modernization project for the eradication of Ottoman cultural, economic, social, and political institutions; and seeks to reclaim Turkey as a regional power (Çınar 2018).

Whereas the AKP deploys themes of Ottoman nostalgia strategically and selectively, its promises of civilizational revival, moreover, seek to repudiate the legitimacy of the Kemalist regime. Kemalism, the founding ideology of the Turkish Republic, understood Western civilization to be universal and aspired to make Turkey a part of it. This goal was to be achieved through imitating European cultural norms and borrowing technological advances. The construction of Turkish nationhood as

9. For information on competing Ottomanisms in Turkey, see Carney (2019), Fisher Onar (2009), and Öngür (2015).

an ethnic identity that originated from Central Asia further excluded the Ottoman-Islamic past while setting up an essentialist difference between Western civilization and local culture (Kadıoğlu 1998, 2).

The primary goal of Kemalist ideology, in other words, was to ensure that Turkey belongs to Western civilization, and this goal was to be achieved through a series of political reforms. By contrast, the Islamic project of civilizational revival argues that Kemalism, by eradicating Ottoman cultural, economic, social, and political institutions, distanced the Turkish people from their true essence.[10] The glorification of the imperial past thus serves as a critique of the Turkish state establishment. In this view, the Kemalist notion of civilization was ill-conceived, as it portrayed the Ottoman Empire as economically backward, defined Islamic cultural values as inferior, and, in doing so, posited that Turkey's "contemporarization" could only be achieved by mimicking the West. But adherents of the Islamic project of civilizational revival claim that Kemalism's focus on implanting European institutions in the name of modernization pushed the country backward instead of propelling it forward.[11]

Civilizational revival further evokes a notion of religion that is less about individual devotion or public morality, but that provides the institutional backbone of the polity.[12] Islam is understood to provide a blueprint for good governance that has been erased, forgotten, or distorted during the modern nation-state era. In this perspective, many, if not all, political, economic, and social problems faced by Turkish Muslims as well as Muslims elsewhere—such as crime, poverty, or violence—are caused by abandoning their civilizational identity and adopting European ways of living, thinking, and governing. It is only by reviving the arrangements

10. Yet, it must also be noted that, much like Kemalism, most Islam-inspired conservative groups in Turkey also take the distinction between the West and the East as a given. For critical readings of the uses and abuses of "civilization" in Turkish politics, see Dalacoura (2017) and Kuzmanovic (2008).

11. For more on neo-Ottomanist articulations of Kemalism, see Christofis (2018) and Ege (2022).

12. On the AKP's pragmatic use of Islamism and neo-Ottomanism, see Gontijo and Barbosa (2020).

exemplified by institutions like waqfs that Turkish Muslims can effectively govern society and the economy.

The Ottoman Empire as a Waqf Civilization

After the AKP came to power in 2002, the idea that the Ottoman Empire was, first and foremost, a waqf civilization was gradually produced and disseminated by a variety of public institutions, namely, bureaus, offices, ministries, and directorates; meanwhile, other organizations, including Islamic NGOs, conservative thinktanks, local associations, and universities, contributed to the process from outside of mainstream politics. Initially, the VGM and the SYDGM partnered with Islamic NGOs and organized a series of conferences in 2003.[13] Panels covered topics such as the governance of poverty according to Islam and the significant role waqfs presumably played in different regions of the Ottoman Empire. A couple of years later, the AKP declared 2006 the national Waqf Civilization Year. In addition to an international conference examining Ottoman heritage through the lens of social policy, numerous activities, such as essay competitions, photography contests, theatrical plays, and walking tours, were organized to generate a "waqf consciousness" in Turkish society.[14] Waqf week celebrations—which ordinarily took place during the second week of May without much participation from the general public—became well-publicized occasions that brought together bureaucrats, politicians, intellectuals, waqf managers, volunteers, and other civil society practitioners. In addition, an increasing number of Muslim intellectuals began to write articles, books, essays, and op-eds examining the civic potential of Ottoman waqfs.[15] Many of these public thinkers gave well-attended speeches

13. These include the Waqf Civilization Symposium (Vakıf Medeniyeti Sempozyomu, Ankara, May 12–13, 2003), the International Waqf Symposium (Uluslararası Vakıf Sempozyomu, Ankara, December 15–17, 2003), and the Poverty Symposium (Yoksulluk Sempozyomu, Istanbul, May 31–June 1, 2003).

14. For instance, see "2006 Vakıf Medeniyeti Yılı" (2006).

15. It is not possible to provide a comprehensive list of nongovernmental publications that discuss the relationship between waqfs, the Ottoman empire, and the Islamic model of good governance in ways that echo AKP's waqf civilization rhetoric. Nevertheless, the

at Islamic associations, thinktanks, and NGOs where participants were informed of the ways in which Ottomans lived, practiced, and spread the Islamic culture of compassion and solidarity.

Through these multiple channels, waqfs were promoted as a model institution for governing the Muslim Social. The waqf civilization rhetoric disseminated a new understanding of waqfs that fundamentally differed from previous political articulations, charitable practices, and institutional arrangements. Waqfs were redefined as social institutions that operate on a voluntary basis, and that address problems without seeking the approval of political authorities or relying on public funds. In this glorified version of the Ottoman past, social problems were solved effortlessly and immediately. Ottoman-Turkish Muslims shared a culture of social generosity, which, it was argued, allowed addressing collective problems through a unique combination of religious piety and mutual solidarity.[16]

The waqf civilization rhetoric provided the forms and formulas through which political authorities comprehended and rationalized the ongoing reconfiguration of Turkey's social welfare institutions. Most of my interlocutors likewise evoked Ottoman nostalgia when they discussed new governmental rationalities that were being implemented by Islamic NGOs and public SYD waqfs. Social imaginaries of civilizational revival thus traveled across sites, groups, and institutions. In the following pages, I discuss how references to the Islamic culture of social generosity, sentimental allusions to the waqf institution, and remarks about the effectiveness of social governance during the Ottoman past saturated this space.

Managers of the Heart

In response to my questions about Islamic charity, my interlocutors would talk nostalgically about the Ottoman culture of social generosity and explain that Islamic institutions were key examples of good governance.

---

following articles and books provide a starting point: Kazıcı (2003), Taşcı (2017), Topbaş (2008), and Öztürk (2005).

16. This paragraph summarizes my work on the distinctiveness of AKP's waqf civilization rhetoric. For a detailed discussion, see Zencirci (2015a, 547–48; 2014, 19).

For example, when I asked Mehmet, the manager of a small waqf in Ankara, about obstacles that he faced in overseeing charity work, he replied:

MEHMET: This waqf business relates to matters of the heart. Did you know that in the Ottoman era, there were waqfs built to provide water to migrating birds? What a civilization! Do you think that such a pure religion, such a compassionate culture, one which deeply cared about migrating animals, would not have been concerned with the needs of the poor and the downtrodden?

ZENCIRCI: What do you mean by "matters of the heart"?

MEHMET: During the Ottoman times, people gave voluntarily. There were waqfs everywhere. Every single needy group was taken care of. Orphans, students, widows, the elderly. These people knew that they were not alone. The rich were not selfish. They had the fear of Allah in their heart. This was also why waqf assets were administered carefully. Trustees understood their responsibility, they kept detailed records, wrote everything down, created long-term plans. They were managers of the heart; in our civilization, this is what civil society is supposed to act like.

Mehmet's golden narrative of the Ottoman past thus conjured ideals of good governance as much as it evoked themes of religious benevolence. He explained the "matters of the heart" in three intersecting ways that fused religious, affective, and managerial languages. The first theme is one of Islamic benevolence, akin to a unified sense of religious responsibility. This unity was possible because the rich shared with the poor willingly, enthusiastically, and "from the heart." Compassion and solidarity, coupled with a deep-seated concern for the well-being of disadvantaged members of society, defined the Ottoman social tapestry. The second theme is one of religion: Islam was the social glue that united the haves and the have-nots around the common goal of societal well-being. Whether the wealthy gave out of "pure" motivations or due to a "fear of Allah," their gifts were generous, nonetheless. The final theme related to the management of waqf assets and properties; as "managers of the heart," Ottoman waqf trustees were administrators who governed effectively and responsibly.

Like Mehmet, many of the people I met at Islamic NGOs and public SYD waqfs—bureaucrats, civil servants, donors, managers, volunteers—frequently invoked the "official" discourse of civilizational revival, but their concerns were mixed with pragmatic considerations about their public legitimacy, as well as the everyday administrative minutia of running an organization focused on poverty alleviation. In the following pages, I demonstrate how these actors comprehended and implemented managerial techniques of good governance, such as collaboration, administration, and accountability, as exemplars of civilizational revival.

State–Civil Society Relations as a Collaborative Partnership

One of the significant claims of the waqf civilization rhetoric pertained to state–civil society relations. The Ottoman-Islamic model of good governance was argued to foster collaboration instead of conflict. This managerial rationality suggested that the Muslim Social was most effective if state institutions and civil society organizations worked together in poverty alleviation efforts (Akyıldız 2003, 107). Although the rationality of collaboration was justified through alternate and competing notions of state power, each discursive claim invoked the heritage of Ottoman-Islamic waqfs. These varied interpretations illustrate the ways in which managerial techniques came to be considered an example of Ottoman-Islamic good governance, further justifying the idea that social problems are best solved through technical solutions.

The AKP called for a collaborative state–civil society relationship by describing Ottoman-Islamic waqfs as social service providers that operated without overburdening the state. For example, in 2018, during a speech he gave for an *iftar* dinner at the Ensar Foundation, Erdoğan said:

> Today, waqfs continue to provide services to our society. These are often services that the state is unable to provide. The inefficient and cumbersome mechanisms of the state, especially when state power is in the hands of those with ill intentions, creates a wide gap between state and society. For this reason, even when the state is strong, even when those

who govern are esteemed, the significance of civil society organizations, especially waqfs, remain important in our civilization. ("Vakıf Geleneği, Kardeşliğimizin En Kuvvetli Bağını Oluşturuyor" 2015)

This is a statement about the role and significance of waqfs in the Ottoman-Islamic civilization. It explains that civic organizations have a function when an otherwise "strong" state is "unable to provide."

Echoing this theme, Muslim intellectuals also defined waqfs as a pillar of Ottoman-Islamic good governance—an example of how civic actors could effectively serve the public good without overburdening the state. Their statements converged on a key point: state institutions and civil society organizations should work together to achieve good governance. Economic historian Ahmet Tabakoğlu (2006) wrote: "Even though the Ottoman waqf system was an independent and democratic form of civil society, it was not really outside the purview of the state" (72). Waqfs were defined as "peculiar civil society organizations of the East" that played a key role in "balancing income inequality in our civilization" (Güner 2004); they were described as a "philosophy of governance" that "integrated state with society so that the state might continue to prosper" (Öztürk 2005, 15) and defined as a model of governance that lacked a "state–society dichotomy." During the Ottoman Empire, the argument went, "state and society were merely two parts of an organic whole," and Ottoman society had a "self-governing" civic dynamism that was nurtured by institutions such as markets, gardens, coffeehouses, brotherhoods, and waqfs (Güneş and Kızılay 2011, 164). In this view, Ottomans had mastered the art of good governance because they delegated public responsibilities to waqfs instead of relying on the centralized "state" to provide social services (Akyıldız 2003, 107–8). Along the same lines, the head manager of the Social Welfare Ministry suggested that the Ottoman Empire was a "waqf heaven," where waqfs took care of public services, such as education, health, and infrastructure, as well as social assistance, social security, and employment programs (Emiroğlu 2009).

Echoing these themes, social service providers collaborated in various ways. Public SYD waqfs and Islamic NGOs shared information and resources, worked together on projects, and, in some cases, even borrowed

2.1 Compassion Market (*Şefkat Mağazası*), which operated through a collaborative partnership between the municipality and the KYM organization, 2010, Gaziantep. Photograph by the author.

vehicles, storage space, and voluntary labor from one another (see figure 2.1). It was common for me to run into someone I met a while ago while visiting another kind of organization, especially if those actors were involved in social service provision in the same district. Often, at the end of an interview, my interlocutors would tell me whom I should get in touch with next, and these suggestions included members of both state institutions and civil society organizations. The ways in which they talked about their collective efforts to eradicate poverty in their surrounding neighborhood almost always emphasized the need for collaboration among sectors.

While the yearning for civilizational revival, and narratives about Ottoman-Islamic waqfs, were constants, what was salient about these conversations was the multivocality of political rationales they provided to justify the logic of collaboration. Despite variation, most accounts calling for civilizational revival venerated central political authority: even when civil society organizations were revered, it was only because of their capacity to serve the state through their creativity and enthusiasm.

Some NGO managers, for example, perceived civil society as a space of innovation. Designing a successful project, which could later be taken up by other—public or private—actors, was seen not only as a measure of success, but also as a form of reviving Ottoman-Islamic institutions of good governance. On this issue, Faruk (the manager of a small Islamic NGO) explained: "Of course, as civil society organizations, we cannot solve every problem. All we can do is to produce models that can later be used by the state and other organizations." Another manager stated:

> Waqfs are not places that just give bread, clothing, or a little bit of money to whomever knocks on their door. In fact, their function is the exact opposite. These institutions would look around carefully, examine their surroundings, and once they have identified problems, then they would come up with a plan to address issues.

Thus, for him, civil society organizations' main advantage was their ability to design specific projects to solve local problems.

Individuals working at public SYD waqfs also embraced the idea that producing and sharing model projects was a form of state–civil society collaboration. Yet, while members of Islamic NGOs argued that effective social programs were more likely to be designed by civil society organizations, waqf employees believed the opposite. In their minds, effective models were best devised in the public domain, and then shared with civic practitioners—that was the value of collaboration. Fatih, a manager of a public SYD waqf in Istanbul, explained:

> Our primary job is figuring out what kind of projects are more likely to produce outcomes. Next, we share these projects, with all the details, plans, and information, with other organizations. Since we are backed by the state, we have a little bit more room for exploration, for innovation. If we make a mistake . . . we can fix it quickly, we can find funds, or get some support. Once we figure out the details, then other organizations can just carry out similar projects.

For Fatih, innovation rather than implementation was to be the main focus of public SYD waqfs. In his view, the state was not cumbersome; rather, its financial strength was what gave public SYD waqfs room to explore. Moreover, these tenets of good governance were drawn from the Ottoman past. "Waqfs were civil initiatives," Fatih said. "The waqf deed specified a task, but beyond that, the trustees could decide what needs to be done. They knew how to respond to changing circumstances." Resourcefulness, speed, and creativity were central to good governance, and these characteristics allowed public SYD waqfs to design successful model projects.

In addition, Islamic NGOs and public SYD waqfs were expected to work together because of their common goals. While Islamic NGOs' relief efforts were argued to be a strategic element of the public welfare regime, public SYD waqfs were likened to civil society organizations due to their shared volunteer spirit. In their case, NGO personnel asserted that their job was to assist the state in fulfilling its public responsibilities. In 2010, Murat, the manager of a small branch of the KYM organization, said:

> Lots of people criticize us; they think we are only giving out handouts. But, let me ask you, when you look at the developed countries of the North, what does the state do? The state provides everything, they even leave milk on their citizens' doorsteps. . . . This is exactly what we are doing here; our job is to fulfill the duties of the welfare state (*sosyal devlet*).

Murat's account illustrates that, for him, the social services provided by the KYM organization were neither a replacement nor a criticism of the Turkish state, but rather an example of the state fulfilling its social responsibility. When elaborating on the topic of state power, he said: "There is a popular saying among us: 'Let the people live so that the state might live on.' What we do is similar, we serve both our people and our state; this way, we contribute to unity and solidarity."[17] By referring to this well-known phrase, Murat maintained that the work done by an organization such

17. This saying, "let the people live, so that the state might live on" (*insanı yaşat ki devlet yaşasın*), is attributed to Sheikh Edebali, who told it to Osman, the founder of the Ottoman Empire. The phrase allegedly became one of the principles of imperial governance.

as the KYM was a form of service, upholding both Ottoman traditions of good governance and extending the scope of patriotic philanthropy. In this interpretation, collaboration was less about competence and more about serving the state.

Managers and workers of public SYD waqfs expressed a similar pro-statist sentiment regarding the role of civil society. For example, Çetin, an enthusiastic manager of a public SYD waqf in Ankara, told me:

> We might be civil servants (*memur*); I know that our salary is paid by the state, but other than that, you need to understand that what we do here is exactly what a civil society organization does. That's why I tell my personnel that they need to be as motivated as NGO volunteers, especially since they work for the state.

In this account, Çetin emphasized the similarities between public SYD waqfs and Islamic NGOs, pointing out that both "worked for the solution of problems, fostered mutual aid, and operated as a bridge between the haves and the have-nots." Civil servants of SYD waqfs had to be as energetic and enthusiastic as volunteers, especially since they were paid to do the work that volunteers did for free.

At first, I found Çetin's argument that there was not much of a difference between Islamic NGOs and public SYD waqfs rather strange. After all, these organizations belong to opposite sides of the public–private divide, and they are subject to different rules and regulations. However, I quickly realized that this interpretation was quite common. Collaboration between public waqfs and civil society organizations was to be expected, as Fatih, an employee of the same public SYD waqf, explained: "All of these institutions are sustained by the waqf spirit; we are inspired by the philanthropic traditions of our civilization. Why should we pretend as if we are separate?" Other managers and employees of public SYD waqfs provided similar arguments: some discussed how the "fascination with the West" had created a "unnatural rift between state and civil society," and others called for "learning how the institutions of our geography are meant to work." Each of these accounts explained the rationale of collaboration in terms of the inherent correspondence between the state and civil society, which, in their eyes, ensured good governance.

Sometimes actors explained the need for collaboration by discussing the relative shortcomings of state institutions and civil society organizations. For instance, NGOs were depicted as establishments that are better equipped to provide social services. Instead of undermining the logic of collaboration, however, this assessment reinforced the idea that good governance requires compliant engagements between government, business, and civil society. According to some actors, the state was capable of effectively addressing social problems, but lacked sufficient financial resources to do so. On this point, Zeynep, a university student who occasionally volunteered at the Istanbul office of the DF organization, told me that she volunteered because she wanted to "assist the state." She believed that it would have been better if the state "could reach all the poor," but since it could not, "charity organizations had to step up their efforts." Others, however, believed that the state, because of politicians' self-interest, was incapable of providing aid in an objective manner. Didem, one of DF's volunteer coordinators, explained this as it related to the Green Card (Yeşil Kart) program, which was introduced in the mid-1990s to provide the poor with access to free health care services. Didem said: "Look at the Green Card program. The reality is [that] even people who drive a BMW might have a green card. Why? Because the state cannot provide aid like we do. They cannot be as effective because they are concerned with immediate political gain." Didem's rendering of collaboration was unique because it involved a critique: politicians gave aid to further their electoral prospects, whereas civic actors understood poor relief in objective, neutral, and technical terms.

Actors from public SYD waqfs tended to justify the rationale of collaboration by discussing the perceived limitations of civil society. Prevalent reasons cited were a lack of financial resources and difficulties in recruiting volunteers. Without direct access to such resources, civil society organizations struggled to envision a sustainable program of poverty relief. Esma, a DF manager, raised this exact point with the following statement:

> In Islam, there is a well-functioning system for this. When a wealthy Muslim creates a waqf, he designates that income derived from rent or the selling of agricultural products will support a soup kitchen, a school,

or whatever else a community might need. If we still had such a system, then we would not have to ask rich people for money in order to sustain our operations.

Like Esma, actors from public SYD waqfs attributed financial difficulties faced by Islamic NGOs to the eradication of Ottoman waqf culture. But while NGO personnel believed that wealthy Muslims could learn to engage in organizational giving as long as there was mutual trust, civil servants of public SYD waqfs felt differently. When I asked Çetin why he reached out to local organizations to share any additional funds or resources (usually donated food boxes that were close to their expiration date, or surplus clothing that did not fit into overflowing storage rooms), he said: "These institutions, they do not have the support of the state like we do. We have to support them, obviously, but it is also good for us to collaborate on these matters so that these boxes are delivered effectively and quickly to those in need." According to him, the state ought to assist civil society organizations to overcome monetary challenges. While affirming the idea that these Islamic NGOs were not exactly like Ottoman waqfs, as they lacked property-based trusts, Çetin also paid homage to the idea that civil society organizations, and not state institutions, were efficient providers of social services. In his view, the rationale of collaboration combined the financial strength of the public domain with the organizational agility and outreach capacity of civil society.

In short, arguments in favor of a collaborative state–civil society relationship involved multiple and, at times, contradictory messages. Despite their multivocality, however, each endorsed a common view that the relationship between governmental authorities and civic actors should be amicable. In turn, everyday actions reinforced these perceptions; through social visits and formal gatherings, actors involved with Islamic NGOs and public SYD waqfs found ways to collaborate. They pooled information, transferred resources, contributed to projects, shared volunteers, and exchanged names of individuals with the requisite political and economic connections. In the end, this collaborative form of state–civil society relations was similar to what scholars have referred to as the "neoliberal NGO discourse" (Kamat 2004; Shivji 2007), a depoliticized understanding of civil society that undermines activism. Yet, instead of being initiated or imposed by Western development paradigms, this collaborative model of good governance was understood as the revival of the Ottoman-Islamic heritage.

The Bureaucratization of Islamic Charity

The idea that traditional waqfs were models of Ottoman-Islamic good governance was communicated to Islamic NGOs and public SYD waqfs through conferences, trainings, and workshops. The project of civilizational revival was regularly evoked to justify the bureaucratization—formalization, professionalization, and institutionalization—of Islamic charity. Across Islamic NGOs and public SYD waqfs, bureaucratic rationalities were perceived as Islamically authentic modifications to poverty governance.[18] In contrast to amateurish and informal face-to-face networks, the Muslim Social was now believed to call for professional attitudes and a solid institutional structure. The cultivation of a religious sensibility toward suffering persisted, though not in its old form in which assistance was provided without much concern about the proper management of funds, the internal procedures of organizations, or attitudes of volunteers. Instead, faith was now seen as a fertile, yet disordered, moral terrain that must be managed through the construction of institutional structures and cultivation of professional demeanors.

Many of my interlocutors brought up themes of formalization, institutionalization, and professionalization when they discussed organizational change. Among Islamic NGOs, these changes were defined as indispensable elements of good governance and a path toward recovering the managerial excellence of Ottoman institutions. Ahmet, one of the mid-level managers of DF, for example, discussed the need for institutionalization with reference to charity efforts that took place after the 1999 Marmara earthquake[19]:

18. On the bureaucratization of Islam elsewhere, see Mohamad (2020) and Müller (2018).

19. For a discussion of how the aftermath of the 1999 Marmara earthquake reconfigured state–civil society relations in Turkey, see Paker (2005).

You need to abide by rules. This is crucial. . . . For example, during the earthquake, a variety of different groups tried to help. . . . I told them, I explained: "You cannot do this by merely distributing what you have. Whichever group you belong to, you need to come together and do this charity work in an institutionalized manner. You cannot be irregular; you cannot just do whatever you please." Rules, records, transparency, regulation—all these things must be implemented.

Ahmet saw the DF as a pioneer of institutionalization, and he held that other organizations lacked the managerial-technical knowledge required to collect donations and distribute aid effectively. In his mind, Turkish civil society organizations had to "do this charity work in an institutionalized manner" because, as he later added: "unlike Ottoman times, most people today do not know how to manage an organization." Thus, for Ahmet, abiding by rules and regulations was necessary not only to gain public trust, but also to uphold the Ottoman-Islamic model of good governance.

Managers of other Islamic NGOs frequently discussed their ongoing institutionalization efforts. When talking about how their day-to-day work changed over time, Mehmet, for example, said: "We have become organized; this is the most significant transformation." One of the key shifts was organizational decision-making. According to Mehmet, they had come to understand that a civil society organization had to have "portable (*seyyar*) units that can make autonomous decisions independent of each other." To this end, they had created units tasked with overseeing "student affairs" or "social assistance." Each unit provided specific training to NGO personnel and volunteers so that they might "gain expertise in their area of management." When talking about these units, Mehmet invoked the administrative structure of Ottoman waqfs:

Remember, waqfs were highly structured. It was part of their architecture. If someone was running the soup kitchen, then that was their focus. If someone was teaching the children, then that was their main contribution. No one tried to do everything all at once. Instead, they learned to do one or two tasks very well.

While Mehmet thought that good governance referred to the administrative division of labor between modular units, others emphasized the need for institutional legitimacy. To this end, DF frequently sought the inspection of external certification agencies, namely, the American Quality Assessors, the Can International Independent Accounting Organization, and the International Organization for Standardization (ISO). These third-party certification bodies audited, evaluated, monitored, and certified internal procedures and operations of the DF organization, as well as several other Islamic NGOs. These audits were conducted in addition to the compulsory investigations of public institutions, such as the Administration Office of Associations (Dernekler Dairesi), the VGM, or the Turkish Ministry of Internal Affairs. Among these various external audits, my interlocutors frequently mentioned the ISO 9002 Quality Management Certificate as a key marker of their NGO legitimacy (*Deniz Feneri Sosyal Yardımlaşma ve Dayanışma Derneği Yıllık Raporu* 2002). Sevda, for example, told me that they obtained this certificate due to their "sensitivity and thoughtfulness," and explained that, in doing so, DF started a "new trend" among Islamic NGOs. She elaborated:

> In my heart, I feel no need for these certificates. I know how carefully we work, how seriously we approach our duties, I see how much our volunteers worry about making a mistake. We make sure to teach them about rules and their responsibilities. We tell them that they need to uphold the procedures of our civilization. We do not seek certificates for our own gratification, but we know that they are useful for other groups.

Sevda's narrative of institutionalization—a revival of Ottoman-Islamic good governance, inspected and certified by Western authorities—exemplifies the way in which a form of bureaucratic rationality was assembled on the ground. In their eyes, the process of institutionalization was primarily about reviving long-forgotten administrative customs of the Ottoman past, even if the process often resembled the pro-Western orientation of the Kemalist modernization project.

Bureaucratization also called for the professionalization of the volunteer force. It was no longer sufficient to have pious people informally mobilize around the cause of Islam while leading a life of service. Rather, volunteers were expected to conduct themselves in a professional manner, realize that this is a "serious job," and, as Sevda, who was one of the volunteer coordinators of DF put it, accept that the organization "is not just a place that they can come and go as they please." Sevda asserted that being a professional volunteer meant treating the organization like a regular job. Volunteers had to keep their promises, stick to a regular schedule, and cultivate formal relationships with other volunteers.

One of the ways Islamic NGOs cultivated professionalism among volunteers was by requiring them to attend a wide range of training programs. NGO personnel and volunteers also attended workshops on supply chain management to ensure standardized internal procedures (Deniz Feneri Derneği 2006). These training programs ranged from one-day events quickly put together by volunteer coordinators at local offices to multi-day events organized at convention centers. In some cases, preliminary training about social projects occurred as part of new volunteer recruitment efforts ("Kimse Yok Mu Derneği'nin Gönüllü Bayan Üyeleri Yeni Gönüllüler Kazanıyor" 2011). While new recruits often had to complete an orientation program before they could begin, even experienced volunteers were expected to participate in various instructional programs on an ongoing basis. Many of these programs combined lectures with informal conversations, sometimes including a talk by an invited speaker presenting on topics such as "project management" or "effective communication skills."

After attending these programs, volunteers often talked about professionalism as the behavioral orientation of a waqf person (*vakıf insan*). In Turkey, this term is generally used to refer to a devout individual eager to share their wealth with others through philanthropic giving.[20] But when volunteers from Islamic NGOs used this term, they were also referring to the type of volunteer work that was done in a serious, "professional" manner. Nur told me that her volunteer experience had taught her that each individual had to "act responsibly" so that the "institution" (*kurum*) can operate in an effective manner and be successful. She added: "I learned that being a waqf person requires one to be serious and reliable. I think that my professional demeanor will give me a higher chance of getting a

20. Also see Işık (2014, 315–16).

job once I graduate from college." Similarly, Emin explained how his ideas about charity work changed since he began volunteering: "Before, I did not realize how much seriousness would be expected from me. But now I understand that one does not have to be rich or influential to be a waqf person, but has to be sincere in each step."

Embracing a professional demeanor was not easy for everyone. Although those who sought to gain "job skills" from volunteering tolerated, or even welcomed, the importance of professionalism, such an emphasis also presented a challenge for those who volunteered merely to enhance their social life by making friends. Aware that a heightened focus on professionalism did not always resonate with volunteers, during one volunteer meeting, Sevda emphasized that a professional demeanor did not mean that they did not care for one another: "We are here to do this service in the most beautiful way. To achieve this goal, we need to abide by rules; let's not forget that we are accountable not only to those who entrusted their donations to us but, more importantly, to Allah." Here, Sevda tried to counter volunteers' feelings that a professional demeanor required them to spend less time socializing with one another. But she also suggested that professionalism was a religious obligation, and that the best way to serve the Muslim Social was to put aside the desire to socialize with others.

Managers' attitudes also shifted in response to this emphasis on professionalization. As Ahmet said: "The work of civil society is a serious business, but today, in our country, there is a lackadaisical attitude. What we need is a professional approach, so that the future of an organization does not depend on this or that individual." Later, when explaining the relationship between institutional endurance and managerial skills, he referred to the role played by *vakfiyes* (waqf charters): "When a founder creates a waqf, their wishes are written down in a *vakfiye*, and a plan for the future of the building, school, or hospital is drawn up. And then, whomever becomes the trustee acts in accordance with this document." In Ahmet's view, professionalism meant acting in a manner that ensured the long-term survival of an institution. He asserted that following rules would make it possible to achieve this goal—in the same way that trustees of Ottoman waqfs adhered to the wishes of the founders.

In addition to Islamic NGOs, SYD waqfs were also objects of administrative reform. As part of the reconfiguration of the welfare regime, the AKP required the SYDGM to audit the internal operations and financial procedures of local offices. Over the years, the SYDGM introduced several decrees that sought to align SYD waqfs with the paradigm of good governance. In 2010, the SYDGM introduced a strategic plan "to form a strong correspondence between institutional identity and the provision of social services" (Cemalettin 2010). The ministry's magazines, as well as actors on the ground, referred to these efforts as a "new rearrangement" (*yeniden yapılanma*) and an "institutional restoration" (*kurumsal yenilenme*). For example, it was declared that "the newly founded forty-three SYD waqfs . . . overcame adaptation problems through focusing on institutional restructuration," and were thereby able to "serve citizens quickly and efficiently" ("Yeni İlçe Vakıflarından Sancaktepe Görevinin Başında: 'Halkın Vakfa Ulaşmasında Hiçbir Sıkıntı Yaşamadık'" 2009).

The institutionalization of SYD waqfs intertwined administrative, spatial, and temporal dimensions as well. Organizational change was part of a larger process of administrative reform that introduced management techniques that were popular in the business sector (Ağartan and Kuhlmann 2019; Demirkaya 2016; Tan 2020). As a result, SYD waqfs were instructed to reconfigure internal procedures and rethink rules governing their interactions with the public, including donors and recipients. As I discuss in detail in chapter 3, SYD waqfs also introduced information systems, adopted communication technologies, and developed strategies for collecting and organizing client data. This process of organizational change flattened and streamlined SYD waqfs. Another aspect concerned the spatial configuration and outward appearance of these welfare offices. Since most SYD waqfs were housed within governorship buildings, they often did not have a dedicated space that amounted to anything larger than a small room. The institutional rearrangement of social assistance programs, however, relocated most SYD waqfs to new buildings, or at least gave them access to several rooms detached from the main building. Other modifications adorned SYD waqfs with a "consumer-oriented" outlook. Many offices introduced take-a-ticket countertop ticket dispensers, seated waiting areas, and walkup counters where applicants could have semiprivate conversations. Civil servants were told that these bureaucratic, electronic, and spatial changes improved client satisfaction by reducing response times. Providing fast and effective service was a key goal. Çetin, when explaining the transformation of their day-to-day operations, said:

> Serving our people is key for us. We do not work like a dusty public office. No employee of this waqf can spend the entire day drinking tea, chatting away, avoiding their responsibilities. Such lethargy, or the usual "go today, come back tomorrow" kind of attitude, is unbefitting for our culture, our civilization.

Similar comments described the cleanliness of the space, having a separate entryway, or being accessible to those who came seeking assistance as ways to achieve managerial efficiency and restore civilizational identity.

Aliye, a social market's female manager, maintained that "People no longer must get up at sunrise to get in line like we used to do at hospital doors during the 1990s. Like our ancestors, we help the poor in a respectful and efficient manner." For her, seemingly mundane aspects of organizational change reestablished a link to the Ottoman past. These managerial adjustments were not just about helping the poor, but also about restoring the glory of imperial good governance.

Like NGO personnel, employees of public SYD waqfs were also increasingly expected to adhere to professional norms. Over the years, several training programs were organized for this purpose. In 2009, managers of SYD waqfs attended a training about social policy, poverty, and problem solving ("Sosyal Yardımlaşma ve Dayanışma Vakıfları Personel Eğitimi Başladı" 2009). In 2010, the Denizli SYD waqf employees received an "education certificate" upon completing their human resources training where they learned about "relationship management techniques, effective communication skills, and how to approach citizens with empathy" ("Denizli SYD Vakfı Çalışanlarına Eğitim Sertifikası" 2010). Although most of these training workshops were planned by the SYDGM, another nationwide body, the SYDV Employees' Association (founded in 2002), also brought waqf employees together to advance their professionalism and improve their outreach to the public ("Kızılcahamam Toplantısı

Gerçekleştirildi" 2010). A professional demeanor was deemed equivalent to serving the poor in a "respectful" manner (more on this connection in chapter 3). Professionalism was also compared to amateurism, which had to be abandoned if Ottoman-Islamic good governance was to be restored. For example, Aliye told me: "I have to pay attention to my relationship with the people who come to collect their aid. Some women come often; I get to know them, their families, their problems, but I cannot be too friendly, or make decisions in an emotional manner." Waqf employees' interactions with applicants called for a professional attitude that relied on objective facts instead of subjective feelings.

Gaining the Public's Trust

In his ethnographic study of faith-based giving among contemporary Muslims in India, Christopher Taylor (2018) demonstrates that "zakat receipts" acquired new meaning as a "material ritual of symbolic community across vast distances" (266). This idea that Islamic almsgiving required formal paperwork was a recent innovation that emerged under the influence of what Marilyn Strathern (2000) aptly terms "audit culture": the notion that an organization should be transparent and always ready for public scrutiny.

A similar transformation was at work in the field of social service provision in Turkey. Managers, employees, and volunteers of the Muslim Social sought to communicate their legitimacy by emphasizing themes of accountability and transparency. When my interlocutors talked about their experience among Islamist activist networks during the 1990s, one of the changes they mentioned was the shifting nature of paperwork. When they organized in "small neighborhoods," Sevda explained, there was not much need for receipts or to "keep track of every single donation or compile a list of people who received aid," because "everyone knew everyone else anyway." By contrast, as organizations grew, they had to make sure that they could "gain the trust of the public." Faced with accusations of corruption and embezzlement, they came to believe that receipts were an effective instrument for gaining the public's trust. The result was the widespread acceptance of the need for accountability to donors, which held that obtaining and organizing information about benefactors and recipients, as well as keeping a detailed record of financial contributions and in-kind donations, was integral to good governance. But, as the significance of accountability to donors became more prominent, less emphasis was placed on downward accountability to benefactors.[21]

A vital strategy for making the flow of money and goods transparent was the act of publishing documents, reports, and budgetary statements. Financial information had to be available and accessible to anyone who might want to examine the organization's expenses. Whenever I visited Islamic NGOs or public SYD waqfs, I would always leave with brochures, pamphlets, and reports that detailed financial transactions. Such documents were a key part of these organizations' publicity materials. They were not only posted online but also distributed to donors, volunteers, and random visitors like me. For example, DF's 2017 activity report included various kinds of information, such as the amount of donations collected, the kinds of aid delivered, the number of countries in which the organization operated, the number of charity projects that were completed, and awards that had been received. This information was presented using tables, Excel spreadsheets, and interactive maps of both Turkey and the world. The crucial elements of these reports were the numbers and statistics: the "I Am Fostering an Orphan" project aided 6,000 orphans located in twenty-one countries; the "Water Well" project built a total of 275 wells in eight countries; and the DF soup kitchen provided 93,726 hot meals to people in need (*Deniz Feneri Derneği Faaliyet Raporu 2017* 2018). Such publications often juxtaposed bar graphs with sensational images of recipients—children, disabled individuals, families, villagers, seniors, and school children, providing an emotional contrast to the quantitative certainty of numbers.

The Assistance Organization Program (Yardım Organizasyon Programı, YOP) was another innovation that was perceived to enhance accountability and public trust. Originally designed by the DF, a variety of other charitable organizations later adopted electronic databases that served the same purpose. By storing relevant information about donors,

---

21. For more on "accountability myopia," see Ebrahim (2005).

recipients, and monetary and in-kind donations, these databases allowed NGO employees to register and categorize recipients, as well as keep extensive notes about their economic situation, their family and employment history, and their specific needs (Işık 2012). During interviews, workers and managers would almost always turn to their computer screens, pull up the YOP, and show me some numbers, lists, or names. As a repository of information, the database symbolized managerial efficiency and institutional legitimacy. Consider this detailed description:

> The DF organization has developed a solid technological approach for managing your donations. Let's say you donate a box of clothing items. This is how our procedures work: our special team will count, register, and separate these items according to their size and kind. They will then prepare an "acceptance of in-kind assistance" document and deliver it to you. Then, our computer system will generate specific barcode numbers which will be attached to each and every donated item. When any of these items are delivered to a family—that is, when they leave the warehouse—the barcode is scanned, and another barcode is generated and attached to the delivery box. This new barcode involves both information about the family and the specific contents of this box. The computer system reads these barcodes together, and hence knows how to connect beneficiaries, patrons, and things. Whenever a donor wants to know to whom we gave his/her donations, we can provide accurate information about the geographical location and economic situation of those recipients. (Deniz Feneri Yayınları 2010)

As this account illustrates, the YOP was imagined as a total interface, seamlessly linking donors with recipients, gifts with needs, and information with care. The computer system was also valued because it allowed volunteers to inform and guide donors. By looking up information stored in the electronic database, a worker was able to quickly determine the material situation of a disadvantaged family. Then, the donor could take specific actions by donating material goods, such as food, clothing, and furniture, or other forms of assistance, like cash payments, all with the intention of improving a family's living conditions.

Hatice, a volunteer at a public SYD waqf, explained that the computer system was beneficial because it gave volunteers a way to call up various kinds of information. Since volunteers spent part of their time working and could often be away for extended periods, being able to quickly locate details about applicants and their immediate needs was of paramount importance. Relating electronic databases to collective care, she reasoned:

> Maybe, back in the day, they would not need to have all this information written down because, you know, people would know each other; in a small area, there would be a waqf, and people would already know which family needs what, who is sick, who just lost their job, etc. But for us, since we are not always here, and since we do not personally know each applicant, the program helps us have the necessary information to help both people who want to give and those that are in need of assistance.

Those tasked with providing care, in Hatice's view, had to be armed with the wisdom of communal knowledge. The lack of familiarity with those who are disadvantaged necessitated access to the information stored in the computer database. A sense of community could develop from having unfettered access to information about recipients.

Sevda also believed that YOP provided access to a sense of community-based knowledge about those who were at a disadvantage. She could check what the organization had available at any time. If someone needed a carpet, she could log on to her computer and find out if the organization already had a carpet. She could also make sure that they always had enough of particular items. More importantly, any donor could request information. If there was a concerned donor, Sevda could log in to the computer system, enter the barcode number, and locate the donated item without leaving any room for doubt. She elaborated: "Everything is open here, nothing is hidden." The electronic database gave her confidence, not only in the eyes of the public, but also in the eyes of Allah. While talking about how she always took notes during the days she volunteered (before she even became a volunteer coordinator), she explained:

> I am not an expert, but I know that during the Ottoman times, they kept detailed records of waqfs and wrote everything down. Of course, they did not have computers back then, but they still cared about doing their work according to a system. Now, it is easier for us because of

technological improvements. I would not want anyone to think that we have been careless with their money; after all, we are working here to advance Allah's path, and we will be held accountable in the afterlife.

For Sevda, the database was a technological improvement that augmented Ottoman-Islamic practices of charity, while Hatice saw it more as something that was indispensable in modern times. At the same time, Sevda's thoughts about moral liability were intertwined with concerns about the afterlife. While the relative weight of these concerns varied from one individual to the next, most actors saw the use of digital and financial technologies as a sign of their religious devotion.

The YOP assigned a specific number to every donated item, in-kind or otherwise, such as a piece of clothing, a pair of shoes, or a can of food; these numbers were then carefully entered into the electronic database. Giving each item a distinctive number allowed users to track these items from the moment of their donation, during their shelf time in the NGO's social market or its warehouse, to the moment they were delivered to those in need. As a result, making sure that item barcode numbers exactly matched those stored in the computer database was a crucial step. For this reason, social market volunteers were regularly asked to do an "inventory count" of items. This was a tedious and boring task that required both physical and mental energy. Emine, who had previously worked as an assistant manager of a commercial supermarket, and who volunteered to "lead the team" during an inventory count, told me that stocktaking required a careful and systematic approach: "I learned the importance of counting and tracking when I worked at the market. You have to make sure nothing is lost, that everything is exactly where it is supposed to be; that way, we can know what we have and what is needed." Overhearing this conversation, Ayşe, the volunteer coordinator for this public SYD waqf, chimed in with a slightly different explanation: "Well, actually, at a supermarket, people are asked to do an inventory count because they are motivated by making money, but here, we want to make sure that we do right by the people whose trust we have painstakingly earned." Uncomfortable with the direct comparison between commercial supermarkets, Ayşe wanted to impress upon me (and young volunteers under her supervision) that inspecting stock, checking barcodes, and making sure that everything matched the information in the YOP was, first and foremost, an act of Islamic devotion. Later, when the volunteers left, she further explained her thinking:

> Yes, it might look like we are doing what is regularly done at shops, but our motivation is different. This building is filled with gifts trusted to us in the name of Allah, much like a waqf, which is Allah's property. We are trustees and, thus, we need to be dependable and make sure that we are diligent caretakers.

Two kinds of trust merged in this account: one between managers and donors, and another between managers and Allah. Accountability connected donors and managers in a manner that deepened both their religious devotion and social relations.

Much like Islamic NGOs, personnel of public SYD waqfs emphasized accountability toward donors. Even though some of their operations were financed by public funds, public SYD waqfs additionally received in-kind and material donations from government-friendly business firms. Developing a trustworthy relationship with potential donors was also perceived as an intrinsic aspect of the Ottoman-Islamic model of good governance, with all that such a model entailed in terms of fostering a collaborative relationship between sectors.

The following conversation illustrates how public SYD waqfs sought to gain the trust of potential donors, especially business owners in their neighborhood. One day in 2010, while I was at a public SYD waqf in Ankara, I witnessed an encounter between the social market manager and employees of a public SYD waqf in another district. As we were folding clothes around a small coffee table in the entrance of the social market, a man and a woman walked in. Aliye quickly got up to welcome these visitors, introduced them to me, and ordered some tea. After greetings and small talk, the visitors explained the main reason for their visit: they also wanted to set up a social market, but they were not sure how to go about it. They had a location picked out, but the chief problem was convincing business firms to donate. The female visitor said: "We really want to set it up as soon as possible. The Governor (*Kaymakam*) is quite enthusiastic; he has been pushing us to take action. Every waqf has one now. And if we don't act soon, we are never going to be able to get in." The manager smiled and said in a calm voice: "You just need to get started." Then, she patiently gave advice about approaching business owners. It was better to ask them what they could donate, for example, instead of asking them whether they could donate. She also suggested that they should go ahead and open the social market once they collected some donations, instead of waiting until they have enough to fill it up. "Once store owners see what you are doing, then they are more likely to trust you."

Relieved by her words, the two visitors left soon after. Aliye later told me:

> We must encourage these businesspeople to trust us, but I do not blame them. It is difficult to trust someone if you don't know what is being done under their roof. That is why we try to be as clear as the water flowing from an Ottoman waqf fountain; we are always open to visitors—we would not want anyone to think that we are hiding something from them.

Other managers and employees of public SYD waqfs also explained the need for educating potential donors about their religious duties. They talked about strategies they used to shift donor's philanthropic preferences which included not only teaching them about authentic practices of Islamic giving but also disseminating more information about the kind of work SYD waqfs undertook. Previously, in the absence of civilizational awareness, cultivating public trust had not been a priority of SYD waqfs. Hakan, an accountant at a public SYD waqf, told me that, despite being a public institution, most SYD waqfs used to operate "quietly," working in a manner that they thought was best, and without feeling the need to explain constantly where they spent their money. But things were different now: "We want to make sure that the public knows what we are up to, not just because of corruption, but also because we want to put an end to the mismanagement of waqfs." Similarly, Aliye had explained that "letting everyone know how much they help the poor" and "being open about their projects and plans" was a key element of their credibility.

Like Islamic NGOs, most SYD waqfs also adopted electronic databases that categorized, tracked, and stored information about donations and recipients. Personnel were expected to be computer savvy, and attended specific training programs that focused on the effective use of new informational technologies. Although this information was meant to be accessible to the public, SYD waqfs, unlike Islamic NGOs, did not advertise internal financial accounts; instead, they reported their activities and monetary transactions to the general ministry. After compiling all of this information, the SYDGM then shared it through conference presentations, press releases, news articles, and ministry publications.[22] These materials featured a mix of nostalgic pieces on the Ottoman waqf civilization; stories about old-fashioned fountains, schools, and mosques; and articles that detailed current internal administrative reforms, social projects, and financial expenditures. Special sections highlighted the achievements of specific SYD waqfs, such as a successful project or an award.

These publications, many believed, communicated the trustworthiness of SYD waqfs. After one of my initial visits, Fatih, a newly appointed manager of a SYD waqf in Istanbul, wanted to make sure that I did not leave "empty-handed," asking his secretary to prepare a collection of brochures, advertisements, and magazines. As I thanked him for sharing these documents with me, he said: "It is crucial for us to gain the trust of our people. If we do not explain what we do, then we cannot really succeed." Fatih also claimed that trustworthiness was a part of civilizational revival: "We cannot restore the glory of our culture, our way of doing things, our waqf traditions, unless we show people what it is that we exactly do, and how we spend our money." These publications provided a glimpse into the everyday operations of SYD waqfs. On the surface, articles were about everyday matters such as funds, expenses, and projects. Embedded within these administrative announcements, however, were themes of civilizational revival: through providing services in an effective and reliable manner, SYD waqfs assisted in the restoration of Ottoman-Islamic good governance, and the establishment of the Muslim Social.

22. Over the years, several official publications disseminated information about the activities, projects, and expenses of SYD waqfs. These include the Dayanışma Dergisi (2008–11) and Yardım ve Dayanışma (2010–11), among others.

Neo-Ottoman Nostalgia for Good Governance

Since the 2000s, ideas about the meaning and function of Ottoman-Islamic waqfs underwent a radical transformation. According to the waqf civilization rhetoric—which was promoted by the AKP and disseminated by state authorities, Islamic NGOs, and Muslim intellectuals alike—the restoration of Ottoman-Islamic waqfs was crucial for solving Turkey's governmental problems. This version of imperial nostalgia blamed the mismatch between Turkey's "Islamic culture" and "Western institutions" for various problems, and instead called for a restoration of Ottoman-Islamic heritage.

In stark contrast to Kemalist ideology, waqfs were no longer considered relics of the past that impeded economic development. Overlooking historical nuances, civilizational revival presented a selective reading of both the Ottoman and the Republican past: whereas the former was a land of vibrant associational and philanthropic life, the latter had expanded state power, thereby stifling the culture of generosity. Instead, novel arguments about waqfs came to the fore: waqfs provided a social balance, acted as a bridge between the haves and have-nots, and organized civic initiatives without seeking assistance from public authorities. In this anachronistic reading, waqfs, for the first time in Turkish history, were portrayed as archetypes of good governance. While claims about the integrative function of Ottoman-Islamic waqfs proliferated, the parameters of proper state–civil society relations gradually altered. The project of civilizational revival called for a bureaucratic and transparent approach that centered public–private partnerships. As rationalities of accountability, collaboration, and managerialism were adopted by Islamic NGOs and public SYD waqfs, the technical contours of the Muslim Social began to take shape. Consequently, for many actors involved in social service provision in Turkey, there was no significant difference between neoliberal arrangements of good governance and Islamic visions of civilizational revival.

The rise of civilizationism is far from unique to Turkey, but most of the scholarship focuses on the ideological and identity-related aspects of civilizationism (Acharya 2020; Ainslie 2021; Brubaker 2017a; Linde 2016). In the Turkish case, by contrast, civilizational revival operated as a social imaginary that restructured mechanisms of governance. This project of civilizational revival, which alluded to the glory of a reimagined Ottoman-Islamic civilization, gave legitimacy to the reconfiguration of the public welfare regime and the incorporation of private charitable giving into the governmental apparatus. The idea that Ottoman-Islamic waqfs provided an institutional blueprint authorized neoliberal rationalities of good governance. Through this assemblage, the increased monitoring of Islamic civil society organizations and public SYD waqfs was portrayed as instances of civilizational revival, instead of the expansion of state power. Moreover, these new institutional arrangements celebrated religious virtues of generosity, yet at the same time justified the technical governmentality of the Muslim Social. Such a blending of Islamic values and managerial rationalities altered the institutional modes and bureaucratic norms of the Turkish welfare regime.

The next chapter examines how the Islamic social project of populist reform justified similar managerial techniques that, this time, focused on enhancing the "autonomy" and "freedom" of recipients while developing a surveillance apparatus that collected information about the poor and carefully governed their encounters with social service providers.

3

Welfare Reform, Populism, and Social Assistance

In 2011, Berna, a mid-level manager of one of Deniz Feneri's main offices, explained her thoughts on the kind of charity work she aspired to with the following words:

> If wealthy people did what they were supposed to, if everyone knew their responsibility, then poverty would disappear. There are lives that are at the extremes today. If I had a magic wand, do you know what I would bring back? Ottoman charity stones (*sadaka taşları*)! During Ottoman times, there used to be these stones at the yard of each mosque, and in front of many waqf buildings. Rich people would leave gold or money in these holes, and the poor would come get exactly what they need without ever touching the rest. They would come at night if they did not want anyone to know about their destitution. Their dignity was preserved. I wish we still had this approach; I wish we were like this today.

She continued, nostalgically: "I joined this organization because I wanted to nurture mutual solidarity." She added, "If you think about it, our organization is kind of like a sadaqa stone, but what we do is not enough." Berna was not the only pious, educated, urban Muslim woman who talked nostalgically and longingly about Ottoman sadaqa stones. Many other actors I met at public SYD waqfs, Islamic NGOs, and municipal governments, and who thus played an active role in social service provision, described their charity work with reference to this obscure architectural edifice.[1] A

---

1. For a discussion of the popularity of Ottoman sadaqa stones in Turkey, see Hattam (2020).

"charity stone" (*sadaka taşı*) refers to a small pillar-shaped structure that was built in the courtyards of some Ottoman mosques and waqfs (figure 3.1). These pillars, standing above five feet tall with a small opening at the top, allowed community members to assist the poor by leaving a small amount of money. Nostalgia for Ottoman charitable practices was so pervasive that some municipal governments even erected new sadaqa stones in public parks to "invigorate this forgotten tradition of Turkish culture" (Özcan 2017).

Far from being a form of personal nostalgia, Ottoman sadaqa stones were promoted as authentic, local, and indigenous models of social service provision. While waqfs were seen as Ottoman-Islamic models of good governance, sadaqa stones were described as anonymous, local, and respectful mechanisms of poverty relief. The image of wealthy Ottomans giving freely and without expecting anything in return, and the needy receiving help in a dignified and secret manner, was a common narrative among my interlocutors, circulating between bureaucrats, civil servants, donors, employees, managers, and volunteers.

Collective yearning toward Ottoman sadaqa stones emerged amid a political debate about the expansion of social assistance programs. As I discussed in chapter 1, starting in 2003, the AKP introduced a variety of new social programs designed to provide in-kind and material aid to those in need.[2] Many of the AKP's opponents argued that these social programs created a culture of sadaqa (*sadaka kültürü*)—a culture of dependency—among

---

2. Two analytical frameworks dominate the scholarship on social assistance in Turkey. The first group includes studies that seek to classify the Turkish welfare regime in a comparative perspective (e.g., Aybars and Tsarouhas 2010; Grütjen 2008; Powell and Yörük 2017). A second group analyzes social assistance programs as mechanisms of political patronage and social control (see Kutlu 2015; Özel and Yıldırım 2019; Yörük 2012). My approach diverges from both analytical frameworks. Instead of focusing on the institutional classification of the welfare regime or exploring the instrumental use of aid programs, I analyze the interpretation of social assistance programs and demonstrate how they acquire meaning and force through an assemblage of neoliberal elements, Islamic references, and populist rhetoric.

3.1 Charity stone (*sadaka taşı*) located outside the İmrahor Mosque in Üsküdar, 2020, Istanbul. Photograph by Jennifer Hattam. Used with permission.

the Turkish poor.[3] Rather than upholding welfare rights, these oppositional voices contend, the government and Islamic NGOs gave "handouts," and social services were merely a tool of political patronage that made the Turkish poor dependent on aid. In the eyes of the political opposition, these new social programs thus represented a "relief-based" notion of poverty governance and one that failed to uphold welfare rights.[4]

3. For insights into the sadaqa culture (*sadaka kültürü*) debates in Turkey, see Buğra (2014) and Zencirci (2015b).

4. Beyond being just a politicized topic, the rights-versus-relief distinction—often mapped onto the sadaqa–social assistance comparison—is deployed by some scholars who argue that the Turkish welfare regime has moved away from a universal rights-based approach to targeted poverty alleviation schemes. Most of these works tend to take sides in a partisan debate even if that is not their intention. While I acknowledge the

By contrast, the AKP and its supporters responded to these criticisms by invoking the social imaginary of populism—or "serving the people." The incorporation of religious sensibilities into the design of social policy, and ensuing shifts in the administration of poverty relief, was argued to be an instance of populist reform.[5] While donors, managers, and volunteers that I met during my fieldwork were ready to give me divergent ideological accounts of the Muslim Social, they unequivocally believed that these new social assistance programs—and their related technologies of experience and information—were distinctive because they epitomized a strong commitment to assisting the Turkish poor in a dignified and respectful fashion.

The idea that these new programs encapsulated an Islamic way of serving the people was a key pillar of the Muslim Social. Regardless of whether these programs achieved their declared goals of "serving the people," what interests me is the fact that a whole host of actors perceived them as such. In their eyes, social assistance programs, and new technologies of information and distribution that accompanied these programs, were part of a larger social project focused on improving the lives of the Turkish "people." To understand these multiple interpretations, I approach populism as a loose and evolving set of discursive appeals and stylistic elements.[6]

---

constitutive power of this distinction in public debates about social assistance in Turkey, this study is not motivated by a defense of any specific approach to welfare policy. If anything, the findings of this chapter illustrate that simplistic dichotomies, such as targeted relief versus universal rights or private charity versus public welfare, fall short of understanding the peculiar characteristics of the Turkish welfare regime. For similar arguments, see Ağartan (2012), Bakırezer and Demirer (2009), Morvaridi (2013), and Öktem and Erdoğan (2019).

5. While the term populism is sometimes used by outsiders to criticize politicians' faulty motivations, the phrase "populist reform," by contrast, refers to the common understanding that interprets and represents a whole host of innovations in the field of social service provision as "service to the Turkish poor."

6. In approaching populism as a social imaginary, I follow scholars who study populism as a discursive—instead of an ideological or policy-based—phenomenon. These include Aslanidis (2016), who studies populism as a "discursive frame" (98); Brubaker (2017b) who defines populism as a "discursive and stylistic repertoire" (360); and Laclau

In doing so, this analysis differs from those frameworks that treat populism as a coherent set of policy tools or understand it as an ideology with static components. While fluid and divergent, populist rhetoric is nevertheless bound by a "core element: the claim to speak and act in the name of the people" (Brubaker 2017b, 362). From this perspective, what matters is not whether the AKP's social assistance programs can be adequately defined as "populist" tools of policy making, but that much can be gained by examining why and how actors themselves interpreted changes in the provision of social assistance as instances of populist reform, and thereby part of the larger Islamic project of serving the people.

For Turkish Muslims involved in social service provision, the political repertoire of populist reform was readily available for making sense of shifts in the welfare regime. The procedures, techniques, and standards that accompanied the expansion of social assistance programs led to a shift in the affective registers and social rhythms of charitable giving and poverty aid in Turkey. In this transformation, several distinctive processes were at work: an emergent concern about the dignity and honor of the Turkish poor, a desire to uphold the autonomy and freedom of recipients, and a governmental aim of making the state more accessible and efficient. However, the goals of those who evoked the language of populist reform were not just to create a dignified experience for recipients, but to do so in a manner that created a balance between the "Islamic" and "managerial" objectives of the state.

In this chapter, I examine the governmental assemblages that accompanied the vision of populist reform by tracing various bureaucratic innovations that sought to enhance the dignity and freedom of the poor. I map how these beliefs and claims acquired meaning in the day-to-day

---

(2005) who describes populism as a series of politico-discursive practices. What distinguishes this analytical framework is an emphasis on studying populism as a fluid set of discursive claims and material practices which constitutes agents and generates meanings, instead of being the outward expression of an inner ideological essence or political style. This analytical framework also invites scholarship on populism to move beyond the democracy-versus-authoritarianism binary, and instead pay attention to the specific political effects of populist discourses, which vary across cultural contexts.

operations of Islamic NGOs and public SYD waqfs, and how visions of populist reform informed ideas and practices of good governance as they pertained to the collection and distribution of relief.

Although the religious significance of sadaqa for Muslims was acknowledged, defended, and endorsed at all costs, at the same time, the ad hoc, impulsive, and non-organized acts of giving—traditionally, the dominant characteristics of charity in Turkey—were gradually abandoned. In this process, two key technologies emerged: (1) technologies of experience, which sought to improve the emotional aspects of recipients' aid experience; and (2) technologies of information, which strove to organize details that had to be known about an applicant to determine their eligibility. New social assistance programs brought the proliferation of both experiential measures—aid packages, social markets, social cards—and managerial procedures—audits, documents, forms, measures, standards—to a conjuncture that altered how the poor in Turkey accessed welfare benefits and how they encountered the state.

Mapping the AKP's Populist Rhetoric

The AKP, like other political parties that use populist rhetoric, combines a language of "economic insecurity" with that of "cultural backlash" in the hope of generating electoral support from the masses (Inglehart and Norris 2016). Drawing from center-right political traditions and Islamic movements, the AKP's populist rhetoric consistently refers to the degradation of Turkish people from rural, conservative, pious, lower-income backgrounds, thereby reinforcing a rigid us-versus-them dichotomy.[7]

7. While I consider AKP's populism as a loose and shifting set of discursive appeals and symbolic claims, an extensive body of scholarship defines the AKP as a populist political party (e.g., Açıkel 2016; Arat-Koç 2018; Selçuk 2016; Göle 2017; Yabancı 2016). Another line of inquiry, by contrast, examines the populist characteristics of the AKP's governmental reforms in policy areas ranging from foreign policy to health services, and from agriculture to the urban environment. For examples of this kind of an approach, see Demiralp (2018), Dorlach (2016), Gürel, Küçük, and Taş (2019), Özdemir (2020), and Özpek and Yaşar (2018). While both sets of studies highlight aspects of the AKP's populist rhetoric, they are more interested in exploring the ideological features of populism

This political rhetoric combines claims about Kemalist elitism, the cultural purity of the "Turkish people," with a promise of economic prosperity. The AKP and its supporters argue that the economic policies implemented by the Kemalist establishment had a major shortcoming: the Turkish state exerted too much control over economic affairs, thereby obstructing the development of a successful Muslim bourgeoisie while also being out of touch with the needs of the popular masses. From this vantage point, only Islamic-conservative political parties, such as the AKP, are seen as capable of fixing this problem of "cultural distance" that hitherto separated the Turkish state from the "people"—a group defined less by their ethnic or religious status and more by their presumed oppression by the Kemalist elite.

The AKP uses and abuses populist themes, such as exclusion, suffering, vulnerability, and religious imagery, through various symbolic performances as well. Erdoğan, even after he has ruled Turkey for almost twenty years, continues to present himself as a victim (mağdur) of Kemalist secularism (Taş 2020; Tokdoğan 2020). He has notably delivered populist messages through public displays of emotion, such as crying while on TV (Aslan 2021). He also communicates his "proximity to the people" (Müller 2016, 43) through embodied performances—for example, by wearing a blue plaid jacket (which symbolizes a "rural-Anatolian" background) during his famous 2014 Balcony Speech.

In addition, the AKP describes a wide range of governmental endeavors as examples of the party's commitment to truly serve the Turkish people. These efforts include infrastructure investments, such as the construction of a third airport and bridge in Istanbul, as well as shopping malls and highways throughout the country. Whenever these megaprojects are criticized due to their environmental impact or lack of architectural design, the AKP responds by combining a language of developmentalism and populism, asserting that large-scale infrastructure projects would fuel the nation's economic growth (Paker 2017). The expansion of the Housing

---

or providing an assessment of "populist" governmental policies without a concern for understanding how elements of populist rhetoric acquire meaning on the ground.

Development Administration of Turkey (Toplu Konut Idaresi, TOKI), which provides subsidized housing to lower-income groups, is depicted as another example of "serving the people" despite the fact that these urban construction projects often enrich top property developers (Arslanalp 2018; Demiralp 2018). The introduction of communications centers—designed to provide a direct medium for Turkish citizens to express their concerns—and the periodic hosting of *muhtar* meetings by Erdoğan himself, are similarly described as good governance mechanisms that allow Turkish people to express their political will (Boyraz 2018; Denli, Öztürk, and Bilgin 2017).

Like these various initiatives, social assistance programs are also portrayed by the AKP as a successful example of populist reform—one that "serves the people" by combining Islamic values with managerial technologies of government. In 2009, Erdoğan responded to Turkish politicians who criticized the expansion of social assistance programs, and who claimed that these programs fostered a culture of dependency among the Turkish poor, with the following words:

> The opposition keeps criticizing us. They have taken up with this sadaqa culture. Sadaqa is an important element of our culture, it is justified, it is legitimate. We are not just a government that distributes coal and bulgur to our people from one election to another. Since we came to power, we have sought and found the poor and gave them everything that they need. This is what being a welfare state means. If the CHP has been unable to accomplish these goals, why is that our problem? They have always been elitist, whereas we are primarily concerned with social justice and equal distribution. ("Kültürümüzde Sadaka Var" 2009)

In this account, Erdoğan presents sadaqa as a legitimate, homegrown, and authentic cultural practice of giving. In similar speeches, Erdoğan, using an Islamic language, has told governors to disregard criticisms about social assistance because, "if a family did not have enough coal to last the winter," he said, "only they would have to answer to Allah in the afterlife" ("Başbakan Sadaka Kültürü Diye Eleştirilen Yardımlar Hakkında Konuştu" 2010). These kinds of speeches presented the AKP's welfare regime as a corrective to the "elitism" of the Turkish state establishment.

Not only did Kemalism overlook the needs of the Turkish poor, but preexisting social programs had treated them in an undignified and patronizing manner. New social assistance programs, by contrast, were able to assist the poor in a respectful and unimposing way, thanks to their cultural knowledge about religious principles of almsgiving, and their competence in incorporating these principles within the governmental apparatus.

Within the context of the welfare regime, the social imaginary of populist reform acquired meaning through themes of respecting the autonomy, dignity, and freedom of the Turkish poor; nostalgic references to Ottoman-Islamic cultures of giving; and a belief in the superiority of new technologies of aid collection and distribution. Before I examine this governmental assemblage, let me first review the ways in which social functions of Islamic sadaqa and Ottoman sadaqa stones were discussed among those interested in reviving these practices to address perceived problems with poverty relief in Turkey.

Sadaqa as a Technology of Social Government

Nostalgic sentiments toward the Ottoman past, a sense of awakened piety about the golden age of Islam, and a belief in the need to improve state–citizen relations in Turkey played a role in the novel articulation of sadaqa as a technology of social government. The religious significance of sadaqa for Muslims was no longer discussed as merely a way for the faithful to deepen their devotion to Islam, but as a medium for guaranteeing collective order and social solidarity within the Muslim Social.

Muslim intellectuals, journalists, and scholars who have published on the topic since the 2000s began to discuss Islamic charity as a medium of government, with less and less attention devoted to the legal and theological aspects of almsgiving in Islam. According to Islamic jurisprudence, social redistribution through zakat was a "a poor individual's right and a wealthy person's debt" (Erdoğan 2013). Sadaqa and zakat were technologies of aid that ensured "social harmony" (Yaran 2016) and "peace" (Aral 2000). In this social order, the wealthy and the poor were united in a voluntary fashion. Muslims who gave some of their money to others could experience "personal happiness" (Ayça 2014), and "reach a balance between the spiritual and material world" (Büyükçıngıl 2015).

Pious Muslims in Turkey were inspired by Ottoman sadaqa stones as much as they were moved by the Islamic injunction to help others in need. A devout Muslim, they came to believe, did not merely give impulsively or to please Allah, but considered the most effective way to fold charitable sentiments into the governmental apparatus. Various actors—from volunteers to managers, from civil servants to donors—reworked and reimagined tenets of Ottoman sadaqa stones as they engineered, negotiated, and contested Islamic-neoliberal assemblages of poverty governance. The following poem, titled "Charity Stones," which was written by Nidayi Sevim (2010), a conservative public intellectual who regularly appears on TV and radio shows to lecture on the glory of the Ottoman-Islamic civilization, represents the main tenets of this reimagined instrument of social solidarity:

> Snow white stone pillars with a cavity
> Many gave but very few took any money
> Those who were wealthy would bring gold
> Those who were not would share their last food
> Those who took were never greedy
> They would never touch the share of others who were also needy
> Located next to mosques, shrines, fountains, almshouses
> Shared the secrets of the destitute in their most difficult moments
> Donors never asked, "to whom?"
> Recipients never questioned "from whom?"
> Where did this beautiful thoughtfulness originate from?
> The left hand shall not know what the right hand gave away
> This principle is fundamental to our civilization's way (Sevim 2014)

In this poem, Sevim argues that sadaqa stones were keystones of the Ottoman-Islamic civilizational order. As discussed in the previous chapter, the imaginary of civilizational revival claimed that each civilization possessed its own institutions, practices, and traditions that are essential to governing society in an effective manner.

As a medium for the collection and redistribution of donations, sadaqa stones were argued to serve numerous social and economic roles. Two main functions that are especially relevant to the focus of this chapter are the claim that sadaqa stones automatically produced a cohesive rela-tionship between the haves and have-nots, and the idea that these edifices protected the dignity of the poor by upholding the principle of anonym-ity. As main anchors of the community, Ottoman sadaqa stones were defined as "examples of an urban culture in which alms were given with-out vanity thereby protecting the honor and dignity of needy community members" (Özcan 2014). The wealthy would voluntarily leave money, and the poor would only take the amount they needed. These architectural structures thus acted as bridges of social solidarity that connected differ-ent segments of society. Sadaqa stones were also described as pure gifts that operated according to principles of anonymity and secrecy because the receiving hand did not see the giving hand. Donors were neither seen nor acknowledged by others, immediately curtailing the desire to show off one's wealth or generosity. Because no one knew whether one was leaving or taking money from the charity stone, the poor were neither embarrassed nor stigmatized. Since everyone could potentially contribute funds, regardless of their social class or financial status, Ottoman charity stones fulfilled certain "psycho-social functions" (Taşcı 2014, 90). These functions included strengthening social solidarity, fortifying the politi-cal order, reducing crime, and preventing class-based conflicts (Yıldız 2012). Sadaqa stones ensured an organic kind of social solidarity that automatically flowed through society. These architectural structures were also defined as "Ottoman ATMs," since "a password was not necessary to deposit or withdraw money, rather, the password was already located in one's heart" (Kartal 2019).

Whereas most people shared a longing for a glorified past, there were differences in the ways in which they understood the ideal relationship between sadaqa and social assistance. Some actors directly involved in social service provision reassessed the dominant features of almsgiving in Turkey, such as its ad hoc, impulsive, unorganized, and informal char-acteristics. Others felt that some aspects of these aid programs—such as the command to collect information about conditions of poverty—were incompatible with Islamic principles of respecting the poor. Even as it came to embody an authentic model of social assistance, sadaqa was modified not just by those who were against social assistance programs, but also by those who most celebrated its distinctive capacity to generate social bonds. The fact that multiple interpretations of sadaqa circulated among actors involved with social service provision in Turkey is relevant not because there is disagreement, but rather because the coexistence of these alternative meanings points to the diversity of Islamic-neoliberal assemblages. Religious values of care and solidarity merged with neoliberal technologies to transform poverty into an object, and certain tenets of charitable giving, such as anonymity and autonomy, were portrayed as technical features that formed the governmental backbone of the Muslim Social.

Technologies of Experience

During the 1990s, I frequently encountered stories about the crowd-charity spectacle in mainstream Turkish newspapers. Highlighted with provocative titles such as "Crowds Got Impatient" and "Stampede for Just a Bag of Rice!," news articles detailed stories of how some wealthy businesspeople visited a shantytown area in the outskirts of Istanbul or Ankara to distribute charitable goods and were met with chaos instead of gratitude. Often, a photograph would accompany such an article, showing the frustrated businessperson (or one of their employees) standing at the back of a truck, trying to distribute goods, such as food, shoes, or school supplies, to an impatient crowd full of women and children. The news article might also talk about a fight that broke out, how long the poor had had to wait to receive just a pair of shoes, or how some recipients ended up with nothing, whereas others received more than what they needed. These scenes were portrayed as an inefficient and undignified way of helping the poor—yet another sign of Turkey's economic underdevelopment and cultural backwardness.

The actual cases of the crowd-charity spectacle are certainly far more complicated than the simplistic portraits of them in the Turkish press. But what makes this crowd-charity spectacle relevant for my analysis is the fact that such scenes were frequently brought up by my interlocutors as the imagined alternative to their own approach to poverty alleviation. For example, Hatice, while explaining how the organization's mobile social market worked, said: "It is not acceptable to load a truck, create a stampede in a crowd, abusing, hurting, offending people. Our mobile market travels to different places, but we do not distribute goods in a rude or haphazard fashion; the quality of our service is very important for us." In her mind, the crowd-charity spectacle was a distasteful and un-Islamic way of distributing aid. Giving and receiving aid was not to be a chaotic experience, but rather a pleasant and orderly one.

Furthermore, the social imaginary of populist reform called for curating a novel form of aid experience for those in need. The goal of social programs was not just the eradication of poverty, but also the assurance of dignified encounters between the state and the poor, as well as the haves and the have-nots. The honor of poor people, moreover, could only be protected if they were allowed to make decisions freely about their material needs. Thus, the aid experience had to obscure the power differential and ensure that recipients experienced a sense of individual autonomy. To achieve these interrelated goals, Islamic NGOs and SYD waqfs experimented with three technologies of aid distribution: the package system, the social market, and the social card. Each of these technologies assembled Islamic notions of charity with neoliberal notions of individual autonomy and free choice. Instead of getting help from others in their neighborhood or kin group, the poor received packages, visited commercial and social supermarkets, and owned and used debit cards. Curating a dignified experience for the poor was an ongoing pursuit of populist reform—a project that continued despite failures, shortcomings, and obstacles.

The Package System

Beginning in the 2000s, the delivery of preassembled boxes of food to the doorsteps of poor people emerged as a new method of social service provision. The package system (*paket sistemi*), as it came to be known, was promoted as a way to reform the aid experience and enhance the dignity of the poor. Thanks to this system, the poor did not have to wait in front of trucks amid a crowd, everyone received the same kind and amount of goods, and the delivery of aid was organized according to a regular schedule. The package system, in other words, accomplished the vision of populist reform, not because more aid was given to more people, but because aid was now distributed in a "respectful" and "efficient" manner.

Today, a variety of organizations, ranging from SYD waqfs to Islamic NGOs and from municipal governments to business associations, distribute aid packages. Although the type and amount of goods vary according to the provider, aid packages generally include nonperishable food items, such as grains, pasta, rice, and canned goods. Most organizations offer aid packages that vary according to the amount or variety of their contents, understanding that larger families may have different needs. Sometimes, the boxes may also contain household cleaning materials or small appliances, or may be distributed alongside heating assistance such as coal. Specialized packages containing stationery and other school supplies may also be included at the beginning of the school year for eligible families. In addition to being used as a standardized strategy of poverty alleviation, package campaigns are also organized during the month of Ramadan and constitute a key part of transnational humanitarian relief efforts.

The package system requires a certain degree of collaboration between sectors. Food items may be donated by a supermarket, or purchased by an Islamic NGO, public SYD waqf, or municipal government, ideally by following the procedures for public auctions. Donors can also purchase an aid package directly from a supermarket, an Islamic NGO, or a municipal government with the understanding that the organization will oversee the delivery of the aid package to a worthy recipient in a dignified manner. Almost all supermarket chains in Turkey offer such prepackaged Ramadan boxes to their customers. These donation drives are often the result of a partnership between a civil society organization and the supermarket chain, where volunteers (often young university students) set up a donation stand in a visible corner of a store. Similar charity stands can be found in other public spaces, such as shopping malls or busy pedestrian streets. These aid packages, in other words, may be financed by a variety of sources, including individual donations, charity campaigns, the public budget, and corporate sponsorships.

Many of my interlocutors believed that certain aspects of the package system were akin to the moral principles of Islamic charity, such as respecting the dignity and individuality of the poor. Concerning the monthly (or bimonthly) delivery of aid packages, one volunteer said, "the families are sure that someone is looking out for them, because they know that the boxes will appear at their doorsteps no matter what. It's just like how the poor in Ottoman times knew that they could always rely on sadaqa stones if they fell on hard times." The package system also allowed for preparing different kinds of boxes for different kinds of families: some people had large families and hence needed more food, whereas other families could get by with a lesser amount. One waqf manager explained the significance of this innovation with the following words:

> When we prepare the boxes, we pay attention to family size and need. Even when, during the Ottoman times, the poor would go to waqfs, maybe they would all get food from the soup kitchen first, but after that, depending on their situation, they would receive different kinds of care. We operate according to the same principle.

News articles, disseminated by public SYD waqfs, Islamic NGOs, and municipal governments, imparted similar messages to the Turkish public. The needy were no longer patronized or objectified because "aid packages were now given without leaving room for chaos, disorder, or a stampede, and in a manner that prevented harm to human dignity and honor" ("Yoksul Ailelere 3 Bin Paket Gıda Yardımı Dağıtıldı" 2011). Moreover, the package system ensured that the poor were assisted "without putting recipients on display" ("İzmir Büyükşehir'den 'İncitmeyen' Yardım" 2014), thereby preventing "a likely public commotion that would hurt the feelings of aid recipients" ("Kayapınar Belediyesinden 3 Bin Kişiye Gıda Yardımı Yapıldı" 2017).

But, as this method of aid delivery became widespread, so did debates about its efficiency and humanity. One set of disputes about the package system concerned the cost of goods, the quality of items, and the inefficiency of delivery methods. CHP municipal governments, who adopted the package system in an effort to mimic the AKP's social programs, were often mocked by pro-government officials for failing to deliver a respectful and dignified aid experience. For instance, when the CHP municipal government of Izmir accidentally sent an aid package to one of the prominent members of the AKP's local body, pro-government officials saw this as proof of the CHP's lack of knowledge about the Turkish poor ("CHP'li İzmir Büyükşehir Belediyesi, AK Partili İlçe Başkanına da Ramazan Yardımı Gönderdi" 2008). In a more recent example, the popular mayor of Istanbul, Ekrem İmamoğlu, was criticized for spending too much of the public budget for financing the municipality's aid packages. Some argued that his inability to offer cost-effective packages demonstrated a lack of governmental skill ("İmamoğlu Bak Ne Paketler Var" 2020), while others insinuated that overpriced aid packages were a sign of corruption and embezzlement ("CHP'li İBB Başkanı Ekrem İmamoğlu'ndan Gıda Paketine 'Fırsatçı' Tarifesi" 2020). These examples illustrate not only how voices from opposite ends of the political spectrum criticized the package system in similar ways, but also that the effective provision of aid packages was widely seen as an index of good governance.

Yet, despite its widespread use, many Turks, even those involved with the distribution of aid in such a manner, thought that the package system did not fulfill its promise. Whereas the package system preserved the dignity of the poor, it failed to provide a "variety of choices," and was thus inadequate in terms of "truly meeting the needs of the poor" ("Kayseri'de İhtiyaç Sahiplerine Ücretsiz 'Market'" 2015). Even if the question of whether shelf-ready goods provided any health benefits was left aside, poor individuals and families had a wide range of nutritional needs that could not be met with shelf-ready, nonperishable goods. Did poor individuals not deserve eggs, milk, poultry, fresh fruit and vegetables, or meat? What if the family needed to buy formula for their newborn? What if a person had allergies or lacked access to a stove? These kinds of questions populated debates about whether the package system was an adequate component of the Muslim Social.

A second set of concerns was about mechanisms of aid delivery. Leaving aid packages at the doorsteps of individuals presented a number of distinctive challenges: ingredients could spoil or get wet; boxes might be stolen or get lost. Perhaps more importantly, the poverty of any individual or family was made public by the delivery of a package, even if they might prefer to keep such information private. The solution to these perceived problems was found in the social market and the social card; these were perceived as superior technologies of distribution and, thus, improved mechanisms for serving the poor, but they also came with their own issues.

The Social Market

Since the late 2000s, many SYD waqfs, Islamic NGOs, and municipal governments have introduced another technology of aid distribution: the social market. Understood as an example of populist reform, the social market was argued to generate a dignified aid experience by allowing poor people to have the final say in what they received and how. These facilities allowed aid recipients to pick and choose consumer goods as if they were shopping at a commercial supermarket. Some of these aid distribution centers used the generic title "social market," whereas others meshed consumerism with social solidarity by using titles such as the Charity Bazaar, Compassion Market, Friendly Hands, Love Boutique, and Heart Connections.

I was invited to see an organization's social market whenever I visited a SYD waqf or an Islamic NGO. Usually located in a smaller room, either within the main building or one nearby, social markets resembled commercial supermarkets in several ways. Unassuming white or brown shelves were mounted on the walls, displaying primarily clothing or food. Each aisle was organized to provide access: clothing items were categorized according to age and gender; coats, shoes, and socks were kept in a different section, neatly grouped according to age, gender, and size. In addition to nonperishable food items such as grains, canned goods, sugar, and tea, social markets offered perishable items such as cheese, meat, milk, eggs, and yogurt. Sometimes social markets even provided household items such as rugs, small furniture, curtains, and kitchenware. Their commercial design was not just limited to the spatial structure and display of items, as many social markets provided shopping carts, had checkout counters, and distributed shopping bags. Each item had its own functioning barcode, contributing more to the illusion of consumerism, as donated items no longer appeared as a gift to aid recipients.

Some social markets differentiated themselves by providing rare consumer items. One employee quite eagerly told me that they had recently started providing menstrual products, adding: "We want to make sure that our people (*halkımız*) can get everything they need." Another employee of a public SYD waqf explained the importance of a "holistic approach to aid," and mentioned that there were many engaged couples who desperately needed financial support. This waqf, therefore, had begun to accept bridal gowns as donations so that they might help poor couples get married—traditionally a highly expensive endeavor in Turkish society.

Unlike thrift stores in the United States or the charity supermarkets of China, Turkey's social markets neither specialized in the resale of second-hand goods nor converted donated goods into cash (Le Zotte 2013; Shue 2011). In-kind donations from retail and food companies stocked these social markets. Many of these companies either were on good terms with the government or were seeking to improve their political connections. Such an organizational setup not only gave the poor access to high-quality consumer products but also lessened the financial burden on Islamic NGOs, SYD waqfs, and municipal governments. The Esenler municipality in Istanbul, for example, announced that the social market was almost free: "the municipal government does not spend a single cent. . . . We only provide logistical support for organization and delivery" (Yağcı 2010). This municipality's social market project even won first prize in a "social municipal governance" contest organized by the AKP in 2010. The lack of public expenditure signified effective governance. Governmental authorities merely ensured that the poor received donations in the most respectful and freedom-enhancing manner. To accomplish this goal, the key was for the state to act as a "bridge between the needy and the manufacturing firms, the donors" ("Beyoğlu Belediyesi Ramazanda Yoksullara Kucak Açıyor" 2015). However, doing so required tremendous administrative effort, as well as the targeted use of public funds. Although donations were free, municipal governments, SYD waqfs, or Islamic NGOs covered startup costs, office supplies, warehouse space, staff salaries, and other miscellaneous costs. Yet, most of these expenses were downplayed to portray social markets as charitable endeavors funded mostly by private donations.

The ideal of a seamless blend between consumerism and social care was evident in how various governmental authorities advertised social markets. In 2010, the general director of SYDGM, Aziz Yıldırım, on the occasion of the opening of the "Love Boutique" social market in Sincan, Ankara, said: "These social market applications are a fundamental component of the welfare state. Our aim is to provide quality products to our citizens without offending their honor. This new social market will also make it possible for our disadvantaged citizens to fulfill their needs as if they are doing their own shopping" ("Sincan'da Sosyal Market Açıldı" 2010). In 2011, the Beyoğlu municipality announced the opening of its social market, proclaiming: "This market is not for people who have money, it is for those individuals who have a need. It is filled with goodness, not money!" ("Beyoğlu Sosyal Market Açıldı" 2010). When a journalist visited this social market in 2014, she referred to it as "one of the rare supermarkets for the poor," and one that was morally superior due to the lack of profit-seeking behavior (Aydıntaşbaş 2014). In 2011, the governor of Muratbaşa, Antalya, similarly explained that the district's new social market allowed "poor citizens" to experience the "joys of shopping" ("Dayanışma Evine Sosyal Market Açılıyor" 2011). The chance to "go shopping without shame or embarrassment" ("Şahinbey'de Fakirin Bayramlığı Sosyal Market'ten" 2014) transformed the poor—in their own minds and in the eyes of the public—into "consumers" and "agents."

Actors on the ground also invoked the language of consumerism—autonomy, choice, self-government. Echoing themes of populist reform, they explained that their goal was to deliver aid in a respectful manner. Erkan, a university student who volunteered at a SYD waqf in Ankara to complete his university's community service requirements, explained his approach as: "I do not get too close, but I make sure that our families know that I am available to help. I want them to feel like they are at a real supermarket instead of feeling like they have no say in the matter." Erkan was reflecting on his duties as a floor salesman. In addition to organizing stock and laying out clothes, he also assisted visitors. In his mind, by simulating the experience of visiting a supermarket, social markets allowed poor individuals to "make their own decisions."

Themes of dignity and freedom were integral to the message of volunteer training sessions as well. During one of these sessions, Fatma, one of the managers of a SYD waqf in Istanbul, explained that theirs was a new approach. Volunteers had to leave behind their assumptions about "traditional charity," because most of what they knew about almsgiving was often based on a misunderstanding of Islam. She wanted to impress on them that a respectful approach to almsgiving was a key part of their faith. She said:

> We do not want anyone to feel they are unworthy. They need to know that we are here for them, we want to help them, and we respect them. Our attitude is just like how, during the Ottoman times, community members would stay back and let the needy pick how much money they needed from sadaqa stones.

In her mind, social markets resembled Ottoman sadaqa stones because both respected poor people's individual autonomy. In a similar vein, Sevda discussed the significance of dignity when explaining why the Deniz Feneri organization refused to accept secondhand clothing. Although some donors were thoughtful enough to wash and iron their used clothes, others just threw their hand-me-downs haphazardly into a trash bag. But, according to her, Islam barred giving such old, worn, and dirty clothes to the poor because doing so would "hurt their pride." Many recipients came to social markets with their children, friends, or neighbors; thus, it was crucial not to embarrass them in front of others. Sevda further elaborated on the value of respect in Islam:

> In our culture, we do not give defective things to the needy. We must give them the best. When I was growing up, my family would always give the finest part of the Qurban meat to elderly neighbors or to poor families with a lot of children to feed. My mom would tell me that our Qurban would not be accepted by Allah if we did not give selflessly and from our heart.

For actors involved in service provision, social markets thus combined anonymity and choice with compassion and solidarity. Consumerist freedom and Islamic ethics were combined in the pursuit of designing a welfare regime that respected the dignity and autonomy of aid recipients.

Yet, in practice, social markets often fell short of these ideals. Stocking the social market with a variety of consumer goods required a steady stream of contributions; even when there were enough donations, companies had a tendency to give food items that were nearing their expiration date. Retail companies, in an effort to manage their excess inventory, often donated shoes and clothes that had been out of fashion for years, if not decades. Mehmet, the manager of a small Islamic NGO in Ankara with a social market attached to it, explained how their social market went back to distributing aid packages, saying:

> Ideally, we want people to pick what they want and then check out these items at the cashier, just like we do when we go grocery shopping. We want them to have the best of everything. But, when it comes to food . . . we sometimes do not have enough to give everyone. So, these days, we had to revert back to the package system.

Mehmet attributed the difficulties of curating a respectful and freedom-enhancing aid experience to a lack of supply. Other difficulties arose in the interactions between managers, volunteers, and recipients. Sometimes the poor were rushed and told to wrap up their "shopping." On other occasions, they were interrupted by managers who explained that they should take less of a certain consumer good or choose something else instead. To address some of these perceived problems, another technology of aid distribution, the social card, was introduced.

The Social Card

Social cards are the latest innovation reconfiguring the terrain of poverty governance in Turkey. In the past decade, the social card technology has been adopted by numerous public SYD waqfs, Islamic NGOs, and municipal governments. Relying primarily on the distribution of preloaded debit cards (with either monetary or point values) to the poor, these cards do not grant direct access to cash. Cardholders may use their points either at organizations' social markets or at select commercial supermarkets. Certain consumer goods—such as tobacco or alcohol—are off-limits. Most cards are given to the female head of a family, and the frequency of recharge depends on a family's needs. Like social markets, most of these cards have names that emphasize solidarity, such as compassion, friendliness, support, and togetherness.

References to financial inclusion, a sense of techno-optimism, and allusions to Ottoman-Islamic cultures of social generosity permeated media representations and public portrayals of the social card. Access to consumer credit was described as a fundamental human right (Roy 2010, 23). Through the use of these cards, the poor could feel "as if they were using their personal credit card" and "enjoy the freedom of shopping" (Yağcı 2010), "have access to an adequate amount of credit that corresponds to their level of need" ("10 Bin Kişiye Sosyal Kart" 2010), and rejoice when they realize that "preassembled food boxes were now replaced with cards filled with money" ("Konya'da İhtiyaçlar 'Sosyal Kart' İle Alışveriş Merkezlerinden Karşılanacak" 2010). There was also a concerted attempt to automatize and streamline the donation process. Whenever a person bought something at select supermarkets, a small percentage of that amount was to be transferred to a "social pool"—overseen by the municipality or a SYD waqf. To attract consumer-donors, supermarkets offered discounts on specific consumer goods if a certain debit card was used. The funds collected in the social pool were then deposited onto individuals' social cards. And if the poor used their social card at select supermarkets, they would also receive a small discount (5% or 10%). In this way, an effortless circle of consumption and generosity was set up.

By piggybacking on the consumer market, social card technologies relieved municipal governments, Islamic NGOs, and SYD waqfs of the extensive logistical efforts that were required to distribute aid packages and run social markets. In addition to their organizational benefits, social cards were also cost-effective and saved time for those distributing aid. "Once we set it up," said one manager of a SYD waqf in Ankara, "the system kind of operates on its own."

The adoption of smart card technologies was, on the one hand, an attempt to showcase technological innovation and modernity (Yıldırım 2018). Yet, on the other hand, this invention was also about shared Islamic values. In 2013, when the government began to implement a version of the social card system and distributed two million social cards, Erdoğan himself explained: "Practices such as zakat, sadaqa, sharing, and solidarity are not just religious concepts, they are what shapes us, what makes us a unitary nation, and what has allowed us to survive for centuries" ("2

Milyon Yoksula Özel Kart" 2013). Erdoğan, like many actors involved in reforming the social welfare regime in Turkey, portrayed financial instruments as extensions of the Islamic spirit of social generosity.

In explaining the benefits of the social card, my interlocutors often emphasized that, from an Islamic standpoint, the social card was superior to both the package system and the social market. One manager of a SYD waqf in Ankara told me that the problem with the package system was that it delivered "every family the same stuff, without a concern for their specific conditions;" they added that "knowing what a family really needs is expected from us Muslims." Another volunteer from an Islamic NGO explained that the aid packages rarely included perishable or fragile items, such as "eggs, milk, meat, or kitchenware," whereas the social card allowed the poor "to get what they need freely at the supermarket," which meant "being true to the spirit of Islam." Others valued the social card for being discrete, thereby avoiding stigma. In contrast to the social market, the social card "kept recipients hidden" ("İhtiyaç Sahipleri İçin Alışveriş Kartı Çıkarttı" 2011), thereby ensuring that their "honor and dignity was protected" ("Sosyal Yardım Kartı Yardımı" n.d.).

While explaining the perceived benefits of social cards, many actors nostalgically invoked Ottoman sadaqa stones, alluding to the anonymity of recipients and the convenience for donors (Yıldırım 2018, 604). Cengiz, a twenty-five-year-old man and an enthusiastic volunteer at a small Islamic NGO in Istanbul, explained the value of anonymity by comparing supermarkets to mosques:

> When poor people walked through the courtyard of a mosque or a waqf, no one would know why they were there; maybe they came to pray, or to meet someone, or something else. If they picked coins from the sadaqa stones, nobody would notice. It was a free space. Similarly, when our families go to the supermarket to use their social card, no one knows that they are deprived, no one looks down upon them.

In his mind, the juxtaposition between a sacred space, such as a mosque, and a commercial venue, such as a supermarket, made sense as long as both allowed for providing aid in a way that respected the dignity of the poor. Other individuals, likewise, saw social cards as an updated version of Ottoman sadaqa stones that made it easier for the wealthy to give. Asiye, an affluent middle-aged woman who had begun to volunteer at her neighborhood SYD waqf in Ankara, explained:

> When individuals with the means visited mosques to pray, they just left some money in the sadaqa stone, without giving it much thought. Now, when I go shopping, just to get the stuff I always get, the card takes a small amount of the money and transfers it to the pool. It just happens automatically.

Since proponents of the social card admired it for its anonymity, there were debates about whether this goal was truly achieved. Would the poor be embarrassed if cashiers or fellow shoppers noticed that they were not actually using a bank card? Would cashiers ever criticize or scorn card-holders for their choices? Concerns about the stigmatization of the poor, in other words, did not disappear with the adoption of the social card. In 2015, the Elazığ municipality was harshly criticized when, in an attempt to announce the new social card system, the municipality distributed photos to the media that depicted recipients (poor women) as they were handed their cards by the governor ("Sosyal Medyayı Karıştıran Fotoğraf: Şov Gibi Yardım Yapılır Mı!" 2015). Another frequently discussed issue concerned the possible misuse of funds. How could one be sure that the poor were buying what they truly need? Lastly, there were concerns that some individuals were able to get two or more cards, since coordination between agencies did not always live up to their ideals.

Like other technologies of aid distribution, this instrument sought to transform aid recipients into autonomous and anonymous individuals. In doing so, it repackaged consumerism into a form of belonging to a distant but caring community. The poor were empowered into anonymous solitary shoppers. Detached from social ties, aid recipients were no longer to be burdened by time spent together during face-to-face interactions—rather, the Muslim Social was to be most prominent in the *absence* of shared bodily presence. Far from being a neutral instrument that served financial inclusion, the social card thus stood at the end of a series of slight mutations through which the pure "Islamic gift" was mediated through axioms of the market. The shift from the crowd-charity spectacle to the package system and the subsequent invention of the social market and the social card were part of a larger transformation that heightened the importance of consumer culture and individual dignity, and the moral value placed on choice and freedom. Moreover, the shift in aid delivery methods occurred in conjunction with an increased focus on determining eligibility. The traditional form of Islamic almsgiving—direct, informal, face-to-face—began to be replaced by the calculation of deservingness, of worthy and unworthy recipients, and of information and statistics.

Technologies of Information

After 2003, the AKP introduced numerous targeted and means-tested social assistance programs (see chapter 1). These programs' legitimacy was largely based on their ability to distinguish between the deserving and the undeserving poor. Finding, recording, categorizing, analyzing, and storing information about the poor was deemed part of a scientific approach to poverty alleviation. Technologies of information, such as the collection of documents, social investigation visits to applicants' homes, and the creation of electronic databases, were thus gradually incorporated into the Muslim Social.

These technologies justified the principle of a theoretically accessible realm of objective truth that exists beyond faith. Instead of relying on their intuition, pious Muslims were now expected to comport themselves as caring but distant experts. Many were drawn to new methods of assessment, but also worried that the emphasis on objective facts contradicted faith-based notions of the true gift. In their mind, traditional Islamic charity was founded upon a humble form of non-inquisitiveness: it was offensive to confront, interrogate, or cross-examine someone who claimed to be in need, and only Allah had access to such knowledge. To seek out exact information about the destitute was thus seen as a religious offense that suggested a lack of true devotion. Despite their reservations, these actors nevertheless participated in the systematic collection of information. Some marshaled interpretations of sadaqa that emphasized personal intuition over objective truth, whereas others claimed that acts of sadaqa always included an implicit calculation about whether the recipient was deserving of aid. Technologies of information were designed, implemented, and negotiated amid these conflictual assemblages of Islamic neoliberalism.

Documents

To serve the Turkish people better, public SYD waqfs and Islamic NGOs were encouraged to improve their internal procedures and increase their knowledge about aid recipients. As a result, the management of print and electronic data became an integral aspect of Islamic charity. Mimicking the bureaucratic power of the state, people I met at public SYD waqfs and Islamic NGOs always made a point of explaining their archival system, sometimes even opening folders and sharing private information about applicants with me. Documents were everywhere: applicants provided them, volunteers organized them, and managers examined them, filed them, and archived them. In what Matthew Hull (2012) calls the "government of paper," documents and documentation became an indispensable element of the Turkish welfare regime.

The Muslim Social organized citizens' encounters with public authorities through a series of regulated steps. First, an individual filled out an application and was then handed a sheet of paper that listed the required documents. Next, the applicant collected these documents, which often required separate trips to various state institutions. Each applicant had to provide a photocopy of their national ID card and a poverty certificate (issued by the *muhtar*), and additional documents were required for different kinds of aid. For instance, those applying for disability benefits had to provide a medical report, whereas requests for a widow salary had to be accompanied by the deceased husband's death certificate, all in addition to the standard documents. Once the applicant compiled all the documents, they were filed in a folder that was assigned a specific number. These folders were often color-coded and categorized according to neighborhoods or to the type of aid that was being requested. Next, depending on the organization, a caseworker, a group of volunteers, or NGO personnel examined the documents to decide if the applicant was deserving of assistance. This was often followed by lengthy discussions among committee members. Sometimes documents were incomplete, so the committee had to request additional information. In other instances, the absence of documentation was overlooked in an attempt to deliver aid in a timely or compassionate manner.

While aware of imperfections, most actors expressed confidence in the documents. They held that photocopied identifications, signed papers, and completed forms provided sufficient information for assessing and addressing need. According to Ahmet, one of the mid-level managers of DF, governing the Muslim Social was not possible without comprehensive documentation:

> Most people do not understand that we have a systematic approach to aid. They think we just go to a neighborhood and give aid to people who are like us. Actually, citizens come to us themselves. Anyone can apply, of course, but we only assist people that meet certain criteria. . . . We do not trust our personal opinion or rely on our religious conscience.

As he compared impulsive, sporadic, and unorganized customs of giving with a methodical approach, Ahmet could be seen as commending a system that puts the burdens of seeking assistance and proving one's level of need on the shoulders of the poor themselves. But, in his mind, there was no contradiction between the Islamic principle of respecting the poor and requesting documents from applicants. "Muslim life is based on quiet systems that work on their own," he explained. "Even though no one asked questions, sadaqa stones worked well because they were surrounded by the community's care and knowledge."

In contrast, other volunteers and managers experienced a certain degree of friction between their task of accessing objective truth and other ways of assessing someone's level of need. Sometimes they were unable to obtain documents and worried about whether they had become too emotionally attached; at other times, they explained that personal intuition was another way to access information. In one of my visits, Mehmet, the manager of a small Islamic NGO in Ankara, opened his file cabinet. It was located behind his desk and consisted of two shelves of manila folders in different colors. "See here," he said, "we have a system in place." He then pulled out one of the folders, opened it, and showed me the front page, which had the applicant's photograph and some basic information such as name, age, occupation, address: "Here, we have a woman who has three children, she only gets a widow salary, she has a very small home—if you had seen it, you would be devastated." Next, he picked up another folder: "Here, we have a man who has lost a finger. He has a medical report that says that he is 32% unemployable. Usually, we are only supposed to give if it is 50%, but this time, we decided to help him, but only for a short amount of time." Whereas he was confident in the deservingness of the woman, he was hesitant, even a bit embarrassed, to admit that a man was collecting aid when he did not seem to have a debilitating illness. In this case, personal feelings had overridden established rules: "We must have decided that he needs the support," Mehmet continued. "Sometimes percentages do not really tell you about their real conditions. We also leave room for giving 'just because,' like we do when we give sadaqa for the sake of Allah." Even as he aspired to rely on technologies of information, Mehmet believed that communal ways of knowing should supplement the information provided by documents.

In contrast, other actors found the emphasis on documents problematic. Many volunteers told me that a true Muslim acted in a humble manner when confronted with material need. Respecting the poor required trusting the person, not the documents they were expected to procure. Of course, information was useful, and helpful even, but knowing an applicant required knowing their community, their neighborhood, their family. Emine, a long-term volunteer at a public SYD waqf, said:

> We are here to serve; Allah will tell you who is truly in need, you just need to look in their eyes. You cannot just order an elderly woman: "Go get this document, show me that you do not own any property, bring your husband's death certificate." To say things like that, it does not suit me; as a Muslim, I would feel embarrassed to act in that manner. . . . If someone comes to you and says, "I am hungry, I need help," then turning them away just because they do not have their documents, that does not fit with our faith. If we really need information, then we can ask their neighbors.

For Emine, personal intuition, religious devotion, and communal awareness replaced the information that one could gather from analyzing documents. Respecting the poor called for a different kind of "data":

one based not on pieces of paper, but on social relationships. According to her, making the needy procure documents was a form of arrogance that was forbidden by Islam. Muslims ought to give freely and with the understanding that only Allah has access to ultimate knowledge about the true condition of the poor.

Here again we see the disputed nature of governmental assemblages, expressed in Emine's belief that true Muslims would not expect the poor to prove their poverty. While comments like these are not necessarily to be understood as examples of resistance to neoliberalism, their utterance does point to ways in which productive tensions were constitutive of the Muslim Social.

Social Investigation

Social investigation (*sosyal inceleme*) was another technology that emerged to collect and verify information about the poor. Teams consisting of NGO personnel, waqf employees, and a mix of volunteers were tasked with visiting benefactors' homes. Often announcing their visits a couple of days in advance, teams tried to complete all their visits in a single neighborhood on the same day. The goal was to cross-check the information provided by the applicant, and fully assess the situation by observing the domestic, economic, and familial circumstances of the household, a process that included taking extensive notes in a form specifically designed for this purpose.

The question was no longer whether a family was truly deserving of assistance, but rather the proper calculation of their level of need through assessing their living conditions according to preestablished categories and standardized metrics. Some forms were extensive and detail-oriented, whereas others were more concise, ranging from two to ten pages, and including as few as fifteen and as many as fifty questions. Despite disparities, all versions of the social investigation form included conventional questions, such as name, surname, birth date, birthplace, mother's name, father's name, address, and so on. In addition to these standard questions, the Deniz Feneri organization's form, for example, included sections for a family's basic expenses, including health, rent, food, bills, and education;

their debt; and whatever social assistance the family might already be receiving. The form also reviewed living conditions. Were they renters, homeowners, or squatters? Did they have electronic appliances? Was their house clean? Were any of the family members sick or in need of medicine? Did the children attend school? And finally, what exactly did the family need: cash, food, clothing, medicine, coal, or furniture? Most of these categories had a checkbox next to it, and additional space for qualitative comments was provided on the back of the form ("Sosyal İnceleme Formu").

To improve technologies of social investigation, the SYDGM introduced a "point system" (*puanlama sistemi*) in 2013, and assigned a numerical value to each category ("Sosyal Yardım Sistemi Değişiyor" 2012) to "develop objective benchmarks" for targeted social programs (Çoşkun and Güneş 2009). In reality, many public SYD waqfs and Islamic NGOs already used a point system in their internal operations. Some of these programs could even sort beneficiaries according to their level of need; that is, they could list applicants from the poorest to those with the least amount of need ("SYD Vakıfları Sivil Toplum Kuruluşlarının Ufkunu Açıyor" 2010). Thus, personnel and volunteers of Islamic NGOs and SYD waqfs—most of whom did not have training in the field of social work— were now tasked with conducting social investigations, assessing the intensity of need, calculating points, and computing percentages.

Many personnel and volunteers felt that they were not really qualified to make such decisions. On this point, Hasan, a manager of a small Islamic NGO, compared the technical expertise of social workers with personal intuition. For him, technologies of information were enhanced by decisions made from the heart. While Hasan found intuition and information to be compatible, others experienced social investigation as one of the most emotionally taxing aspects of their charity work. Some volunteers thought that their lack of expertise restricted their ability to properly assess a situation. For instance, Sibel, who frequently conducted visits to the recipients' houses, complained: "We are not social workers; unfortunately, we do not have the training, so we hope that we are being fair to both these poor families and to those who have trusted their donations with us." She turned to Elanur, a twenty-one-year-old university student who, as part of her volunteer training, had recently begun to accompany

Sibel during some of these house visits, and asked her: "What do you think of our approach so far?" Elanur, surprised that her opinion was sought, thought for a second, and then shared her experience:

> You can see easily that they really need the help, but you have to take a step back and assess the situation. That was hard for me. You see, in my family, we just help people. . . . But this is an organization, so it makes sense to ask for documents, fill out forms, and write down how much is given to whom and for what reason . . . The approach here is very systematic.

Most volunteers struggled with the emotional demands of social investigation and found themselves conflicted about whether they were helping the poor in the proper "Islamic" fashion. Some, like Elanur, believed that religious principles of giving were lost when technologies of information came into use. Others felt that the poor were put on display since their private information was accessible to many. "In Islam, poverty is not something to be embarrassed about," explained one NGO manager, "but I still worry about whether we are doing right by them when everyone knows so much about their situation." In these instances, volunteers' spiritual devotion conflicted with the emotional distance required by managerialism, but they operated jointly, nonetheless.

Moreover, many actors acknowledged that there were limits to how much (or how accurately) the poor could be known. For example, many DF volunteers told me that most poor women lied about their marital status. Since widows and divorced women were more likely to get assistance, it made sense for female applicants to present themselves as single parents who lacked the support of a male breadwinner or an extended family network. One volunteer explained how most applicants would send their husbands to a relative's house when they expected a visit from the social investigation teams. This was a concern, but there was not much to do about it because volunteers could not "always know what is going on." Another manager of a SYD waqf said: "people are known to lie," and explained: "We cannot possibly check everything one says or does. . . . We almost always err on the side of abundance; they might be liars, but only Allah can judge their situation."

Social investigation operated amid these concerns over the accessibility of truth. When confronting "dishonest" or "sneaky" applicants, actors tasked with dispensing goods felt conflicted. While they used social investigation forms, they did not always make decisions according to established criteria, often relying on their personal intuition or religious devotion instead of "objective truths" about poverty. Such a blending of spiritual affections and technical measures highlights another way in which Islamic neoliberalism was assembled via contestations instead of coming together in a seamless fashion.

The Social Assistance Information System

These efforts to generate, analyze, and interpret information about applicants culminated in the creation of the Social Assistance Information System (Sosyal Yardım Bilgi Sistemi, SOYBIS). SOYBIS promised a "total information capture"—a key characteristic of computerized and digitized welfare regimes (Dencik and Kaun 2010). Like other Turkish e-governance initiatives, electronic information about poverty was deemed to improve state–citizen relations.

At the beginning of my fieldwork, some actors were already discussing the need for a more systematic approach to govern social service provision. They had come to believe that the compilation of documents was not sufficient for determining eligibility. For example, Hatice told me in 2009 that it would be beneficial if the state created a "shared database." She explained that some applicants worked in the informal sector and others had casual day-labor jobs, which meant that these individuals did not have traceable income since they were not registered through the social security system. In her view, a "system" would prevent recipients from abusing organizations: "We cannot control everything, nobody can, but if there were a [unified government] database, then it would prevent people from unfairly collecting assistance."

I was first introduced to what such a database might look like during a visit to the SYDGM in 2010. Ali, a civil servant who worked in the Social Assistance office of the ministry, explained the various steps of the application process. Then, he asked me to provide my national ID number so that he could enter it into a pilot program on his computer. He was able to access information about me, such as whether I owned any property or owed any taxes. After we examined these private financial details on the computer screen, he explained:

> Each waqf will eventually have access to this system. Once the applicant provides us with their national ID number, we can pull up all kinds of information about their economic situation. . . . We have all the information we need to objectively assess an application. That way, we will only give to those who are truly in need.

This pilot database was initially called the "Identity Sharing System" and was partially funded by the World Bank, Ali elaborated. Would everyone have access to this information eventually? Ali was not so sure: "We cannot just hand this information over to any civil society organization. I mean, these are important documents, but I am not really sure how the system will work when it is fully integrated (*bütünleşik*)." An integrated system required all aid organizations, including SYD waqfs, NGOs, and municipal governments, to enter information about recipients, the amount and kind of aid given, and the duration of the provision. Interoperability and communication between organizations was to ensure full access to accurate information.

Implemented over three stages from 2010 to 2012, the SYDGM promoted SOYBIS as an improvement upon earlier mechanisms of determining need. According to Hayati Yazıcı, the state minister who oversaw the operations of the SYDGM at the time, SOYBIS was a prime example of modernization; previously, the burden was placed on applicants to "prove their need" by collecting various documents and "taking a bus from one state institution to the next, waiting in line at thirteen different places so that they can provide answers to twenty-eight different questions"; but this "primitive" approach was now abandoned ("Devlet Bakanımız Hayati Yazıcı 'Sosyal Yardım Sadaka Değildir'" 2010). VGM General Director Adnan Erdem similarly explained that SOYBIS allowed the "swift assessment of applications with just one click" and was thus able to eliminate those instances where an individual might try to obtain aid from multiple organizations ("Bütünleşik Sosyal Yardım Hizmetleri Projesi Çalıştay Toplantısı Yapıldı" 2008).

Actors expressed conflicting opinions about the truthfulness of information stored in the database. They also held opposing views about whether SOYBIS represented an Islamic notion of care, charity, and community. Some believed in the accuracy of the information stored in the database. In their minds, the database was a manifestation of a scientific approach to poverty. Metin, a middle-aged man and the head manager of a SYD waqf in Istanbul who had been trained as a social worker, trusted SOYBIS to provide much-needed guidance. His discussion of how SOYBIS combined developmentalist, populist, and Islamic goals is exemplary of this stance held by many:

> This is something we have wanted for a long time. But it requires planning and a vision. What is the point of development if it does not benefit those who are most in need? Allah blesses our efforts; the more information we have, the better we can serve our people. We need to know everything that happens in our area, just like the leaders of the past: they would know who came to the sadaqa stone to get what they needed at dawn, without being seen, and who frequented the sadaqa stone even though they already had enough.

Metin reasoned that an information-based approach to determining eligibility was not antithetical to Islamic notions of charity. He downplayed the significance of anonymity, instead emphasizing that sadaqa stones provided access to information about the needy. He thereby normalized the way SOYBIS, like other technologies of information, probed recipients' private lives. The poor had to be observed and assessed, regardless of whether information was retrieved via communal ties or technological means.

In contrast to Metin, Nebahat, a clerk at an SYD waqf in Ankara, who had recently completed a preliminary training organized to educate SYD workers about various aspects of SOYBIS, found the emphasis on information problematic. While reflecting on what she learned at the training, she explained:

> There was a lot of focus on numbers: calculate this, enter that, make sure everything goes into the right box, how to find what you are looking

for, that kind of stuff. It was helpful, sure, but what can you really know about someone's condition by looking at their national ID number? If our job is to serve, then we need to listen, otherwise you would give some comfort maybe, but there would be no closeness. When one gives sadaqa, when one is trying to help another person, you need to be affectionate. I mean, I think it is also important to form a human relationship when you do this kind of work, but that was not something that came up much [in the training].

For Nebahat, a SYD waqf had to be a place of heartfelt intimacy, not cold facts. She prided herself on rejecting short conversations in favor of learning about the mundane details of clients' everyday lives. Until recently, however, she did not actually consider the lengthy conversations that she had with them to be an issue. But now she was asked to focus on data entry instead of spending her time chatting with applicants—most of them were women whom Nebahat had come to know well. She found it difficult to "act like a stranger," but felt that a professional demeanor was expected from her.

In short, while the populist social imaginary portrayed an information-based approach to poverty alleviation as a vital feature of Islamic charity, actors' involvement in technologies of information wavered between confidence and enthusiasm on the one hand, and unease and hesitation on the other hand. Keeping one's distance instead of developing close personal relations became the preferred manner for those tasked with governing the Muslim Social, except the imagined distinction between collective wisdom, individual faith, and factual evidence was much more permeable on the ground (also see Alkan-Zeybek 2012).

Regulating Aid, Governing Poverty

Instead of a retrenchment of the welfare state, a fundamental shift in the government of poverty occurred in Turkey: the replacement of "disorganized" almsgiving and "inefficient" welfare with a governmental apparatus that systematically reorganized mechanisms of aid delivery. Inspired by the social imaginary of populist reform, Islamic NGOs and public SYD waqfs reimagined traditional forms of almsgiving in ways they hoped would serve the Turkish poor more effectively. Many pious Muslims described new social assistance programs as a way of improving, humanizing, modernizing, and, in a sense, reforming Islamic charity. Yet some actors remained uneasy about these myriad changes, feeling that some elements of the Muslim Social were not truly Islamic. Nonetheless, even when they were unsure, they took part in the design and implementation of various technologies of aid. These contested viewpoints about whether their faith condoned, mandated, or tolerated inquisitive methods of assessing need were part of the governmental assemblages that made up Islamic neoliberalism.

The governing of poverty took shape via two great threads of political knowledge: technologies of experience, which created "market-like" and "dignified" mechanisms of aid delivery, and technologies of information, which systematically distinguished between the deserving and undeserving poor. Poor relief was no longer a chaotic experience, but a curated one. Informal attitudes (of recipients, managers, donors) and disorganized mechanisms (concerning the selection of beneficiaries or the distribution of items) were no longer considered to be genuine responses to the problem of poverty, but were rather seen as an anomaly that must be folded back into the governmental order. At the juncture of these two technologies of aid, and as a shared element, I have highlighted the rise of techno-politics and managerialism among Islamic NGOs and public SYD waqfs. The mismatch between dehumanizing techniques of surveillance and compassionate techniques of experience aside, these technical interventions often fell short of their goals: knowledge was never sufficient to determine deservingness; recipients frequently lied about their conditions, subverted rules, and challenged expectations; and social markets often could not deliver an autonomous and dignified experience to benefactors. Nevertheless, these technologies worked in tandem to transform the Turkish poor into a "unified object of intervention" (Dean 2010, 87). Actors working in public institutions and volunteering in NGOs were portrayed as "politically neutral artisans" (Ferguson 1994a, 178). These individuals were equipped with a comprehensive arsenal of tools such as documents, forms, surveys, questionnaires, and electronic data about aid recipients, and they used these technical instruments to reimagine the meaning of Islamic charity in what they considered to be a pro-poor direction.

The standardization of monetary and in-kind donations and the rearrangement of social interactions transferred poverty governance into the technical-managerial realm. Moral-religious concerns were not entirely replaced, but reformulated in technical terms: respecting the spiritual dignity of the poor called for recognizing their individuality and freedom, while Islamic charity operated as a caring form of surveillance. These techniques of governance were structured around a double process: the disappearance of the crowd-charity spectacle and the elimination of subjective feeling. In the process, donations became semi-commodities, losing some of their "hau"—the spiritual component that, according to Mauss (1967), transforms ordinary things into gifts that carry the traces of their original owners. At the same time, anonymity gave these gifts a higher spiritual meaning. Donors gave anonymously, and recipients did not have personal interactions with their benefactors. Paradoxically, it was exactly the lack of a face-to-face relationship that was argued to generate emotional intimacy between the haves and the have-nots.

The question of how to create social bonds and assist the needy in a properly Islamic fashion, coupled with concerns over the objectification of the poor, are present in other dimensions of the Muslim Social. In chapter 4, I turn to the social imaginary of humanitarian responsibility to examine the interplay between religious notions of transnational community and the construction of the Muslim poor as a "deserving Other."

4

Humanitarian Responsibility and the Muslim Poor

Scene 1

Ankara, 2007. I took the public bus from downtown Ankara to get to Ümitköy—an upper-class suburban neighborhood that connects to Kızılay, Ankara's downtown, via an ever-expanding highway used by an increasing number of commuters. As I stared out the bus window, I saw a series of billboards: one that announced the opening of a new shopping mall, another that provided a visual list of grocery items on sale at a nearby supermarket, and yet another that publicized a children's festival organized by the municipal government of Ankara. Among these, a minimalist billboard is the one that grabbed my attention the most: the word "Goodness" (*İyilik*) was written over a white background with light-blue letters. Upon closer examination, I noticed the name of a prominent charity organization, Deniz Feneri, on the bottom-right corner. The billboard contained no other words, symbols, or images. Assumed to be self-explanatory, Goodness cultivated a sense of humanitarian responsibility among middle-class commuters and encouraged giving time and money to distant strangers.

Scene 2

Ankara, 2009. I was traveling from Ankara to Istanbul to conduct interviews with volunteers of Islamic NGOs. As I walked around the Ankara intercity bus terminal, waiting for the departure time of my bus, I noticed a large charity advertisement on one of the walls put up by Kızılay (Turkish Red Cross) in preparation for the upcoming Qurban holiday. The image was composed of symmetrical squares, each including a close-up picture of a smiling person's face. Young and old, these individuals were presumably all from different places. When I stood in front of this billboard, they directly met my gaze. I wondered: Do these images represent donors, recipients, or do they belong to the organization's personnel? Unnamed, divorced from context, and separated by invisible lines, their photographs nevertheless communicated a sense of community.

Scene 3

Istanbul, 2011. I was walking on a busy pedestrian street in the Taksim district, somewhere close to the famous Galata Bridge. I noticed an enormous billboard painted on the side of a building. A smiling boy, dressed in what appeared to be traditional African clothing, smiled and waved his hand. This was an advertisement for an orphan sponsorship program that was managed by the IHH organization. This cheerful boy looked with anticipation and demanded attention from passersby. The call to action was located at the bottom corner: "Send a text, make a phone call, or donate online," the ad said, "it has never been easier to support an orphan." Details such as the child's name, background, and circumstances were absent, but the sentiment was clear: as Turkish Muslims, we can and should do something to alleviate his suffering.

Each of these images illustrates the role that media advertisements play in the production of Islamic humanitarianism. During both my fieldwork and my subsequent visits to Turkey, I increasingly encountered images of suffering and calls to solidarity in public spaces, such as city centers, streets, and shopping malls on a daily basis. In addition to public billboards, Islamic (as well as secular and liberal) NGOs use a variety of other mediums, such as TV commercials and newspaper ads, to solicit donations. What explains the proliferation of these images and slogans in public spaces across Turkey? What transformed the notion that poverty and destitution are delicate personal matters and that Islamic charity should thus remain an undisclosed act of goodwill? What kinds of governmental assemblages enabled public displays of material need and social responsibility to become an ordinary aspect of urban life? And what are the effects of this public visibility for how social belonging is felt, experienced, and understood?

The widespread use of these advertisements illustrates a shift in the aesthetics of humanitarian communication in Turkey. The rise of organized, formal, professional Islamic charity coincided with the emergence of a distinctive humanitarian imaginary that sought to "socialize" Turkish Muslims "into those ways of feeling and acting that are legitimate and desirable" (Chouliaraki 2013b, 44). As has been the case elsewhere, Islamic humanitarianism altered collective understandings of destitution, need, and poverty and prescribed rules concerning the proper modes of charity, responsibility, and solidarity (Brankamp 2020; Chouliaraki 2013a; Mitchell 2017; Piotukh 2015; Reid-Henry 2014). The resultant neoliberal-Islamic assemblages of humanitarian responsibility operate not as a reflective mirror of a preexisting community, but as a productive force that constructs moral positions, creates political subjectivities, generates emotional structures, and produces knowledge about one's own selfhood and imagined others (Barnett and Weiss 2008; Bornstein and Redfield 2011; Fassin 2011; Malkki 2015; Mitchell 2016; Ticktin 2011). Innovative charitable images, slogans, and advertisements played a constitutive role in the production of humanitarian responsibility among pious Muslims in Turkey.[1]

1. The driving question of the scholarship on Islamic humanitarianism concerns the moral universe of aid work: Do Islamic NGOs operate according to the liberal principles of Western humanitarianism, such as neutrality, partiality, and universality, or do they instead adhere to an alternative framework that seeks to foster a sense of Islamic communitarianism? In seeking answers to this question, some scholars argue that Islamic humanitarian organizations are fundamentally different from Western aid organizations, and claim that the former are motivated by jihad instead of universal suffering (see Burr and Collins 2006; Levitt 2006). The idea that there is a fundamental difference between Western and Islamic humanitarianism is shared by some anthropologists who see non-Western charitable practices as a critique of the implicit assumptions of humanitarianism concerning agency, temporality, and the ideal gift relationship (see Bornstein and Redfield 2011; Mittermaier 2014; Scherz 2013). Other scholars, by contrast, celebrate the ways in which Muslims have adopted the governmental techniques of international aid organizations (see Benthall 2011; Benthall and Bellion-Jourdan 2003; Kroessin and Mohamed 2008; Petersen 2015). These perspectives, however, are primarily concerned with what Islamic humanitarianism is, instead of how it is constructed or what it does. By contrast, I examine how notions of humanitarian responsibility are generated, enforced, and negotiated, with a specific focus on the shifting governmental assemblages of Islamic values and neoliberal elements.

In this chapter, I examine how the communicative repertoire of Islamic humanitarianism in Turkey imagines the Muslim Social through a focus on the representation of deserving Muslim Others in advertisements and strategies used for inciting emotional responses. As critical media scholars have argued, charitable advertisements construct new subjectivities, formulate distinctive social imaginaries, reconfigure notions of belonging, and convey new ideas about the responsibility of individuals vis-à-vis one another (Boltanski 1999; Chouliaraki 2010, 2013b; Cooper 2018; Cottle and Nolan 2007; Dogra 2013; Fehrenbach and Rodogno 2015; Orgad 2013; Seu and Orgad 2017). Studying the discursive and visual politics of Islamic humanitarianism provides a lens for analyzing how various campaigns generate social identities, engender affective connections, and produce new understandings of religious belonging among Turkish Muslims and their imagined Others.

Within this broader line of inquiry, two aspects of what is often referred to as "neoliberal humanitarianism" are especially relevant for the purposes of this book: the role media advertisements play in the commodification of deserving Others, and the production of social belonging through the elicitation of emotional responses from spectators. Scholars working on this issue highlight that many humanitarian campaigns, endeavors, and interventions often perpetuate neoliberal elements, such as individualization and privatization, and disseminate pro-market values, such as accountability, competitiveness, and entrepreneurship, thereby making certain ways of thinking, feeling, and acting possible while precluding others (Daley 2013; Kapoor 2012; Mostafanezhad 2014; Oomen, Martens, and Piccoli 2021; Sözer 2020; Turner 2020). This literature examines the charity–media nexus by focusing on how advertisements represent the "deserving Other," articulates new languages of solidarity, and frames the moral obligations of prospective donors (Daley 2013; Desai 2019). These scholars find that one of the problematic aspects of humanitarian advertisements has to do with the objectification and commodification of "deserving Others" through sensationalist displays of suffering and need. At the same time, humanitarianism excludes as much as it includes, by distinguishing between "lives to be saved and lives to be risked," and in doing so, gives "specific value and meaning to human life" (Fassin 2007,

500). This chapter demonstrates that Islamic NGOs and state agencies in Turkey are involved in a similar politics of life in which they classify, sort, categorize, and separate out whose lives matter and whose do not, and do so in the name of helping others.

Another key issue relates to the ways in which the visual politics of humanitarianism references and, in turn, generates a wide range of emotional attachments between spectators and distant strangers. A main goal of humanitarian communication is to generate "intimacy at a distance" through reconfiguring parameters of philanthropic ideas and altruistic practices (Orgad and Seu 2014). While the emotional valence of humanitarian advertisements varies greatly—from pity to solidarity, and from guilt to mutual care—the communicative repertoire of humanitarianism is mainly about inciting emotional reactions through the strategic placement of images and slogans. In addition to reifying differences between the self and the Other, constructing the boundaries of a moral community, and espousing a worldview where the proper response to suffering is contributing to humanitarian campaigns from a distance, neoliberal humanitarianism also operates by curating an experience of emotional intimacy for responsibilized donors.

Following these insights, in this chapter I first map the communicative repertoire of Islamic humanitarianism to demonstrate the distinctive features of this humanitarian brand. Focusing on several transnational humanitarian campaigns that seek to help "Muslim orphans" and "fellow Muslims," I make two interrelated arguments. First, while advertisements used by Islamic NGOs and governmental agencies seemingly promoted a cohesive, egalitarian, and nonhierarchical community of believers, visual representations of distant suffering still enforced a savior–victim dichotomy. Second, the communicative repertoire of Islamic humanitarianism in Turkey focused on creating emotional intimacy for prospective donors by using specific tropes of the "deserving Other," such as orphans and fellow Muslims in need. Each of these representational styles, I further demonstrate, was inscribed with specific modes of emotional appeal, ranging from cheerfulness to anger, and from compassion to pity. The following analysis therefore posits that the Muslim Social was constructed and understood at a transnational scope through a series of intimate (but also distant) attachments between benefactors and their imagined Muslim Others. Before turning to this analysis, let me first provide information about the background assumptions and main claims of the Islamic social project of humanitarian responsibility as it originated in Turkey.

Humanitarian Responsibility

The Islamic social project of humanitarian responsibility suggests that Turkish Muslims ought to share their wealth and resources with other Muslims—and some non-Muslims—even if they are distant strangers. By grouping diverse individuals, communities, and geographies, this responsibility implies that Muslims, by virtue of their shared religious beliefs, have an obligation to alleviate each other's suffering. In doing so, this imaginary redefines Islamic practices, traditions, and values of almsgiving as timeless examples of developmental and humanitarian aid, thereby glossing over the variance in relations (kin vs. non-kin), scope (proximate vs. distant), and type of authority (patriarchal vs. transnational), which ordinarily differentiate humanitarian and faith-based forms of giving.

The very idea that Islam dictates its believers to alleviate the suffering of distant Others is part of Turkey's self-designation as the leader of the Muslim world. This geopolitical vision has found one of its key expressions in Ahmet Davutoğlu's neo-Ottoman foreign policy vision. A key figure in Islamist politics, Davutoğlu was Turkey's Minister of Foreign Affairs (2009–14) and later the prime minister of Turkey (2014–16). In his scholarly work as well as in his political career, he proposed "neo-Ottomanism" as a foundation for humanitarian diplomacy.[2] This pan-Islamist and expansionist foreign policy doctrine sought to reformulate Turkey's "geopolitical imagination" (Çelik and İşeri 2016, 432). Instead of defining

---

2. Humanitarian diplomacy refers to governmental and NGO-based provision of aid for purposes of enhancing the soft power of the donor country. In the Turkish case, humanitarian diplomacy often referred to a transnational vision of Islamic community, thereby making foreign diplomacy an integral aspect of Islamic humanitarianism (Davutoğlu 2013; Murinson 2006).

Turkey as a peripheral country or an extension of Europe, Davutoğlu considered the nation a "core country" of a newly conceived region that included Africa, the Middle East, and the larger Muslim world (Özkan 2014). One of the ways in which the AKP sought to establish Turkey as a regional powerhouse was through an expansion of humanitarian relief and developmental aid to countries with minority- or majority-Muslim populations. In addition to governmental organizations, such as TİKA and AFAD, Islamic NGOs were also tasked with carrying out overseas campaigns in countries ranging from Niger to Pakistan, and from Bosnia-Herzegovina to Turkmenistan (chapter 1).

Turkey's humanitarian efforts—assistance, emergency relief, diplomacy, and peacebuilding—were based on the premise that economic success and religious solidarity operated in conjunction. Developing profitable commercial relations was only possible if core countries, such as Turkey, were aware of and capable of meeting the needs of disadvantaged populations. This shared but contested geopolitical imaginary called for an alternative pact among Muslim-majority countries and promised not only an increase in economic opportunities but also a sense of belonging. Building on themes of civilizational revival, humanitarian responsibility championed the familiar theme of Turkey as the protector and savior of all Muslims.[3] Erasing the exploitative and unequal dimensions of Ottoman imperial rule, this dual narrative of "civilization" and "humanity" painted Turkey's search for new markets in a favorable light (Deringil 2003).

A key element of this Islamic social project was the imagined opposition between transnational Islamic relief efforts and Western/Christian humanitarianism.[4] Portraying themselves in competition with Western/

---

3. For more information about the racialized aspects of Islamic humanitarianism in Turkey, see Güner (2021) and Venkatachalam (2019). Also see Yeşil (2023) for an analysis of the instrumentalization of Muslim suffering in AKP's global communication initiatives.

4. I am aware that Christian and Western humanitarianism do not refer to the same phenomena. The reason I am using this term is only because my interlocutors perceived it as such. In their eyes, even secular Western humanitarian organizations were primarily motivated by Christian proselytizing efforts.

Christian organizations, many of these actors believed that Islamic ways of helping others were superior due to the presumed lack of power differentials among Muslims. Whereas Western/Christian aid led to the objectification of the poor, Islamic humanitarian and developmental relief efforts were said to respect the humanity of recipients.

Narratives about Western/Christian aid and concerns about the proselytization of fellow Muslims instilled feelings of obligation and solidarity. For many Turkish Muslims, the ability to provide disaster relief and humanitarian assistance to distant corners of the world was experienced through mixed languages of religion, nationalism, and compassion. Many of my interlocutors expressed a desire to be as successful at international relief efforts as global aid organizations, and were curious about charitable giving in other religious and cultural contexts. For example, Faruk, a mid-level manager of a KYM branch in Istanbul once told me:

> As Turkish civil society organizations, we want to be one of the first to arrive whenever there is a disaster. We want to represent our country in the best possible way. During the 1999 earthquake, people from all over the world came to help us; why shouldn't we be allowed to help others?

Similarly, when Ayşe, for instance, asked me about charitable giving in the United States, I told her that I believed that Christians gave as often as Muslims. She responded:

> I know; once I went to a church, and I watched a ceremony. At the end, everyone left some money in a small basket. No one seemed to take any offense. But that is not how it is for Muslims. If we collect donations, everyone thinks something else is going on.

By "something else going on," she was referring to allegations of corruption and links to violent organizations that are often brought up against Islamic charities. Ferhat also brought up perceived differences between Christian and Muslim charity; he wanted to know "if Christians learned charity from Muslims, or if we learned it from them"—a question I did not have an answer for. These individuals, as was the case with many of my interlocutors, conceived of Islamic humanitarianism in opposition to Western/Christian aid organizations. In their minds, faith-based giving was no longer a local or even nationwide activity, but rather a transnational enterprise. As they came to think of themselves as global altruists, they felt that there was a double standard in the field of humanitarianism. As Faruk's and Ayşe's accounts illustrate, they believed that no one questioned if Western NGOs or Christian groups showed up in distant corners of the world to help or solicited donations for that purpose. But, when Muslims did the same, they were met with suspicion and disbelief.

Despite this imagined opposition, Turkey's humanitarian discourses, practices, and interventions often mimicked the cultural logics and representational strategies of Western humanitarianism.[5] This resemblance was a result of the fact that the communicative repertoire of Islamic humanitarianism repackaged languages of religious solidarity and notions of the deserving Muslim poor into easily consumable images and emotionally resonant slogans.

The Communicative Repertoire of Islamic Humanitarianism

As the use of print and visual media for humanitarian purposes became widespread, the Turkish state and Islamic NGOs produced a distinctive humanitarian brand by manufacturing new languages of religious solidarity and visual representations of need and suffering.[6] This novel communicative repertoire elicited and governed ways of compassionate feeling and responsible action. The Islamic project of humanitarian responsibility acquired force as activists, bureaucrats, civil society practitioners, and laypersons began to think about social bonds and moral obligations in novel ways, with all that is implied for the construction of collective identities and representations of the Other. In particular, conceiving the Muslim Social at a transnational scope required new ways of representing and understanding traditional concepts of Islamic charity.

5. For a similar discussion of Muslim organizations mimicking Western aid practices, see Baron (2014).

6. The term "humanitarian brand" describes the use of market logics by humanitarian campaigns and organizations, and specifically refers to processes of crafting a public identity with a specific moral message and distinctive social purpose (see Vestergaard 2010).

The Islamic reimagination of Turkey's humanitarian responsibility drew from a vast repertoire of terms associated with religious notions of charity, deservingness, and mutual responsibility. In addition to themes drawn from Islamic cosmology, this communicative repertoire made strategic use of secular, liberal, and patriotic slogans to appeal to a wider range of potential donors. Consequently, these representations produced a new vocabulary for understanding humanitarian responsibility in religious terms by summoning their audiences to reconsider scriptural norms and cultural practices that have traditionally governed Islamic giving in Turkey.

Media advertisements frequently used religious terms, such as al-fitr, sadaqa, qurban, and zakat, to elicit donations from the Turkish public. These were no longer practices of faith-based giving that took place between friends, relatives, or neighbors, but rather a humanitarian act of generosity. By referencing the importance of *ibadet* (worship) and *hayır* (philanthropy), TV commercials narrated heartbreaking stories of suffering, need, and destitution among orphans, sick children, and elderly women and called upon Muslim publics to feel and act. Circulating in Islamic charitable campaigns' advertisements, these repetitive phrases sought to provide an immediate answer for why potential donors ought to give. On the one hand, this communicative repertoire argued that there was no fundamental difference between giving to one's immediate kin and helping those in one's immediate vicinity by assisting distant strangers. On the other hand, one did not have to be deeply religious in order to give: merely caring for the suffering of others was sufficient. This dual meaning was crucial for these humanitarian advertisements to succeed— both for their messages to resonate with their multiple audiences and to collect funds from potential donors.

The *ümmet* (*ummah*) was one of the frequently used slogans in charitable advertisements. Traditionally, the term *ummah* refers to all Muslims who, regardless of whether they are dead or alive, are believed to be bound by a transhistorical religious-spiritual connection. However, since the nineteenth century, this term has become analogous to the idea of a "Muslim world," a kind of pan-Islamic solidarity of Muslims around the globe (Aydın 2017). When used as a "style of humanitarian appeal" (Chouliaraki

2013b, 55), the ummah similarly communicates a monolithic notion of the Muslim world as categorized along lines of religious difference. These advertisements thus convey a sense of religious belonging to prospective donors: offerings are not just for distant strangers but rather for an imagined community of co-believers.

Although references to a global community of co-religionists were most prevalent, advertisements stressed that Turkish Muslims were responsible for helping non-Muslims as well. Since Islam is a universal religion, the argument went, Muslims have a global responsibility to "the entire universe, and not just to a clan, tribe, ethnic, linguistic group, the members of a certain race, or a geographical area" (Taşgetiren 2009, 6). These kinds of commercials and posters emphasized vocabularies of mutual care and shared humanity, but still interpellated their audiences primarily as Muslims.

In addition to providing religious grounds for why one ought to contribute to these charitable campaigns, advertisements also included slogans that refer to notions of collective belonging, such as "brotherhood" (kardeşlik), "sharing" (paylaşım), "friendship" (dostluk), and "goodness" (iyilik).[7] While allusions to an imagined community perpetually oscillated between themes of global universalism and religious particularism, this communicative repertoire nevertheless provided a moral compass for visualizing the Muslim Social at a transnational scope.

Another key element of this communicative repertoire was representations of the deserving Muslim Other. Advertisements for humanitarian campaigns drew from Quranic notions of populations who were deemed eligible for charity, while redefining conventional objects of humanitarian care through an Islamic language. In these advertisements, certain images were amplified not only because of the level and intensity of need,

---

7. For example, Deniz Feneri identifies itself as the "Goodness Movement of the Century," uses the slogan "Make a Sacrifice in the Name of Friendship" when soliciting donations for the Sacrifice (Qurban) holiday, and refers to its charity sale events as "Goodness Sales." The IHH frequently refers to brotherhood in its campaigns, publishes a children's magazine titled Goodness Mail, and provides children with a "Good Child Certificate" in exchange for small monetary donations.

but also because these categories were assumed to resonate with the religious sensibilities of the Turkish public. Three words were common in humanitarian advertisements: the needy (muhtaç), the unjustly treated (mağdur), and the downtrodden (mazlum). These three terms were more common than the Turkish word for the poor (*yoksul*), but were interchangeably used to refer to the deserving objects of humanitarian aid and religious compassion. The word *muhtaç* was used in reference to individuals who were too proud to ask for help. These imagined worthy recipients were also often referred to as *ihtiyaç sahipleri* (those who are truly in need). By contrast, the term *mağdur* referred to victims of unjust treatment—to people whose destitution or misery did not come as a result of their own personal decisions. In a similar vein, mazlum referred to people who were pushed to the margins of society. Although they were desolate and helpless, they did not raise their voices against their oppressors; they suffered in silence.

In short, the communicative repertoire of Islamic humanitarianism creatively combined references to traditions of religious charity, languages of Islamic solidarity, and representations of deserving Others with visual strategies and styles of appeal that are regularly used by Western humanitarian organizations. Each of these advertisements operated as part of the broader "social technology of belonging" (Berlant 2004, 6) to the Muslim Social. The transnational scope of the Muslim Social was generated through the interplay between humanitarian representations, Islamic customs, and perceptions of a world shaped by religious difference. However, the use of themes drawn from traditions of Islamic charity had a peculiar effect: the production of easily consumable images that not only overlooked complexities of suffering and solidarity, but also generated morally circumspect norms of emotional intimacy.

Poverty Images and Affective Messages

Certain groups of people fit the image of the ideal recipient for pious Muslims. Although the construction of the poor is in accordance with Islamic cosmology, there is still a formidable gap between Quranic categories of the deserving poor and those considered as worthy recipients by contemporary Islamic NGOs in Turkey. Two categories of the deserving poor—orphans and fellow Muslims—were most frequently used. By combining religious imagery with representational styles and emotional messages drawn from global aid organizations, the Islamic social project of humanitarian responsibility construed the Muslim Social at a transnational scale of belonging. While this governmental assemblage fostered emotional intimacy between co-religionists, the communicative repertoire of Islamic humanitarianism perpetuated differences between Turkish Muslims and their imagined Others.

The Muslim Orphan

While the belief that Muslims have a humanitarian responsibility to orphans residing in distant lands is a recent invention, assisting orphans has always been considered a religious duty by Muslims.[8] In addition to the fact that the Prophet Muhammad was an orphan himself, several other Islamic texts stress the importance of providing emotional and financial support to orphans (Benthall 2011, 103). Beyond its religious connotations, orphan care has played several political functions. For example, in the late Ottoman Empire, concerns over the well-being of destitute, orphaned, and marginalized children justified the legitimacy of modernization efforts (Maksudyan 2014; Özbek 2003).

It was only in the 2000s that Islamic NGOs began to organize orphan-focused transnational campaigns as part of the larger project of humanitarian responsibility. While these campaigns referred to Islamic practices of assisting orphans, they called upon and fostered fundamentally different kinds of social bonds and ethical norms. In Turkey, traditional forms of orphan care were provided as an extension of patriarchal authority to children of kin—the orphan became part of the extended family. By contrast, orphan sponsorship programs constructed an obligation to children of distant strangers, thereby marking orphan care a religious obligation that includes children beyond one's immediate kin. In the absence of face-to-face interactions, these humanitarian campaigns sought to generate

8. Islamic law defines orphans as children who have lost a father (*yetim*), whereas children who have lost a mother are not considered orphans because they are assumed to receive care from their fathers (see Baron 2014, 24–25).

affective attachments between benefactors and recipients through the use of specific media strategies.

Among these NGOs, the IHH has been quite successful in creating a humanitarian brand in transnational orphan care.[9] This organization was founded in 1992 when a group of Islamist activists in Istanbul got together to organize aid to Bosnian Muslims.[10] This is the reason the IHH refers to itself as the first Islamic humanitarian NGO in Turkey. In addition to orphan-focused campaigns, the IHH organizes overseas projects during the month of Ramadan for the Qurban (Sacrifice) holiday, and carries out several developmental programs. IHH's humanitarian brand aligns well with the AKP's foreign policy outlook, and AKP diplomats often interfere to protect IHH volunteers if problems arise during humanitarian missions.[11]

One of the first orphan campaigns that the IHH organized was for Afghani children who lost their parents due to the 2001 US invasion.[12]

9. While IHH is the leading Islamic NGO in transnational orphan care, other Islamic NGOs in Turkey have also begun to organize similar orphan campaigns, albeit at a smaller scale.

10. The IHH was formally registered in 1995. Between 1992 and 1995, it largely operated as an informal group, bringing together Islamist political activists.

11. In May 2010, the IHH organized the Gaza Freedom Flotilla (*Mavi Marmara*), which resulted in the death of nine volunteers and an international crisis between Israel and Turkey.

12. During this campaign, Turkish Muslims were presented with "negative images" of Afghan orphans and were asked to join aid efforts with reference to a language of moral responsibility. The IHH uploaded real-life photographs of Afghani children onto their website. Taken by Turkish activists who had traveled to Afghanistan to provide humanitarian aid and assistance, these photographs capture children in their daily lives: playing with their friends, sitting together with their relatives, and walking down the roads of their village. Although most of these photographs hinted at the prevalence of misery and impoverishment, they communicated the sense that these children belonged to a specific local community and cultural geography, even if they may have lost a parent. In other words, the children were not represented in a fashion that divorced them from the reality of their everyday life. The figure of the "Muslim volunteer" was also strangely absent from these images. Sometimes, a group of activists appeared together in a photograph where they have a concerned and solemn look. They seemed to be content, but

During this campaign, assisting Afghani orphans was portrayed as part of transnational political solidarity that exceeded the borders of the nation-state. By contrast, most of IHH's orphan campaigns today operate as an extension of the Turkish government's humanitarian diplomacy. In these campaigns, the IHH combined Islamic values of orphan care with prevalent themes of Western humanitarianism, such as the idealization of the orphan-child as an innocent and worthy aid recipient (Manzo 2008; Zarzycka 2016). These representations positioned Muslim orphans at the center of Islamic humanitarianism. While revered, the Muslim orphan was also caught in an aesthetics of spectacle and suffering. Audiences were moved by the capitalist desire to consume, as much as they were motivated by a religious motivation to help.

As of 2023, the IHH administers thirty-eight orphanages in various countries such as Afghanistan, Bangladesh, Burkina Faso, Ethiopia, Indonesia, Pakistan, Philippines, Somalia, Thailand, and Uganda. Although the organization has built residential orphanages in Turkey, most of its focus is transnational, with particular emphasis on countries in Asia and Africa. On their website, the IHH (n.d.-b) explains their orphan-related mission:

> The majority of the world's orphans today are located within oppressed geographies of Islam. These unprotected children are susceptible to a variety of threats such as human trafficking, organ trafficking, drug abuse, crime, prostitution, begging as well as the risk of becoming child soldiers and workers. Many Christian missionary organizations reach millions of orphans located in Muslim countries and are eager to use them for their own interests. At IHH, we do our best to protect thousands of orphans in many of these countries. We work endlessly in order to support these children until they can support themselves by providing a variety of services such as lodging, health care, education and food. We want them to be able to live in their own country, grow up

---

they were not "happy," nor did they seem to be "empowered." (This discussion is based on the author's analysis of IHH's 2002 website, which can be accessed through the Wayback Machine: https://archive.org/web.)

amongst their own kin without being separated from their own culture. We build residential orphanages for those children who have lost their own parents and who do not have the support of any close relatives.

With this style of humanitarian appeal, the IHH compelled Turkish Muslims to act upon their faith. Orphans were portrayed as at-risk populations facing physical harm, moral degeneration, and Christian proselytizing. The IHH legitimated its activities by stressing how specific projects are embedded within a holistic approach to orphan care. The goal of protecting these orphans from Christian humanitarian organizations, as well as Western adoption agencies, is stated in explicit terms. Such allusions to the link between Western humanitarian assistance and religious conversion sought to grab Turkish Muslims' attention by producing a moral panic over religious identity.

Even so, the communicative repertoire of Islamic humanitarianism privileged a positive portrayal when it came to the representation of Muslim orphans. IHH's orphan-focused campaigns sought to cultivate a series of positive feelings. Many orphan campaigns used symbols such as "smiles," "hearts," and "love." These orphan projects had titles such as "An Orphan for Each Heart," and "I wish I had a family in Turkey who cares about me." Various IHH advertisements emphasized the significance of belonging using slogans such as "family," "humanity," "brotherhood," and the "world." The suffering of orphans, and the humanitarian responsibility of Muslims, was curated through a series of "positive" experiences that were manufactured between the orphan and the donors/sponsors: the charitable act was valued not only due to its otherworldly benefits, but also because it created an emotional bond between distant members of the Muslim Social.

For instance, in 2014, the Organization of Islamic Corporation (whose headquarters are in Jeddah, Saudi Arabia) declared the fifteenth of Ramadan as "World Orphan's Day." This declaration came as a result of IHH's petition and activism. One of IHH's campaign images announced the declaration of World Orphan's Day with the slogan "The World Will Smile if Orphans Smile (*Yetim Gülerse Dünya Güler*)!" (figure 4.1). In contrast to "shock-effect" styles of representation that signify the "Third World child/

4.1 Web advertisement for IHH's orphan sponsorship campaign. The slogan at the top announces: "The World Will Smile if Orphans Smile! On World Orphan Day, children smile with you." The text at the bottom announces that the Islamic Cooperation Agency has declared the fifteenth day of the month of Ramadan as World Orphan's Day. Used with permission.

orphan"[13] through an iconography of hunger, pain, and suffering, in this image the IHH uses a "positive image" of the Muslim orphan as a confident and happy person.[14]

In this image, real photographs of six cheerful and vibrant children (three girls and three boys) are situated under the slogan. Dressed in traditional clothing from different countries, these orphans are presented as a cohesive group, even though it is clear that each photograph was taken at a different time and place. Adjusted, reframed, and manipulated, these photoshopped images are presented as if they provide a direct link to an

13. For an informative historical overview, see Briggs (2003).
14. For a discussion of the differences between "shock-effect" and "positive" styles of humanitarian communication, see Chouliaraki (2013b).

existing group of Muslim orphans. But such a community is summoned into being through the call for acting upon one's humanitarian responsibility. Orphans are made into objects of care at the juncture of representation and responsibility. The caption affirms this message: "Are you ready to reach out to 204,000 orphans who live in 45 countries with our 636 projects? Then, text 'orphan' and send a message to donate."

Like the children in UNICEF brochures, Muslim orphans are presented "alone, without parents, without an explanation of their circumstances, and without context" (Bornstein 2011, 124). But what could potentially be a disturbing picture—a child alone with no adult to provide care—is transformed into an invitation for developing a sense of belonging and familiarity. Their clothes communicate that these are not Turkish children, but come from different cultural, ethnic, and national backgrounds. Nevertheless, they still belong to a Muslim geopolitical imaginary. The ad simultaneously calls upon the idea of a universal humanity and a Muslim ummah through juxtaposing the trope of the smiling child next to a call for generosity during the month of Ramadan. This humanitarian aesthetic has a very low tolerance for agony, replacing spectacles of suffering with possibilities for engagement with cheerful children.

Thus, and this is true across all forms of media representation of orphans, the desire to avoid "compassion fatigue" fails to generate a political awareness of the structural conditions that result in the plight of children across the world.[15] What we instead have is a positive image of a happy orphan/child who does not even seem to need our help. What the child offers the spectator is not a chance to eradicate suffering but a chance to partake in humanitarianism's capacity to generate mutual happiness. This "sanitized imagery is no more or less 'realistic' than that presumed to be 'negative' imagery" (Darke 2004, 102). Nevertheless, positive images do not need compassion to generate happiness or well-being. Orphaned children are already cheerful and content, but by taking immediate action,

---

15. For a discussion of the role of orphans in Western humanitarianism, see Bornstein (2011) and Cheney and Rotabi (2017).

Muslim spectators can share their joy and happiness. What the Muslim orphan offers, then, is a promise of emotional well-being and a sense of belonging to a reimagined Islamic community.

Another key feature of IHH's child-focused campaigns was the premise that Turkish children had to be educated in the art of helping distant strangers. For example, since 2013, a new partnership between the IHH, the Directorate of Religious Affairs, the Education and Science Workers Union, and the Turkish Ministry of Education has been put into effect to oversee an ambitious orphan sponsorship campaign that matches specific classrooms in Turkish schools with orphans in various countries (*Her Sınıfın Bir Yetim Kardeşi Var Projesi*). Classrooms participating in this project are expected to contribute a small amount of money to sponsor an orphan who is located in Turkey or abroad. According to the organization's website, in the 2016–17 academic year, more than eight thousand Turkish classrooms participated in this campaign and sponsored more than twenty thousand orphans around the world (IHH n.d.-a). In response to criticisms that this campaign provided Turkish children with an "ideological education," the IHH claims that the goal of the campaign is to build "moral character" while "empowering Turkish children to solve world problems" (Karabağlı 2015). Thus, while the overt goal was to help orphans of the Muslim world, this campaign, like other orphan-focused aid efforts, sought to generate a sense of humanitarian responsibility at a young age.

The pedagogical benefits of orphan sponsorship were integrated into each and every step of the campaign. When a classroom signed up to sponsor an orphan, the IHH sent them a package that included the following items: a brochure, a coloring book, a flag of the orphan's country, a poster, stickers, a second coloring book for preschoolers, a form that includes information about the sponsored orphan, a world map, and a brochure discussing "the Prophet Muhammad's Love for Children" (IHH n.d.-a). These promotional materials were then used by children and displayed in classrooms. Caring for Muslim orphans, which engendered feelings of compassion and responsibility, became part of the ordinary rhythms of education.

To cultivate emotional intimacy, this campaign also matched each classroom to a specific orphan. To this end, each classroom received an "orphan summary information form" (*yetim özet bilgi formu*). This form included a photograph of the sponsored child at the top-right corner and a brief list at the bottom that provided information about where the orphan is from, where they currently live, their age, their file number, whether they have any siblings, how long they have been sponsored, and the exact date when their father died. Sometimes, the picture of the orphan hung in a corner of the classroom—a constant reminder to Turkish children about their humanitarian responsibility to Muslim children elsewhere. As part of their education, children learned more about the sponsored orphan's country, history, and economic conditions. Each form included a brief paragraph with more information about the orphan's country and everyday life. The form about an orphan boy named Muhammed from Sudan explained how "the region's ethnic differences" and "rich resources in Darfur" brought "Western intervention." As a result, "Muslims in Sudan struggle with hunger, poverty, and health problems, as well as other problems that are created by famine and civil war" (Ministry of National Education: IHH Orphan Project n.d.). Another form provided information about Omar, an orphan from Egypt:

> Since the 2013 Egyptian military coup, many civilians, including women and children, have been killed. The Western world, despite the difficulties that Egyptians face, has failed to develop an adequate response, thereby allowing the violation of human rights by the military regime. As a result, many Egyptian children were orphaned. This is why the IHH has added Egypt to the list of supported countries. (IHH "Albüm—Atatürk Ortaokulu," n.d.)

As these two examples illustrate, these forms usually provided more knowledge about the country than they did about the child. In so doing, these documents narrated a story about how Turkish children ought to see the Muslim world, and how they should conduct themselves as caring humanitarians who can alleviate the suffering of other Muslim children. By combining Islamic themes with humanitarian styles of representation, these forms provided a unique kind of geographical education that taught Turkish children how to see the world through a lens of humanitarian responsibility.

The orphan information form was also part of the package given to individual donors who wished to sponsor an orphan. Many managers and volunteers perceived this form as a valuable technology of intimacy. This point was explained to me by Bülent, a manager in his late fifties who had been part of the IHH for more than a decade. He held the conviction that "If our people could see the situation with their own eyes, if they could see the suffering and poverty that these children face every day, then they would know that their meager donations are being put to good use." He had just returned from a trip to Aceh, Indonesia, and was referring to the orphans he had met there. He elaborated by explaining the relationship between information and intimacy with the following words:

> Since our sponsors cannot visit these countries, we have to provide information that can overcome the feeling of distance. Seeing a photograph of the child, knowing his name, learning a little bit about his daily life. . . . These kinds of information are necessary to keep donations flowing. Why would people want to give money if they know nothing? It is human nature to crave intimacy (*yakınlık*) after all.

For Bülent, the orphan information form was a tool for generating a sense of social proximity that could potentially overcome the alienation brought on by geographical distance. Emel, an IHH volunteer who had recently finished her undergraduate degree, articulated a similar observation:

> In the past, we lived in small neighborhoods; everyone knew each other. If a child had lost her father, then Muslims would step up to the plate. But today, we live in a different age. The Muslim world is very large, but today we can also reach those who are far away.

Hence, for Emel, the geography of the Muslim world was both an opportunity and a challenge. She added: "Providing information to those who want to help is crucial. Otherwise, they will not feel the goodness that emerges from their benevolent worship, they will not know that those mazlum children thank them in their prayers." By framing the orphan information form as a vehicle for generating mutual goodness, donors were to conclude that their humanitarian responsibility was well received by the recipients. At the same time, orphan information forms, like the social investigation forms that I discussed in chapter 3, understood information as a prerequisite of social intimacy. In both cases, forms identified, categorized, and organized details of the recipients' lives, making such specifics accessible to potential donors and the Turkish public.

Not unrelated to the assemblages between the technical and the emotional was an increasing belief in the capacity of "small" actions to create social change. IHH's campaign materials emphasized that Turkish children were not to despair in the face of the enormity of this task. The following excerpt from one of IHH's videos illustrates the intersection of agency, social change, and humanitarian responsibility:

> Actually, humans love good deeds more than they like bad deeds. If we can stay away from bad behaviors and compete in goodness, then we can diminish the destructive effects of natural disasters, lessen the intensity of war, and overcome illness and poverty. . . . That is, if we change ourselves, then we can also change the world. We believe that the goodness in children's hearts can solve many of the world's problems. You are the ones who will create a humanitarian Turkey and a beautiful world. Because goodness is what will change the world. (IHH 2017)

Apart from the absence of an explicit reference to religious themes, this description shows that IHH's orphan campaign also sought to educate Turkish children about their personal power and individual agency. Here, the helping child was construed not as a moral subject who gave in order to please Allah, but as an individual agent who was not only responsible for but also capable of making the world a better place. The cultivation of intimacy, hence, was made possible through an assertion of individual agency. For instance, one of the key slogans of IHH's orphan campaigns was the "butterfly effect":

> It might not yet be possible for you to make a better world on your own. But you can still engage in superhero acts that might have a butterfly effect. By saving a little amount from your pocket money, you can address a need of an orphan, or realize one of her dreams. . . . You only need to look into your own heart in order to see and reach out to

the other, because only good deeds can travel the world by overcoming obstacles. (IHH 2015b)

This excerpt offers a perspective on religion and the world in which children (and adults) are capable of helping other children and providing happiness to others and are able to do so without expecting anything in return. Giving to others, hence, is no longer seen as a form of self-sacrifice, or as a restriction of material pleasures, but as the road that leads to a more fulfilling life and the creation of a new world that is "full of goodness." This humanitarian discourse has implications for ideas about social change as well. The promise of the "butterfly effect"—referring to the meteorological notion that small changes can lead to large-scale systemic transformation—means that Muslims, as individuals, must begin by acknowledging the impossibility of solving the world's problems and, consequently, become empowered with the belief that each and every one of them can create social change. Moreover, the most fundamental elements of humanitarian responsibility, believed to exemplify the qualities of a devout Muslim, rely on the cultivation of a series of emotional experiences that create positive feelings such as joy, happiness, and emotional well-being.

Fellow Muslims

From the perspective of Islamic scripture, neither refugees nor victims of disasters are considered to be especially deserving of aid. Nor is developmental aid necessarily understood to be a fundamental tenet of the Islamic faith. Yet today, many Muslims in Turkey believe that they have a responsibility to other Muslims who experience suffering and impoverishment due to conditions of underdevelopment, civil war, or natural disasters. The Turkish government's and Islamic NGOs' transnational efforts are simultaneously driven by a desire to gain legitimacy in the international area, motivated by an attempt to match the influence of Christian organizations in Muslim-majority countries, and are justified with reference to a transnational community of fellow believers. Through their participation in transnational aid, which included travel to various countries, as well as extended stays to oversee the construction of dormitories, mosques, school buildings, wells, and food distribution events that took place as part of Ramadan and Qurban campaigns, many Turkish Muslims began to see themselves as global humanitarians. But the construct of a "fellow Muslim in need," although emphasizing equality among Muslims, was nevertheless not immune to the workings of power and the reproduction of differences.

Here I focus on the images of suffering and affective themes that are present in the visual representation of Niger and Syria in humanitarian advertisements. Both countries have emerged as prominent recipients of humanitarian aid from Turkey, and both frequently appear in mainstream media as deserving Others whose suffering and need ought to be addressed immediately. Although these countries face quite a different set of challenges, the humanitarian lens reduces their complex histories of political conflict and economic disenfranchisement to a social problem that can be addressed through the successful cultivation of emotional intimacy and the effective management of transnational aid. By teaching pious Muslims how to imagine themselves as capable, empowered, and accountable for ameliorating the suffering of distant strangers residing in Niger and Syria, as well as in other places, the project of humanitarian responsibility reinforces the notion that Turkey is the savior/leader of the Muslim world and, by extension, depicts Arab and African Muslims as helpless victims. Put differently, the humanitarian ideal of a monolithic Muslim world not only overlooks but also perpetuates hierarchies and differences among Muslims.

Niger: Civilizing Compassion for the Truly Needy

After the AKP came to power in 2003, the Turkish government gradually developed a strategic interest in a number of African countries that, in addition to Niger, include Chad, Ethiopia, Somalia, and Sudan. Several public institutions, often in partnership with Islamic NGOs, have provided unprecedented amounts of developmental aid to these countries ranging from the provision of basic necessities such as food, medicine, and water, to the construction of dormitories, hospitals, orphanages, schools, and water wells. The government also opened a number of new embassies on the African continent and has set up local centers to support Turkish businesspeople and civil society practitioners during their visits (Özkan 2012). Qurban campaigns have also played a key role in the construction of humanitarian responsibility to African Muslims. In TV commercials and YouTube videos, Qurban animals purchased by the donations of Turkish people are often juxtaposed with ceremonies that distribute Qurban meats to populations in Africa, thereby creating a visual effect that generates emotional intimacy between Muslims despite geographical distance.

Campaigns organized in the name of helping African people use a style of humanitarian appeal that invokes a nonhierarchical relationship between fellow Muslims. For instance, one of TİKA's projects, a student exchange program that sent young Turkish people to complete volunteer programs in several African countries, was titled: "The Bridge of Brotherhood between Volunteer Hearts" ("Gönüllü Yüreklerin Kardeşlik Köprüsü" 2018). Such an emphasis on brotherhood was reiterated by Erdoğan who, during his 2013 visit to Niger, said: "We have come here with a spirit of brotherhood, not one of colonialism." Referring to one Niger-focused campaign that was organized in 2018, the head manager of a small Islamic NGO explained:

> As civil society organizations, we are honored to use the donations of Turkish people to provide humanitarian assistance in mazlum and muhtaç geographies of Islam. Instead of colonizing these lands, our task is to build and uplift these geographies and to do so by reviving our ummah awareness that dates to the Ottoman times. (Musa, Karacaoğlu, and Tok 2019)

In this expression of humanitarian responsibility, Turkey's strategic interests in African countries were portrayed as an alternative to Western colonialism. A sense of duty to deserving Others was generated by appealing to Turkish Muslims' self-identification as part of a global ummah and by marking African populations as belonging to the innocent and needy geographies of Islam.

While Africa has come to occupy a distinctive place in Turkey's humanitarian imaginary, Niger occupies an even more central position. All the Islamic NGOs that I visited, regardless of their organizational scope or financial resources, organized fundraising campaigns and oversaw developmental and humanitarian projects in Niger. Many Islamic NGOs also narrated the Nigerien cause through media products, such as brochures, CDs, magazines, media advertisements, pamphlets, TV commercials, and YouTube videos. Humanitarian assistance to Niger was also a frequent topic of mainstream TV channels, such as state-owned Turkish Radio and Television Institute's (Türk Radyo Televizyon Kurumu, TRT) stations, which often provided extensive coverage of recent developments (e.g., Kuzey Haber Ajansı 2013).

When I inquired what prompted their interest in Niger, my interlocutors echoed the government's humanitarian rhetoric: the country faced extreme poverty, low levels of literacy, high birth rates, famine, and underdevelopment, which was why Turkish Muslims were called upon to do something to help their fellow believers. But, while referencing a transnational community of Muslims with equal standing, the communicative repertoire of Islamic humanitarianism visually expressed Niger through an aesthetic of extreme poverty, where aid was represented both as an intimate experience of religious belonging and as a power-laden act of engendering development.

Rather than promoting faith-based community in the name of religion, Turkish Muslims were tasked with improving the livelihoods of Nigerien people through designing and implementing long-term developmental projects that focused on education, health, and infrastructure. The developmental-humanitarian narrative reinforced the structure of economic inequality that underpinned the transnational imagination of the Muslim Social. Nigeriens were depicted as distant Others experiencing true destitution (*muhtaçiyet*) despite their pure innocence (*mazlumiyet*). But while such a representation cultivated feelings of compassion by reinforcing the gap between "saviors" and "victims," it also stripped Nigeriens of their political agency and simplified their complex reality into one of rural underdevelopment and industrial backwardness.

The first set of campaign advertisements represented Niger through a picture of rural crowds. Photographs captured villagers in their everyday life: men sitting in front of their huts, children playing in fields and on dirt roads, women cooking or drawing water from a well (IHH 2015a). These representations framed Niger's main problem as one of economic backwardness and material scarcity. Differences between individuals, families, groups, villages, cities, and regions were overlooked in favor of monolithic representations of agricultural underdevelopment. In this way, Nigeriens were subsumed into nameless members of a rural population. Their suffering was attributed to a lack of industrial development. While no information about the history of Western imperialism or European colonialism in the country was ever provided, the implication was that Niger's lack of resources required immediate attention from Turkish Muslims if they were serious about protecting African Muslims from Western NGOs.

Situating people in their daily environment, going about their lives without a concern for the humanitarian gaze, created a specific visual effect of *muhtaçıyet*: the people who were truly in need were also the ones who were too proud to ask for help. In contrast to Muslim orphans, who appeared happy and met the gaze of the spectator, in this group of images, Nigeriens were rarely depicted as looking directly into the eyes of the audience. It is not that they were averting their gazes with embarrassment, but that they were merely busy with the demanding tasks of agricultural life. The facial expressions were diverse, ranging from concerned to hopeful, desolate to delighted. Although there was a certain sense of manufactured messiness in these images, they were not chaotic as, for example, images of Syria were.

A second set of images brought Nigeriens closer to the foreground of the picture, allowing the spectator to see them as individuals instead of as nameless members of a crowd. These kinds of pictures almost always involved Turkish aid workers, who were often shown as distributing aid packages to villagers, spending time with families, or playing with children (see Deniz Feneri Derneği 2016). Some of these scenes also simulated the moment when the gift exchange took place: aid workers handing off bags to women in front of traditional huts, villagers waiting in line to receive food packages, and opening ceremonies for newly constructed huts, clinics, school buildings, and water wells were common tropes (see Dost Eli Derneği 2021; Deniz Feneri Derneği n.d.; Anadolu Ajansı 2017). This second set of images positioned the viewers closer, making the audience a witness to the aid workers' activities and interactions. By capturing instances of giving and by highlighting practices of care and compassion, these representations brought the innocent, needy, deserving Other into closer view, thereby generating a sense of emotional intimacy between spectators and benefactors.

But it was only a third set of images that provided close-ups of Nigeriens' faces: depictions of a smiling Turkish aid worker surrounded by smiling individuals looking directly at the gaze of the audience.[16] Like their Western counterparts, these photographs were taken in the style of "selfie-humanitarianism" and sought to communicate a sense of camaraderie. In contrast to the first set of images, which depicted Nigeriens as faceless members of an agricultural society, photographs that juxtaposed the aid worker with recipients allowed the spectator to see benefactors as separate individuals who were eager to meet one's gaze. While these images communicated a sense of physical closeness and emotional intimacy, in doing so, they also supported an expression of solidarity that reinforces the commodification of the deserving Other (Koffman, Orgad, and Gill 2015).

These images, which portrayed Nigeriens as impoverished villagers enduring the dire circumstance of agricultural life, justified the need for humanitarian action. Through this narrative frame, Turkish Muslims were responsibilized into caring and capable actors who must do something to address the problem of extreme material deprivation, and to do so in the name of Islam. This development-focused style of humanitarian appeal, however, exclusively highlighted the philanthropic actions of aid workers— and by extension Turkish donors—rather than acknowledging the on-the-ground agency of Nigeriens themselves. As such, these representations drew from Western colonial imagery, which constructs Africans as noble savages and portrays Westerners as enlightened saviors who brought "civilization." While attempting to protect African Muslims from the activities of Western NGOs, the Islamic social imaginary of humanitarian responsibility reinforced similarly hierarchical perceptions of the world.

16. For examples of this trope, see "Nijer'e Cansuyu" (2013).

Syria: Paternal Care for the Oppressed

The political conflict in Syria had not yet begun when I conducted the initial fieldwork for this book. But, after the onset of the Arab Spring in 2011, and especially after 2013 when a full-fledged war broke out in Syria, the situation of the Syrian people—both those who migrated to Turkey and those who remained within Syrian borders—became a key humanitarian responsibility. In fact, no other international event has been as divisive and transformative as the Syrian conflict has been for Turkey's voluntary sector. Since the beginning of the conflict, the AKP has developed an "open-door" policy toward Syrian refugees and has been granting them a "temporary protection" status since 2011 (İçduygu 2015). With this status, Syrian refugees receive ID cards that give them access to certain social services, such as health care and education; hence, they are no longer considered to be "undocumented" individuals.

As of 2023 approximately 3.7 million Syrians reside in Turkey, making the country the host to the world's largest refugee population (Eder and Özkul 2016). The majority of Syrian refugees are relocated to twenty-two government-run refugee camps in areas close to the Turkish–Syrian border. Since these camps always run at full capacity, most refugees have also migrated to urban centers, such as Ankara, Istanbul, and İzmir. In fact, 90% of refugees live outside of camps. Yet neither the government's humanitarian efforts nor its "open-door" policy has been sufficient to accommodate and integrate Syrians into Turkish society. Syrian refugees and migrants face a wide range of challenges in their everyday life, ranging from prejudice to deportation, from discrimination to violence, and from perpetual unemployment to treacherous labor conditions (Baban, Ilcan, and Rygiel 2016; Canefe 2016; Lazarev and Sharma 2017; Yıldız and Uzgören 2016). Further, many Turkish people believe that refugees are damaging the Turkish economy, and a large majority are opposed to aiding Syrians (Erdoğan 2015, 4). Although some have settled and sought regular employment and housing in Turkey, most want to get into the European Union (EU) using various channels such as applying for asylum or paying smugglers. The influx of Syrian refugees has been a divisive topic for European countries as well. In an attempt to slow down the arrival of refugees and migrants, in March 2016 the EU signed an agreement with Turkish authorities. This controversial EU–Turkey accord allowed Greece to return "all new irregular migrants" back to Turkish authorities in exchange for increasing the number of Syrian resettlements in Europe and providing additional funds to support Turkey's humanitarian efforts (Collett 2016).

While aid to Syrian refugees is Turkey's main priority, Islamic NGOs and state agencies also organize campaigns for people living in Syria. Despite differences in emphasis and tone, the communicative repertoire of Islamic humanitarianism represents Syria through the prism of oppression. The humanitarian crisis is marked as a form of injustice against innocent victims. This humanitarian imagery largely represents Syria as a child trying to survive amid chaos, political conflict, and war. Such a visual arrangement evokes protective feelings of compassion among the Turkish public, encouraging them to transform their anger into humanitarian action. By infantilizing Syria, however, this style of humanitarian appeal perpetuates the savior–victim dichotomy and obscures Turkey's military involvement in the ongoing war.

In most advertisements, Syrians are referred to as defenseless victims of *zulüm* (un-Islamic oppression). Some posters emphasize that ordinary Syrians are being oppressed (mazlum) at the hands of Syria's minority Alawite sect—the oppressors. For example, humanitarian advertisements often refer to Syria's president, Bashar al-Assad, as *zalim* (tyrant). By referring to Syrians as innocent victims of oppression, the communicative repertoire of Islamic humanitarianism is able to deploy a wide range of strategies for eliciting emotions and collecting donations from the Turkish public.

This framework has resonated with Turkish Muslims who are accustomed to Erdoğan's political rhetoric about the Sunni–Shia conflict in which Turkey is portrayed as a leader and protector of Sunni Muslims. The oppressed–oppressor dichotomy is present in several other humanitarian projects that originated in Turkey, such as those that were organized to assist Palestinians in Gaza or the Rohingya population in Myanmar. These campaigns suggest that there is an urgent need for humanitarian solidarity, not only because these Muslims are facing ethnic cleansing, persecution, occupation, violence, and war, but also because these atrocities are being committed by non-Muslims. Although such a construction has drawn attention to the plight of some Muslim populations by portraying Muslims as victims of unfair treatment, it has excluded other conflict situations where Muslims themselves inflicted violence on people—both Muslim and non-Muslim. In the case of Syria, this style of humanitarian appeal has ignored some key details: the fact that the oppressors were also Muslim, the fact that the Syrian civil war was one that was largely being fought between rival Muslim groups, and perhaps more importantly, the fact that the Turkish government contributed to the perpetuation of the conflict, and hence was complicit in the suffering of Syrian people. But these nuances and complexities have been overlooked in favor of a humanitarian discourse that simplified the Syrian war through the prism of tyrannical oppression.

Other campaign ads about the Syrian conflict portrayed the ongoing military conflict through blown-up and blurred images of destruction. Some commercials were presented as a collage of photographs that appeared to be shot in different locations. The juxtaposition of ruined buildings, collapsed homes, dark and isolated streets, dust, and debris generated a visual effect of chaos and catastrophe. These were either real photographs of war-torn Syrian cities, towns, and villages, or photorealistic representations that had a similar visual effect. This sense of violent fragmentation was exacerbated with single photos of human suffering located in front of the buildings. Figure 4.2, which depicts an advertisement titled "War Impacts Them the Most," is illustrative of this trope. A blown-up picture of a hurt child is positioned against a black-and-white background of destroyed buildings and dismayed crowds. The child is crying by herself. There is no one to comfort her. The contrast between the pain of the lonely child and the indifference of overwhelmed adults invites the audience to act. Other advertisements also made use of images of children crying and alone, or of anguished mothers trying to save their children from collapsed buildings and street violence. Men rarely appeared in these photographs, and if they did, they were depicted as Turkish aid workers who were carrying children away from danger or distributing aid to civilians. In contrast to the portrayal of Muslim orphans as joyful children, Syrian children were represented as sad, scared, and

SAVAŞ EN ÇOK
ONLARI ETKİLİYOR
Suriye'de zalim esed'in Halepteki
bombalarından kaçmış insanların yaşadığı
Azez ve Çobanbey bölgelerindeki kamplara
un ve battaniye ihtiyacı var

'SURIYE' yaz
3851'e
gönder
5 TL
bağış
yap

4.2 Web advertisement for a small Islamic NGO's campaign for Syrian refugees. The slogan at the top reads: "War Impacts Them the Most: Those who ran away from Tyrant al-Assad's bombs in Aleppo are now staying in camps in Azez and Çobanbey. They need flour and blankets!" The script at the bottom left adds: "Type 'Syria' and send [a text message] to 3851, donate 5 Turkish Lira." Advertisement by Çare Derneği. Used with permission.

miserable. These anguished figures called for the urgent fulfillment of humanitarian responsibility.

Another frequently used style of humanitarian appeal was one that focused on the urgent need for providing necessities—such as blankets, flour, and milk—to Syrians. This group of advertisements circumvented the ongoing military conflict, and instead focused on issues like cold weather or hunger to communicate the need and suffering of Syrian people. One set of campaign materials used negative imagery of children (sometimes with their mothers) enduring the cold weather. Popular slogans included "Don't leave Syria/n children out in the cold," and "Syria/n children shall not go hungry" ("Suriye'ye Kış Yardım Kampanyası" 2019; Enson Haber 2014). The constant switch between "Syria" and "Syrian children" created feelings of protection while infantilizing the Syrian Other. The emphasis on necessities—such as providing food and warmth—also arranged the act of giving as a requisite part of a close relationship. Another set of advertisements used a representational strategy that was borrowed from commercial advertising: providing a list of commodities alongside information about how much it costs to donate that specific item (Ahmet Yesevi Derneği 2018). Some campaigns even named projects providing cold-weather clothing for children a "Winter Collection," thereby associating the act of helping Syrian children as part of seasonal consumption habits ("Kış İyilik Koleksiyonu" 2020).

In addition to the use of images of Syrian children that communicated a hierarchical power relationship, another common humanitarian vocabulary was one of fellowship (*kardeşlik*), which combined familial notions of intimacy with religious values of solidarity. Most ads referred to Syrians as "our siblings," both inviting Turkish Muslims to act as if Syrians were a member of their family, and signifying the idea that Turks and Syrians were religious fellows (*din kardeşliği*). For example, an IHH advertisement from 2018 juxtaposed the slogan "My Syrian sibling should not go without bread" with the black-and-white photograph of a vexed little boy holding a plastic bag—presumably containing bread—that has a visible IHH logo on the front (IHH 2018). In this ad, the clear picture of the little boy is situated against a red background with blurred details, the contrast signifying the need for urgent action. Another campaign organized by the Religious Affairs Foundation (*Türkiye Diyanet Vakfı*, TDV) positioned the slogan "Fellowship Does Not Stop at Borders" (*Kardeşlik Sınır Tanımaz*) on top of a wintery background with pictures of two children standing away from each other ("Erzurum'da Suriye Kış Yardımı-Erzurum Müftülüğü-Türkiye Diyanet Vakfı" 2022). The spectator is invited to notice that the children are not dressed properly for the cold weather. The image of three shivering children is juxtaposed with a smaller picture in the bottom right that depicts a group standing next to a bunch of donation boxes and appearing thankful. The juxtaposition of freezing/miserable versus warm/content children might appear unsophisticated, but the emphasis on winter—and not war—as a common enemy nevertheless enables these kinds of ads to conjure up familial notions of intimacy.

Calls for helping "our neighbors" were also a common trope within this style of humanitarian appeal that emphasized paternal care. Regularly used phrases in these sets of advertisements—such as "I cannot sleep when you go to bed hungry," and "I cannot go to bed if you are cold"

4.3 Street billboards, 2015, Ankara. The one on the left reads: "This Love Is Ours, These Legends Are Ours, These People Are Ours: This Country Belongs to Us All." The middle one declares: "One Nation, One Flag, One Country, One State." The one on the right announces: "Our Friendship Does Not Stop at Borders. The Turkish nation cares for the forsaken, stands up against tyrants, and protects the innocent." Advertisement by Çare Derneği. Photograph by the author.

(Kesin Karar 2022)—made an implicit reference to a well-known hadith by the Prophet Muhammad: "Those who go to bed full when their neighbors are hungry are not one of us." These slogans claimed that geographical proximity called for a similar kind of responsibility that one usually reserved for one's neighbors. This style of humanitarian appeal portrayed the border between Turkey and Syria as akin to the intimate relationship one might develop with people living close by. In figure 4.3, emotional intimacy is represented through the portrayal of a smiling Erdoğan, who is gently being kissed by a young Syrian child. While the slogan calls for an acknowledgment of equality between neighbors, the contrast between the adult/Turkey and the child/Syria undermines the egalitarian language of fellowship. But perhaps that is exactly the point: by donating to charitable campaigns for Syria, pious Muslims in Turkey were to act upon their responsibility, an Islamic-neoliberal assemblage that produced feelings of moral superiority as much as it conjured notions of religious duty.

Media, Belonging, Community

With the rise of organized charity, many Islamic NGOs in Turkey began to use media technologies to develop a distinctive social imaginary. For each charity campaign, they came up with a memorable slogan that combined humanitarian images with Islamic idioms. They employed newspaper advertisements, urban billboards, and TV commercials to convince potential donors to help distant strangers, and did so in the name of religion, brotherhood, and humanity. Certain categories of the deserving Muslim poor became familiar among Turkish citizens as they began to feel a sense of social belonging to a transnational community of co-religionists.

While portraying humanitarian responsibility as an indispensable component of Muslimhood, discourses and practices of Islamic humanitarianism configured faith-based giving into an intimate relationship that occured between distant strangers and was mediated by NGOs or governmental institutions. Adherents of this project believed that they merely juxtaposed images of poverty and suffering with languages of solidarity that already existed among members of the Muslim Social. But these visual representations and styles of humanitarian appeal did not operate according to a logic of illustration, but one of production. Representations of the Muslim Other—the poor, the orphan, the fellow believer—as I have shown in this chapter, appropriated formative dichotomies of Western humanitarianism, such as savior–victim, civilized–savage, and capable–helpless, thereby replicating cultural hierarchies and power differentials. Although the project of humanitarian responsibility pitted the notion of a pristine Islamic community against a destructive vision of the West, in so doing, Muslim humanitarians mimicked those patterns of perception and emotion. The use of print and visual media to generate emotional attachments, however, led to the commodification of the deserving Muslim Other. At the same time, this vision construed transnational religious identity as a form of affective belonging. Connections between Muslims were forged through a vocabulary of emotions ranging from love and pity to compassion and brotherhood.

Envisioning a transnational Islamic community by way of a shared religious brotherhood is a nuanced and contentious process. It is complex and, as this chapter also demonstrates, images and emotions that are prevalent in humanitarian campaigns are neither endemic to "Islam" nor impervious to neoliberal elements. Indeed, they are often manufactured in a haphazard and inconsistent fashion. The absence of a singular notion of Islamic community, the diversity of poverty images and affective structures, and the fact that the production of the Muslim Social lacks a singular logic, however, does not diminish the power of this social imaginary for those who feel responsible to distant strangers. But, at the same time, despite their unwavering belief in a collective identity that is shared among Muslims around the globe, such a sense of belonging is the product of an ongoing process marked by power and difference. A closer examination of humanitarian campaigns reveals the types of stratification that are called upon to fabricate the illusion of singular Islamic community. These processes of categorization and exclusion further complicate the idea that actors relate to the Muslim Social in a similar and uniform fashion. Most interestingly, we see that the contested ways in which actors experience faith-based service does not prevent but rather compels them to participate in volunteer programs. This puzzle is explored in depth in chapter 5.

5

Spiritual Sanctuary
and the Muslim Volunteer

On a sunny day in April 2010, I attended a volunteer meeting of the Deniz Feneri organization. The meeting was held in preparation for a charity sale (*kermes*) that was being put together for Mother's Day weekend. About twenty-five middle-aged women were sitting in a semicircle on chairs in a large room at a community center. Located next to a park in Ankara, this community center had a small free clinic and a soup kitchen. Addressing the volunteers, Leyla, the volunteer coordinator, began her speech with an Arabic prayer followed by a Turkish one. Leyla was a conservative woman in her early forties who had been unable to pursue a higher education degree since she wore a headscarf.[1] Although she had been active in the Islamist movement during her twenties, her political involvement was later interrupted by marriage and raising children. But once her children were older, she had begun to volunteer at Deniz Feneri, and was eventually hired as an outreach and volunteer coordinator.

On this day, her goal was to convince participants to bake goods, make crafts, and spend their time at the upcoming charity sale. She began her conversation (*sohbet*) by discussing the role of faith in Muslim life,

1. Beginning in the 1980s, Turkish women who wore the Islamic headscarf were banned from entering the grounds of public universities and state institutions because the headscarf was seen as a symbol of political Islam by the country's secularist-military establishment. After more than two decades of political contestation over this issue, the headscarf ban was lifted by the AKP in 2013. For more information, see Cindoğlu and Zencirci (2008) and Çınar (2008).

emphasizing that it was difficult to live a pious life in today's modern society, and that Muslims had to find better ways to rise to that challenge. Delivered like a religious sermon, her speech had a dramatic effect, enhanced with well-placed pauses and the use of nonverbal language. Looking around the room, I could see that many of the women were nodding in agreement, while others were praying silently, or crying softly. After a lengthy discussion about the importance of volunteer work and giving in Islam, Leyla concluded her speech with the following words:

> Turn to your hearts. There you can find the strength and inspiration to be a beautiful Muslim. It is not easy to accomplish such a journey, but it is what we must strive toward. We live in a time of "me," during an age of consumption. Now, there will always be the rich and the poor; who will have what kind of a destiny depends on Allah's will. Some people might think this is not fair, but our religion has a solution to inequality. We need to look deeper into our souls if we want to be a beautiful Muslim; we need to discover our potential. We can find our true selves only if we are kind to others.

In this account, being a beautiful Muslim pertains to both the material and spiritual dimensions of human existence. The beauty of Islam is to be found through engaging with others in one's community, a process through which Muslims can "discover their potential" and "find their true selves." In this neoliberal-Islamic assemblage of volunteerism, giving to others is not just conceptualized as a moral obligation or as a religious command, but also marked as an act of self-improvement. Capitalizing on existing anxieties about piety and modernity (and often exaggerating them), Leyla's stories aimed to, as Nikolas Rose (1990) put it, "act upon the choices, wishes, values and the conduct of the individual in an indirect manner" (6). These kinds of religious conversations about the place of volunteer work in a Muslim's life promised what, in this chapter, I refer to as a spiritual sanctuary. This Islamic social project sought to protect Muslims from excessive individualism by articulating Islam as a haven of peace and tranquility. Faith-based volunteer work emerged as one site for the modern Muslim individual to experience collective forms of subjectivity, while simultaneously centering the idea of the human person as an autonomous, individualized, and self-directing actor. By privileging a notion of Islamic community that was consonant with assumptions of liberal individualism, these conversations, interventions, and programs produced Muslim-neoliberal subjectivities. Individuals were not only responsible for alleviating poverty but were additionally capable of accessing their "true selves" through acts of charity.

The spiritual desire to establish a new sense of individuality exemplifies tenets of "neoliberal subjectivity": a phenomenon where seemingly ordinary activities—cooking, exercise, DIY culture—operate as a technology for "free, enterprising subjects" to "govern their own self-development" (Binkley 2014, 4). Persons are called upon to comprehend their own emotional well-being as a governmental enterprise that only they can access and configure, thereby integrating private, inner, psychological life into the folds of government (Dean 2017; Scharff 2016).[2] While most scholarship on neoliberal selfhood focuses on the spread of market-based values such as competition, calculation, and material gain, the emphasis on the enterprising self who is not only responsible for but also capable of their own well-being departs from such an approach, instead inviting us to consider how seemingly anti-market or non-market spheres of activity may also be part of neoliberal assemblages.[3]

The proliferation of volunteer programs amid economic liberalization is perhaps one of the best examples of this governmental assemblage. Despite celebratory accounts of civil society that see volunteerism as a harbinger of democracy and development, governments also benefit from the proliferation of volunteer programs that encourage actors to solve collective problems by taking private action (Bloom and Kilgore 2003; Eliasoph 2011; Hemment 2012; Hyatt 2001; Ilcan and Basok 2004; Mostafanezhad

2. For work that explores the relationship between entrepreneurial subjectivities and spiritual quests in Turkey, see Cengiz, Küçükural, and Gür (2021), Sayan-Cengiz (2020), and Şehlikoğlu (2021).

3. For literature that considers neoliberal subjectivity through the lens of competition and monetarization, see McGuigan (2016), Vassallo (2020), and Verdouw (2017), among others. For scholarship on neoliberal subjectivity in Turkey that adopts a similar approach, see Türem (2016).

2014; Rosol 2012; Simpson 2005). The process of "neoliberal volunteerism" involves the transfer of social responsibility to private actors, endeavors, and organizations, as well as the infusion of business-inspired rationalities into volunteer work. Suzan Ilcan and Tanya Basok (2004), for example, explain that "the task of government today is . . . enabling, inspiring, and assisting citizens to take responsibility for social problems in their communities, and formulating appropriate orientations and rationalities for their actions" (132). Far from being a venue for grassroots activism, most formal volunteer programs thus operate as a site for the production of model citizens that can address social problems in an orderly fashion (Pak Lei Chong 2011; Rozakou 2016). The celebration of volunteer work, moreover, privileges individualism over collectivism, emphasizing free will, autonomy, and initiative at the expense of other ways of understanding and acting upon the commons (Ganesh and Mcallum 2009). For instance, Jon Dean (2015) argues that the rise of "instrumentally motivated volunteering," as exemplified in volunteers' joining social projects to hone transferable skills, enhance their chances of gainful employment, or improve their emotional well-being, is an example of the "individualization and marketization of everyday community life" (140).

These neoliberal elements have also affected the relationship between religious subjectivity and volunteer work in Muslim-majority contexts (Jung, Petersen, and Sparre 2014; LeBlanc 2020; Mittermaier 2014; Vicini 2020). Although the desire to be a considerate person (as opposed to a self-indulgent materialist or hedonistic egoist) has played a central role in the Islamic revival (Deeb 2006; Hirschkind 2006; Mahmood 2005; Schielke 2009; Van Doorn-Harder 2006), new volunteer programs depart markedly from earlier experiences of community volunteering and political activism. While building on longstanding principles of charity and service, contemporary Islamic volunteer programs increasingly emphasize ideals that are valuable in the market, such as accountability, competitiveness, skills training, and long-term development, thereby illustrating the blending of Islamic values and neoliberal ethics in the field of volunteerism.

The spiritual sanctuary project that forms the subject of this chapter resembles the ethos of these volunteer programs. But, the following analysis suggests that volunteer experiences, interactions, and subjectivities in Turkey were not entirely determined by the governmental objectives of this Islamic social project either. In order to unpack this complexity, I follow scholars who recommend studying neoliberal volunteerism by paying attention to the affective dimensions of volunteer encounters and experiences as well as to the production of subjectivity (Bornstein 2012; Fleischer 2011; Griffiths 2015). Neoliberal elements such as accountability, self-interestedness, and competitiveness certainly permeate the field of volunteerism in Turkey, as is the case in other Muslim-majority contexts. Yet, at the same time, individuals assembled, comprehended, and valued their personal involvements and social relations in divergent ways, thereby transforming the field of neoliberal-Islamic volunteerism in that very process.

This chapter focuses on the governmental assemblages produced by faith-based volunteerism in Turkey and traces how new volunteer programs contributed to the formation and operation of the Muslim Social. Governmental authorities, NGOs, and Muslim intellectuals promoted volunteerism as part of a larger project of providing a spiritual sanctuary. This far-ranging project sought to protect the Muslim individual from the detrimental effects of capitalist modernity, but in doing so, reaffirmed the free-standing, autonomous, self-sufficient individual as its main agent. Volunteer work was construed as a path for Muslim individuals to improve their emotional well-being, pursue religious salvation, and contribute to social solidarity. Nevertheless, volunteers' encounters and experiences were neither merely "Islamic" nor "neoliberal," but acquired meaning through divergent moral, political, and religious registers, as volunteers sought emotional intimacy in their volunteer work. Neoliberal-Islamic assemblages of volunteerism were thus experienced in remarkably different ways by individuals as they sought to make sense of their volunteer experiences and encounters with the "deserving Other" through affective languages of patience, tolerance, and hope.

Spiritual Sanctuary

Most Islamist movements promise to heal Muslims from the perceived ills of modernity, such as crime, depression, illness, suicide, and social isolation. In this rendering, Islamic devotion protects Muslims from moral depravation and prescribes a path toward achieving happiness in this world and the next. While the discursive construction of Islam as a spiritual sanctuary varies across time and space, similar claims are made. Modernity poses an existential risk to Muslims—both in terms of their individual faith and their collective presence—and overcoming such a challenge requires a spiritual journey that one must embark upon; only those Muslims who have had the courage to undertake this journey are the ones who can find "true Islam" and live a spiritually fulfilling life.

In most instances, Islam as a spiritual sanctuary is defined as the opposite of capitalist modernity. Muslims are to find spiritual healing by renouncing materialism and individualism. The Muslim individual is interpellated as someone who can experience a spiritually enhanced form of modernity by seeking refuge in Islam. But even though such anti-capitalist themes are prevalent, the project of spiritual sanctuary is not one that retreats from modernity. Rather, the goal of ensuring Muslims' well-being is best understood as a set of responses that are shaped by their object. Thus, while spiritual sanctuary constructs a vision of Muslims as communally oriented beings, and presents modern capitalism as a mode of being that is antithetical to the values and principles of the Muslim Social, this project, at the same time, draws from the very categories and principles that it seems to denounce. Whereas the project of spiritual sanctuary purports to reject individualism, it also reinforces the freestanding agency of Muslims by marking the individual as the main subject of this project. Put differently, the Muslim individual is construed as someone who could experience a spiritually enhanced form of modernity by seeking refuge in Islam.[4]

An example of this paradoxical reification of individualism concerns the relationship between faith and mental health. Beginning in the 2010s, a popular debate among religious TV programs, Islamic YouTubers, and Muslim magazines was organized around a thought-provoking question: "Can a Muslim experience depression?" (*"Müslüman Depresyona Girer*

---

4. For discussions on the relationship between Islam, selfhood, and spirituality, see Deeb (2006), Gökarıksel and Secor (2012), Hirschkind (2006), Jassal (2014), Mahmood (2005), Schielke (2009), and Simon (2009).

mi").[5] While some traditional voices argued that depression was primarily caused by a weak devotion to Allah, most commentators explained that the opposite was true: only the dearest subjects of Allah were bestowed with the spiritual test of depression (e.g., Akten 2017; Demireşik 2015; "Müslümanlar da Depresyona Girer" 2021; "Müslüman Depresyona Girer Mi?" 2012). Religious scholars encouraged depressed Muslims to seek medical attention from doctors with an Islamic sensibility, so that religious values and psychiatric recommendations would not contradict each other (Bayancuk 2019). Doctors, talking on TV programs, declared depression a "sacred illness," and some even explained that depression was an opportunity to liberate oneself from the hold of a narcissistic ego and to deepen one's faith (Akyovalı 2018). Others argued that depression was a "worldly test" (*imtihan*) and encouraged Muslims to find ways to meet this challenge without retreating from society—be it through prayer or by helping others (Ağırakça 2018; Doğramacı 2017). These various recommendations reinforced the idea that Muslim individuals needed spiritual healing and suggested that such healing could be achieved by embarking on a religious journey of self-discovery.

Since 2003, the AKP also took up the mantle of providing a spiritual sanctuary for Turkish Muslims through carefully orchestrated discourses, interventions, and programs designed to govern the conduct of individuals with themselves, with others, and with society at large. A subdued moral panic over spiritual corruption pervaded a variety of domains ranging from family life to education, and from gender relations to youth lifestyles. This grammar of moral corruption was alternatively communicated through references to religion, nationalism, and the health of the social body, often combining neoliberal elements with Islamic-conservative values. For example, Erdoğan's pro-natalist discourse, which encouraged all Turkish families to have a minimum of three children, was justified through a fabricated moral panic over population decline (Korkut and Eslen-Ziya 2016). In a similar vein, the AKP government's disdain toward

---

5. Pious Muslims in Turkey experience higher levels of mental health stigma when they seek counseling services (see Çağlan and Göcen 2020).

women giving birth by cesarean section instead of "naturally" combined gendered expectations of conservative womanhood with concerns over the purity of the Turkish nation (Altunok 2016; Cindoğlu and Unal 2017). The need for spiritual healing was also expressed through the political rhetoric of raising a "pious generation" (*dindar gençlik*) who were to replace problematic youth identities in Turkey such as "atheists," "socialists," "drug-users," "thieves," and "alcoholics" (Alemdaroğlu 2021; Lüküslü 2016). In various speeches, Erdoğan emphasized that the conservative-democratic youth would act as a guard against the erosion of the social fabric, and as an impetus for reviving Turkey's spiritual power.

In addition to youth- and family-related discourses and policies, the AKP relies on a wide range of volunteer programs to govern the private lives of Turkish citizens.[6] Starting in the early 2000s, Islamic NGOs and various governmental agencies began to organize formal volunteer projects (chapter 1). At the same time, most public SYD waqfs encouraged university students to volunteer their time so that they might receive community service credits or add a line to their resume. These programs assist various groups in need, ranging from school children to the elderly, and from patients to the poor and disadvantaged. While some managerial techniques were introduced to enhance the aid experience of recipients (chapter 3), various training programs focused on the professionalization of the volunteer workforce (chapter 1).

To put it differently, the governmental aim of the Muslim Social was not just to serve the poor, but also to provide a spiritual sanctuary for those in need of emotional healing and social connections.[7] This governmental apparatus imagined a political machinery of "social projects" that mobilized a voluntary network of Muslim individuals. At every street corner, in every poor neighborhood, in every provincial town, there were to be groups of people playing with children, visiting the sick and the elderly,

6. For an insightful analysis of how state-run volunteer programs combine neoliberal elements with post-socialist themes, see Hemment (2012).

7. In addition to providing spiritual benefits, volunteer programs also serve as a conduit for religious engineering and constructions of active citizenship (see Bee and Kaya 2017; Çakmaklı 2015; Işık 2021).

teaching in literacy programs, and distributing food to the hungry. Each "problem" was to have its own project, and each volunteer was to choose a "social cause" that was dearest to their heart. This neo-Tocquevillian dream of associational vibrancy made practices of social care visible to the public. These projects, regardless of whether they achieved their ambitious goals, transformed volunteer work into an observable element of social life—no longer buried within the private moral space of one's relationship with Allah.

Assemblages of Volunteerism

Volunteering as a formal altruistic endeavor is relatively new in Turkey, in contrast to longstanding traditions of generalized philanthropic donations (*hayırseverlik*), service to one's community (*hizmet*), and forms of collective involvement that occur in the context of grassroots movements (see Akboğa 2017; Campbell and Çarkoğlu 2019; Şimşek 2004). A concerted effort toward bureaucratization, formalization, and professionalization of volunteer work emerged as a result of new understandings of NGO legitimacy (Can 2013). Most civil society organizations adopted internal procedures—formal rules as well as less formal guidelines—to govern the behavior of volunteers and manage their interactions with the larger public. In contrast to the amateurish, informal, and mission-driven nature of earlier volunteer efforts, these volunteer programs are cause-specific and project-based. As a result, most NGOs in Turkey began to spend as much time and energy recruiting and retaining volunteers as they did serving their beneficiaries.

When religious publications that emphasize the need for Muslims to give their time and money for the well-being of society are examined, the concurrent expression of self-oriented and pious motivations emerges as a commonality between them.[8] Charity was no longer to be given in secret, but was to play a key element in the governance of the autonomous Muslim self. Numerous texts elaborated on the religious injunction

8. On how Turkish Muslims negotiate the tensions between self-oriented and religious motivations, see Işık (2021) and Vicini (2020).

to give with reference to several themes, such as personal giving (infak), benevolence (iyilik), and worship (ibadet). These concepts were defined, reinterpreted, and expanded upon by academics, religious scholars, and conservative thinkers in relation to the pursuit of helping others. For instance, Osman Nuri Topbaş, a Sufi leader with a large following, explains that "even someone who lacks the material means can find ways to perform infak in a proper fashion" (Topbaş 2008, 82). Another theologian claims that "an orientation toward the well-being of others" was the "golden rule of Islam," and recommends religious education to enhance the spirit of volunteerism (Ege 2011, 12). Other intellectual figures highlighted that each Muslim has the spiritual potential to be a "waqf person," defined as someone who "loves all of God's creatures equally [and] heals the sick" (Narince 2004, 16).

These Islamic articulations were enhanced by New Age and self-help rhetoric that echoed claims of popular psychology. One text claimed that the psychology of happiness required a distinctive mindset: "Think of your good deed as an investment for the future and be assured that your efforts will be reciprocated in the most bounteous and beautiful way!" (Topkara n.d.). Individuals could "become happier through increased emotions of trust," and "feel better" about themselves (Tarhan 2007, 29). This kind of emotional healing was possible due to the "scientific connection" between "personal happiness and helping those who were less fortunate" (Kuş 2007, 34). Western doctors and experts were often quoted about their insights into the "science of happiness." One article, titled "Help Others, Defeat Depression," referred to research conducted at an unidentified American university, which purportedly showed that "Depression can be overcome by developing positive personality traits such as helping others and being kind. . . . Experts explain that focusing on other people's problems helps individuals feel better about themselves" (Deniz Feneri Derneği 2012). Another article exploring the relationship between religion and volunteer work asserted that people were more likely to volunteer if they understood helping others as an avenue for achieving their life goals, such as happiness (Ege 2011, 12).

What united these claims was the notion that volunteering was both a path toward eternal salvation and a medium for self-healing. The plight of the Muslim individual was a common topic of discussion in the publications of Islamic NGOs as well. Consider this excerpt from an article published in the bulletin of a provincial NGO:

> Our social conceptions are changing every day. New ideas are inscribed into our brains: "If you are bored, go shopping; if you are unhappy, buy something; if you have money, then spend it; if you are going to wear clothes, then buy brands; you deserve better." These messages create a cultural confusion. We are told that we need all these commodities, we are asked to spend our lives in shopping malls. We are not against need; we are only against wastefulness. What is presented to us as modernity and civilization are actually the codes of a civilization that is founded upon consumption, hedonism, and exploitation. Real freedom does not mean that we get to choose what we can buy. That is not how we should express ourselves; true freedom entails self-government. Let's not forget that we can only truly be ourselves if we live according to our own beliefs, ideas, and values. And for this to occur, we need to remind ourselves that we are part of a civilization composed of people who cannot go to bed if they know that their neighbor is hungry. (Oruç 2010, 19)

This account, which combined an emphasis on individual freedom, a critique of Western modernity and consumerism, and a civilizational awareness, illustrates the scope of Islamic-neoliberal assemblages of volunteerism in Turkey. Likewise, most managers and volunteer coordinators were aware of their volunteers' mixed motivations, and paid attention to their personal stories. In response to a question about volunteer motives, Leyla explained that many people joined the organization when they were going through a hard time, even if they would not readily admit it:

> It is the product of modern life. Some of our volunteers are depressed, others are going through a divorce, whereas another group feel like money and success have not brought them happiness. They come here to feel good even if they often say that they are only pleasing Allah. Of course, we welcome them all with open arms.

Aysun expressed a similar acknowledgment of volunteers' mixed motivations. A mid-level director who worked at the TDV, she explained why Muslims joined civil society organizations with the following words:

Those who come here tell us: "I feel happy here. I feel hopeful." As an organization, we act as a remedy for loneliness. People suffocate in modern life. Charity organizations can remedy the lack of community; in fact, they can do better than traditional religious brotherhoods. Those places expect submission from their members; people are supposed to stop thinking about themselves; they are not allowed to be free. But a Muslim can be free without living a lonely life.

According to Leyla and Aysun, most of the people who were drawn to Islamic NGOs and volunteer work were those who were seeking an answer to their personal troubles. My experience with various volunteer groups affirms their insights. Some of the older volunteers were retired and did not like feeling "useless," others were trying to come to terms with death and illness, whereas another group craved socialization and just wanted to "get out of the house." Young volunteers also mentioned complex motivations such as overcoming boredom and depression, acquiring social skills, making friends, and learning about business opportunities. Beyond these material benefits, many volunteers likewise reported an overall improvement of their general well-being: they began to feel "content," saw their life in a "new light," and learned to be "thankful" for what they have. These worldly concerns were often explained through religious idioms. Some volunteers discussed the merits of helping others by using verses from the Qur'an, such as "Whoever does a good deed—We will increase for him good therein," and "Whoever does a good deed—it is for himself; and whoever does evil—it is against the self" (Qur'an 42/23 and 45/15). Others talked about how, for them, religious devotion (ibadet) was primarily about ethical formation by telling stories about the lives of the Prophet Muhammad and his companions. Yet another group elaborated on their personal motivations through expressing a nostalgia toward Ottoman waqfs, which, in their eyes, presented an Islamic model of compassion.

Muslim volunteers thus emphasized a religious mode of cultivating subjectivity, and were drawn to the idea that Islam provided a sanctuary for nurturing emotional well-being. The existence of such pious incentives was suggested as proof of their other-oriented, selfless, and respectful approach, even though individualistic motivations were as widespread as spiritual and otherworldly ones. The following section discusses the governmental assemblages between religious devotion, communitarian values, and neoliberal elements of individualism by turning to experiences and encounters of volunteerism as narrated by three individuals.

Giving Time as Experience and as Encounter

Many of these volunteer programs meant to align personal desires with governmental outcomes by defining volunteer work as an indispensable element of faith and citizenship. However, volunteers' on-the-ground experiences were neither coherent nor predictable. In the following pages, I present three personal narratives of individuals who, through their volunteer experience, at times reclaimed, and at other times transcended, the contours of neoliberal-Muslim subjectivity. For these individuals, volunteer work operated as a site for enacting their own religious, moral, and political visions of self, belonging, community, and faith. Although their experiences varied, each narrated their encounter with the "deserving Other" through an emotive language that nevertheless aligned with the spiritual sanctuary project. While Ayşe saw volunteer work as a self-reflective practice that allowed her to deepen her faith through patience, Mert conceptualized giving time to others as a chance to experience a sense of shared humanity that went beyond ethnic, cultural, and religious difference. By contrast, Emine approached Islamic charity through a vocabulary of hope, which she contrasted with the sense of desperation she felt in the face of pervasive injustice. While the emotional iconography of their narratives and the articulation of Islamic values and neoliberal elements varied, each experienced a sense of personal transformation as a result of their volunteer work. Their stories, therefore, illustrate both the complexity of Islamic-neoliberal assemblages as well as the appeal of the spiritual sanctuary project for a wide range of groups.

Case 1: Volunteer Work as Patience and Piety

This first case exemplifies how, despite the individualist ethos of the spiritual sanctuary project, an orientation toward Allah might still operate as the primary frame for volunteer work. For Ayşe, the volunteer experience was mainly about fulfilling her religious duties. She understood Islamic giving as an occasion to deepen her faith and perceived her faith to require a commitment to moral refashioning. Her encounters with the muhtaç (truly deserving poor) were not just about relating to a community of strangers but rather afforded a rare opportunity for experiencing the divine. Any challenges she faced in this journey were a test of her patience and had to be endured with grace and submission. While forging a sense of intimacy with recipients—and with her own faith—was still a defining element of "becoming a beautiful Muslim," Ayşe's spiritual journey was largely marked with strong ethical and pious undertones. Her story therefore illustrates the extent to which the Muslim Social actively enlists conservative, devout Muslims to the spiritual sanctuary subject, while also demonstrating that moralizing notions of Islamic charity are not entirely eclipsed by neoliberal forms, practices, and languages of self-oriented volunteerism.

Ayşe was a young woman in her mid-thirties who had been volunteering at Deniz Feneri for approximately four years. Among all the volunteers that I met, she was one of the most conservative individuals; she approached every aspect of her life as a chance to become a better Muslim. The oldest child of a family who had migrated to Ankara from a rural Anatolian village in the 1980s, Ayşe had only finished middle school, though her two younger brothers had both received a high school education. She told me that she would have wanted to continue her schooling, and that she had always been a hardworking student who had "enjoyed learning." Her parents, however, had not been as supportive of her wish to attend high school as they had been of her younger brothers. Ayşe did not attribute the difference to gender, as she reasoned that her parents had not yet known how "things worked in the city" when she was of school age, but they were able to provide guidance to her siblings by the time they were fourteen years old. Besides, back in the village, girls rarely continued their schooling beyond the primary-school level, and her parents needed her help at home. As the oldest child, she was expected to cook, clean, and take care of her brothers.

Ayşe began to volunteer at Deniz Feneri through someone she met while performing her hajj duty (in 2005). It is highly unusual for someone as young as Ayşe to have already completed her pilgrimage. Hajj is compulsory for all Muslims if they have the means to afford such a trip, but

Muslims in Turkey, like Muslims elsewhere, often wait until they are older to complete this religious duty. In addition to financial constraints, Muslims might postpone their trip due to the expectation to lead a more modest life afterward; one might quit drinking or begin covering her head, for instance. When I asked her why she had chosen to complete this trip at a younger age, Ayşe said: "I wanted to please Allah, do what is asked of me when I still can; who knows whether I will have the opportunity later on?" Even though Ayşe was primarily motivated with fulfilling a religious duty, she also worried that her eagerness had been inappropriate: "Patience is a virtue, I know that, and I try to live my life in harmony with this principle; I pray that Allah forgives me. Maybe I should have been more patient and waited before going to hajj. I sometimes worry that I may have been a bit arrogant." On the one hand, this account illustrates one of Ayşe's key beliefs: religious obligations, if done in a self-centered manner, may not "count," so one needs to be aware of their motivations and overall demeanor. On the other hand, her concerns about whether she had acted in accordance with the maxim of patience illustrate the weight she placed on fortitude in her conception of religious piety.

This orientation toward Allah and the afterlife was prominent in Ayşe's understanding of volunteerism. Before volunteering at Deniz Feneri, Ayşe did not have much experience with community work. But since she grew up in a neighborhood where "everyone cared about everyone else's needs and difficulties," she had learned how to be mindful about others from people in her family. Her grandmother, for example, frequently came up in our conversations, especially in those moments where Ayşe wanted to elaborate on what volunteer work meant for her. Ayşe's grandmother had passed right after Ayşe returned from completing her hajj duty. The loss of her grandmother was hard on Ayşe, and these difficulties were exacerbated by the fact that she had to adjust to the realities of a post-hajj life, which included, among other things, covering her hair with a black headscarf and wearing a long black jacket as a sign of her modesty. (Ayşe dressed modestly even before her trip, but often wore colorful dresses and head coverings.) But Ayşe was also inspired by her grandmother's generosity and fortitude. "A wise woman," who had to raise her five children on her own after her husband passed away at a fairly young age, Ayşe's grandmother initially found it difficult to adjust to life in the city after having followed Ayşe's parents. Eventually, however, she became someone that everyone, at least most of the young women in the neighborhood, sought out, often to ask advice about familial and religious matters. Although not an educated woman by any means, Ayşe's grandmother became a community leader. For Ayşe, her grandmother's generosity was her most inspiring quality:

> My grandmother had a big heart: she cared about other people, and she never hesitated to give, she always shared with others who were in need. Many times, I have seen her invite people to our house, and later to her house even if there was not enough food for us. Somehow, she would find a way to create plenty of food, everyone would be satisfied; that is how bountiful (*bereketli*) her hand was.

Ayşe's rendering of her grandmother's generosity—first in the village and later with her neighbors in a lower-class neighborhood in Ankara—demonstrates how Ayşe imagined community as a small group of people who had intimate, face-to-face relations and were brought together by reciprocal gift relations. The bounty of a feast, of giving when there was nothing to give, underscored a trust in Allah's divine will and an orientation toward community.

In fact, for Ayşe, material wealth had nothing to do with whether one could be generous toward others. Volunteer work was thus the perfect opportunity for those Muslims who had time but not enough money. We once had a chance to talk about this topic at length during a charity sale event in Ankara. As we were standing between decorative carpets, old audiotapes of religious sermons, and Islamic self-help books, Ayşe explained what infak meant for her:

> İnfak means that you need to be a beautiful Muslim. I mean, even a smile, a nice word can count as infak. But if someone has a lot of property, then they might give more, so I always pray to Allah: "*Yarabbi*, please let me earn lots of money so that I can give more." But even in the absence of money, we can still give, and spread goodness. I sometimes do handcrafts, I knit sweaters or sew hats. I also volunteer here; there is always something one can do. The effort might be miniscule, but it is still recognized by Allah.

For Ayşe, volunteering was first and foremost about Islam and living a conservative, devout, and modest life. Certainly, engaging in these volunteer activities provided Ayşe benefits that could be defined as "this worldly" (*dünyevi*): this volunteer work gave her the opportunity to socialize and a reason to get out of the house. By joining the organization, she not only made friends but also exercised authority over younger, less-experienced volunteers. Yet, as she rendered her own story, Ayşe emphasized the affective experience of patience and endurance over self-oriented benefits such as happiness or self-improvement. Put differently, in an effort to portray herself as a devout Muslim, she downplayed the personal advantages of volunteerism.

Since Ayşe had begun to volunteer at Deniz Feneri shortly after her grandmother's unexpected death, she had initially thought of her work as a form of charity (hayır) that she did in her grandmother's name. At first, she worked in the communications department, reading letters sent to the organization by people seeking material assistance. This was a challenging task, and Ayşe found it difficult to read these letters in a detached manner (as she had been told to do). With sympathetic eyes, she told me: "You would not believe what people write. They often write on old, crumpled pieces of paper. You read their words, and you know that they really need help, they need someone to bring them food or medicine, often they just need to know that they are being cared for." Reading these letters gave Ayşe a new appreciation for the importance of enduring difficulties: "I learned to be patient. Seeing such pain and suffering is difficult, but I am doing my part and I am doing what Allah wants from his subjects (*kullar*)."

The emotional experience of patience also shaped Ayşe's encounters with the deserving poor. For Ayşe, the "real" poor were those people who were muhtaç (truly needy) but were too proud to ask for help. She wanted to "find the truly poor," because she believed that helping the real poor was what Allah asked from his most devoted believers. In her mind, the poor were the dearest in Allah's eyes: they were not burdened, but blessed with material deprivation. This conservative approach to the poor found its expression in a popular phrase that Ayşe also used: "The poor do not really need our pity; in reality we are the ones in need of their compassion so that we might be blessed with the keys of paradise." This phrase inverted the hierarchical relationship between the haves and the have-nots; the wealthy may appear to be the ones with power, but their salvation depended on the kindheartedness of the poor. She was not against aiding those who actively sought it, but she believed that finding the truly deserving poor would deliver wide-ranging spiritual and religious dividends.

After working in the communications department, Ayşe began to spend most of her time in the social market. She believed that this new position was a better fit for her. Unlike her position in the communications department, she did not have to make decisions about whether someone was eligible to receive aid. Only preapproved applicants were allowed to visit the social market. She was relieved. "After all," she told me, "only Allah could make the final decision on such sensitive matters." Ayşe was uncomfortable with making decisions about the poor because she felt that she was not well-suited for administrative tasks. In her words: "I did not start volunteering so that I can file papers, calculate numbers, organize letters, and things like that. May Allah forgive me, but I clearly do not have the aptitude for that kind of work." Instead of working in departments that focused on management, Ayşe preferred to spend her time with aid recipients because, as she told me, she "craved that kind of emotional intimacy."

I went to visit Ayşe at the social market on a day that turned out to involve a training session for new volunteers. As one of the most experienced volunteers, Ayşe was tasked with showing the ropes to a group of new volunteers. On that particular day, two younger women were assisting Ayşe as part of their training. Over morning tea, I learned that both women were college students, and their primary motivation for volunteering was to complete their service requirement. Both were studying education, and their university had recently made it compulsory for them to do service-learning. The day began with dusting shelves, followed by emptying boxes of children's clothes. As we worked, one of the younger volunteers, Funda, who was studying to be a preschool teacher, told me: "I like helping other people because the happiness on their face makes me happy as well." Overhearing our conversation, Ayşe intervened with a slight tone of disapproval: "There is nothing wrong with Muslims enjoying happiness; Allah certainly does not want us to be miserable. But here we try to focus on being beautiful Muslims." Ayşe's definition of volunteer work required a solemn but affectionate approach to the poor. The remainder of the day, I watched Funda as she carefully governed her emotional demeanor under the watchful eyes of Ayşe. Funda laughed less, joked less, talked less, and assumed a solemn and quiet attitude when she interacted with visitors.

As this interaction shows, new members often saw volunteer work as a path to fulfillment and happiness. But Ayşe believed that this kind of approach did not truly align with Islam:

> Volunteer work changes you, no doubt about it. But the goal is not to become happier or feel better about yourself. For a Muslim individual, the purpose of charity is to develop an intimacy with the poor, with Allah, with your own faith. You are supposed to change by looking inward, with patience and prayer. It is hard work.

In this construction of moral selfhood, Ayşe emphasized qualities such as contemplation, endurance, and humility. But, while she believed that a beautiful Muslim's ethical orientation should be toward the afterlife, she still related to others and to her own self through a language of liberal individualism. In fact, volunteer work—which she saw primarily as an individual religious practice—provided a venue for her to practice and refine moral dispositions that were integral to her own interpretation of beautiful Muslimhood. While Ayşe's assemblage of Islamic neoliberalism might appear as if it is not "neoliberal enough" due to the absence of an explicitly self-oriented narrative, the fact that she articulated her moral quest as a spiritual journey that can only be completed by a stoic sense of individual contemplation suggests otherwise. Like other Islamic social projects examined in the previous chapters, the appeal of the spiritual sanctuary lay not in consensus about the proper balance between Islamic values and neoliberal ethics, but rather in the openness of the project's diverse interpretations of religion, multiple notions of relating to the deserving Other, and distinctive experiences of emotional intimacy.

Case 2: Tolerance in the Name of Humanity

The second case presents a narrative of volunteering as a medium for accessing and experiencing a sense of shared humanity. Expressed by

Mert, a young Turkish man with a strong attachment to Turkish national-ism, this narrative illustrates the potential of volunteer work to transcend questions of identity that often plague and divide the Turkish citizenry. He articulates giving time to others as a valuable encounter that allows both parties to connect beyond their cultural, ethnic, and political dif-ferences. Mert tells the story of how he was internally transformed while serving school-age children. He learned the value of fundamental human qualities that cut across differences. While he was not as devout as Ayşe, Mert's story of self-transformation was also tied to his faith, specifically his realization that Islamic service was about practicing tolerance toward others. In addition to deepening his faith, volunteer work provided Mert with self-oriented benefits, such as overcoming depression and feeling more confident in his abilities. Mert's narrative, therefore, demonstrates how Islamic values and neoliberal themes may be salient even when they are not central to volunteer subjectivity.

Mert was a twenty-eight-year-old man who had gone to college in an Anatolian city to study electrical engineering. College had not been par-ticularly challenging; he had even enjoyed living in a smaller city after having grown up in Istanbul. Mert came from a Sunni Muslim family, but, as he told me, no one in his family was very religious. For Mert, this meant that while his grandparents prayed five times a day, his father only went to the Friday prayers, and that his parents would consume alcohol, only giv-ing it up for the month of Ramadan, during which they fasted earnestly. Ideologically, his family was closer to the Nationalist Action Party (MHP) than to the AKP; hence, most of his family members believed in the ethnic purity of Turkishness. Although his family did not have any particular qualms about Erdoğan or the AKP, when I met him in 2010, Mert, like his father, told me that the AKP had been too lenient on the Kurdish issue (a view he most likely dropped later).

Before he left for college, Mert's parents advised him to "stay out of trouble" and focus on his studies. Getting his degree, thus, had been Mert's primary goal, but at the same time, throughout the first year of college, he met people from different walks of life, and had interactions with nationalists, Islamists, and, on rare occasions, even with leftists. Although Mert presented himself as someone who was not "political," he expressed strong opinions about campus politics. He thought that left-ists, on account of their support for the Kurdish cause, did not actually care about "Turkey's real problems," and were a bit "romantic" when it came to their ideas about human nature. He was not very fond of the Islamists he met during college, either. All they did was constantly pray together, often inviting Mert to come to the mosque or participate in other kinds of events. Mert rarely joined them, but regularly attended Friday prayers on his own. Additionally, Islamists' gender ideology was too strict, and college was a place where women and men were supposed to interact with one another and get to know each other. At the time, I learned later, Mert had an Alevi[9] girlfriend and, hence, did not think that their relationship would be approved in "those circles." His parents were actually glad when they eventually broke up because, as Mert explained: "They do not think that people from different faiths can have a long-lasting marriage, but that was not why we broke up. We just could not agree on a plan for the future."

At some point during college, Mert had found himself spending a lot of time with like-minded nationalists. His only reservation about this group regarded their propensity toward protest and violence. From an ideological standpoint, Mert agreed with their views on the superiority of Turkish national identity and was similarly uncomfortable with the asser-tion of cultural, religious, and political differences as espoused by Alevi, Kurdish, and leftist groups. But he began to withdraw from this group after one of his roommates was injured. Often, these nationalist students would get in fights with leftists, frequently over simple matters such as what someone said in a class discussion. Mert had nursed his roommate and had closely witnessed his suffering while he was at the hospital and, later, during the long healing period at home. He already had reservations about this group's propensity toward violence, but this event shook him to his core:

9. Alevis are the largest religious minority in Turkey and often face political oppres-sion and social exclusion. While technically they fall under the Shi'a denomination of Islam, they follow a fundamentally different interpretation than other Shi'a communities.

My roommate was in so much pain, and, of course, he could not tell his parents, so we had to take care of him, which I am happy to do, but it was a stupid kind of suffering. Did he convince anyone? Did he change anyone's mind? No, he just proved that he was strong, that he was a man, but it served neither our nation nor our religion. And, what's worse, differences were hardened.

As this excerpt illustrates, Mert was critical of this kind of nationalism, not only due to the use of violence but also for being too rigid. He realized that most people were obsessed with protecting their own identity, instead of reaching out to those who were different from them. This was when Mert entered what he referred to as a "difficult period." He did not want to hang out with his usual friends, he fell behind on his coursework, and, most mornings, he did not even want to get out of bed. "When I looked around," he explained, "everything seemed gray. I thought everyone was fighting about futile things, I did not see the point of going on as if nothing had happened."

Desperate to "feel better," Mert decided to join a volunteer-run university club. "That decision changed my life," he said. This club originated during the 1999 Marmara earthquake, when students mobilized to collect donations and delivered them to disaster victims. But by the time Mert had joined, the organization had rebranded itself, now bringing together college-age students with primary-school children so that the former could tutor the latter on subjects such as math and English. Every Saturday morning, Mert would get on a bus with fifteen to twenty other students and go to the same school, where they were each responsible for instructing a small group of children. The "weekend camp," as it was referred to by the college students, lasted about half a day and involved in-class instruction followed by outdoor play. As he recounted those early days, Mert proudly said that he surprised himself by not missing even a single weekend session. This was not because the club expected its members to approach these weekend camps as they would their "real job," but because Mert had realized that regular attendance was crucial for gaining the trust of the community. Most importantly, Mert continued to show up because he did not want to disappoint the children:

At first, I just got on the bus on Saturday mornings, went to my assigned classroom, and taught them some math. Nothing complicated, but I remember trying to come up with fun examples that would complement what they were normally taught. But, how shall I put it? Of course, education is helpful, and certainly these children need all the support that they can get. But what most of them want, really, is just some love and attention. Someone to hear them, someone to listen to them. And you cannot create that kind of familiarity if you just go one or two weekends and then stop showing up afterward. I think I kept going back because I did not want to disappoint them, and I did not want to disappoint myself either. And, more importantly, there was also a nice emotional connection; we all felt it.

For Mert, a self-oriented vocabulary of volunteer work was interwoven with visions of egalitarian friendships with innocent children.

After participating in the weekend camp for a couple of months, Mert realized that many of the young boys, maybe because they lived in "rough neighborhoods" or maybe because of "poverty," often put up a tough act to protect themselves from heartbreak. "These children are mazlum, but despite all their difficulties, they are full of love (*sevecen*), but they first need to get to know us." For Mert, mazlumiyet denoted a sense of innocence as well as a longing for social connections. "The parents of these children," Mert explained, "are not only poor, but they are also exhausted. Often, they have many children, and so they cannot really pay attention to each and every one of them." Such an articulation of childhood as innocence thus emphasized the socio-emotional needs of children and downplayed economic differences. Mert, of course, knew that most of the children's families lacked financial resources, but, as he put it, he did not want children to perceive their relationship "as if it was just about money." For this reason, he never brought gifts to children. But many of the other volunteers, either because they wanted to gain the children's favor, or because they felt pity toward them, often distributed small gifts, such as chocolate, gum, or toys, at the end of the class period. Mert understood their rationale but thought that such gestures, instead of closing the gap, exposed economic differences between the volunteers and the children. He elaborated:

I realized very quickly that these children are very smart and very sensitive. If they realize that you are only there to give out chocolate or toys, they will take those gifts, but they will keep their distance. The only way to gain their trust is if they know that you truly enjoy spending time with them. You cannot fake intimacy; you must feel it from your heart.

Mert came to this realization partly while playing soccer with the kids. During breaks and after the completion of the classes for that day, some volunteers would join the children to play in the schoolyard. "It was nothing special," Mert explained, "but it brought us together. We were part of a team, just having fun together." While playing soccer, Mert got to know Yusuf, a fellow volunteer who was a couple of years older, who Mert respectfully called "*abi*" (older brother). A serious young man, Yusuf abi was not particularly friendly to newcomers. While most volunteers spent their time socializing with one another during breaks, Mert noticed that Yusuf abi spent his break time playing soccer with the children. At the end of the day, he also conversed with mothers who came to check on their children. "He was genuinely interested," Mert told me, and added: "he was dedicated to teaching the children and wanted to make sure that they got something out of all of this." But many of the other volunteers, Mert noticed, were just there for "their own benefit;" some wanted to meet other people, others sought a line on their resume, while most were volunteering their time to fulfill a community service requirement—that is, they were motivated by individual gain. But Yusuf abi was different. In addition to his "respectful and caring approach," Mert admired Yusuf abi's orientation toward religious service. Since he had never mentioned religious issues, Mert was surprised to run into Yusuf abi at the Friday prayers. Afterward, they went to have lunch at a nearby restaurant and chatted about volunteer work. To Mert's surprise, Yusuf abi's story was one of Islamic salvation. Mert recounted their conversation:

He told me that his primary motivation was to please Allah. That spending time with children, understanding their problems, [and] educating them was part of his way of serving humanity in the name of the *da'wah* (*dava*). I never thought of him that way because he never brought up religion or political issues when he was with the children.

After this conversation, Mert began to see Yusuf abi as a model volunteer. They continued to spend time together on the weekends, and Mert observed how Yusuf abi calmly engaged with the children and how he carefully communicated with their parents, "never looking down on them or judging them," he explained. In his eyes, Yusuf abi embodied a way of acting on "our lost humanity." This encounter, in turn, gave Mert the tools to combine his faith and his volunteer work in a way that he had not considered before. Adopting a nonjudgmental outlook that respected difference was better than confronting others with disdain and violence.

During his time with the weekend camp, Mert found two kinds of community: a community of like-minded students who wanted to "make a difference" instead of engaging in never-ending political debates, and a community of disadvantaged children who gave Mert a new appreciation for his religion, Islam, and renewed his faith in humanity. Mert's articulation of community thus appeared to be quite paradoxical on the surface. Whereas students were divided along political lines, these irreconcilable differences, he believed, disappeared when everyone mobilized around a common cause. And whereas most of the children he tutored were ethnically Kurdish, Mert came to believe that their shared religious beliefs made it possible to overcome potential areas of conflict. Over time, Mert gently forged an emotional bond with the children, and in the process of spending time with them, whether in the classroom or while playing soccer, he started to feel better: "they restored my faith in humanity. This was a helpful period for my soul," he longingly explained. "Maybe I should have been a teacher instead of an engineer."

For Mert, the capacity of volunteering to connect people from different backgrounds superseded the possibility that acts of giving time and money might reinforce a sense of separation between self and other. In his eyes, being a beautiful Muslim required bonding with others at a deeper level. When explaining the importance of social connections among diverse groups, he shared: "People need each other. Our religion recognizes that humans cannot live on their own; that's why we say, 'people are mirrors of one another' (*insan insanın aynasıdır*)." In this account, Mert mentioned mutual need and reciprocal learning as vital aspects of Islam. It was this understanding that allowed him to relate to those he helped without judgment or prejudice. But, at the same time, Mert acknowledged that volunteer work had improved his personal well-being. In addition to giving him a sense of purpose during a difficult time, Mert also noted: "Doing this work taught me many things. I became more confident, I learned that I could solve problems. I used to be a little shy." In contrast to Ayşe's disapproval of perceiving giving time as a path to happiness, Mert was not bothered by the potential personal benefits of volunteer work. He recognized that most middle-class residents of urban cities were drawn to volunteer programs because they were looking for a deeper meaning in their lives. He believed that spending time with school-aged children and helping them—albeit through bounded, structured, and preplanned activities—was beneficial both for the givers and the recipients of time.

Upon graduating, Mert moved back to Istanbul to live with his parents. After a period of unemployment, he found a job at a computer software company. Even though he had family and friends, he initially felt isolated and was depressed for quite some time. Before finding a job, he joined a civil society organization, the Educational Volunteers Foundation of Turkey (Türkiye Eğitim Gönüllüleri Vakfı, TEGV), a secular-liberal organization connecting adult volunteers with disadvantaged children in addition to providing a wide range of sponsorships for educational purposes. In fact, he told me this personal narrative on a day that I accompanied him to one of TEGV's education parks in Istanbul. Mert appreciated the activities organized by TEGV, but this volunteer program did not provide him with a sense of fulfillment like the one that he experienced while volunteering at the university student club. Nevertheless, Mert continued to volunteer, even after he found a job. For Mert, volunteer work performed several functions. Spending time with children gave him a sense of connection, helping his loneliness. Even if he was not able to forge the same kind of friendships, spending time with children allowed him to fondly remember the challenging but transformational aspects of his college years. Lastly, he was able to spend time with volunteers who often expressed different political views and had disparate ethnic backgrounds, but who nevertheless came together to educate children who were the future of Turkey, which reminded Mert of their deeper social connections.

In contrast to Ayşe, who foregrounded the relationship between herself and others in a religious axis, Mert articulated volunteer work through a vocabulary of shared humanity. Participating in volunteer programs allowed him to develop empathy toward people who came from different walks of life, who belonged to various ethnic groups, or who had dissimilar political ideas. Gaining confidence in his own abilities, expressing faith in everyday life through small acts of giving, and connecting to others whom he saw as different than himself were key elements of his volunteer iconography. The soft language of humanity allowed Mert to avoid a sense of religious zeal, while also providing a venue for charting his own spiritual journey that promised self-healing through encounters with innocent children. In this sense Ayşe's and Mert's volunteer experiences were similar: both pursued this work to enrich the "self-to-self" relationship, and both believed that they increased their self-awareness through spending time with deserving Others. Individualism and communitarianism blended in their narratives, albeit in significantly divergent ways.

Case 3: Between Disappointment and a Sense of Hope

This last narrative explores the persistence of the "political" within Islamic-neoliberal assemblages of volunteerism. While Mert's story represents an apolitical interpretation of volunteer work, this case features a young woman (whom I will call Emine) who gave her time to deserving Others but who also desired to instigate political change against injustice and inequality. For Emine, the main issue that separated people was the gap between the haves and the have-nots. She believed that Muslims should strive to ameliorate this problem. While she was part of various civic groups, she also painstakingly acknowledged that activist movements often fell short of accomplishing their goals. In her desperation, she turned to volunteer work. While aware of these programs' limited impact, Emine's sense of optimism was momentarily revived since she felt like she had "made a difference." That she sought and found emotional healing through her volunteer work, and that it was this kind of self-transformation that allowed her to continue her political activism, places this case squarely in the realm of the Muslim Social while also illustrating its limited reach.

Emine was a young woman and one of the more well-spoken individuals that I met during my fieldwork. A high school teacher in her mid-twenties, she was the youngest child of an educated urban family. Her father was a university professor in Islamic theology, and her two older sisters and her mother had received their bachelor's degrees in social science-related disciplines. All three sisters were married, but while her sisters' marriages had been arranged through relatives, Emine had met her husband in college. In contrast to her sisters' weddings, which Emine found extravagant, her wedding was a small ceremony, because neither she nor her husband liked to "show off." Emine believed that Islam ordained a frugal and modest life, and she explained to me that she preferred to spend money on more useful things. In contrast to her older sisters, who spent "too much time at the shopping mall," Emine almost never used makeup and wore unassuming, simple clothes with plain colors. Even though all three sisters veiled in public, Emine explained to me that they had quite different personal styles:

> They like dressing up and buying fancy things. It does not matter how expensive an item is, they feel it is worth it if is a brand of some sort. If I were to criticize them, they would say that Allah allows Muslims to own quality items. And then, one of them especially, posts all this stuff on her Instagram; she is trying to become an influencer, I guess. It is still kind of modest, but it always comes down to money.

For Emine, her sisters represented a kind of religiosity that was overwhelmingly influenced by consumerism, social media, and Islamic brands. In this respect, her disapproval of her sisters' lifestyles resembles the trope of the "*süslüman*," a term that combines "*süslü*" (dressy) and "*Müslüman*," and is often used to criticize Turkish Muslim women who, despite being veiled, act "freely" in public by smoking tobacco, mingling with the opposite sex, and wearing excessive makeup (Yarar 2021). While Emine was not interested in policing women's public behavior through conservative appeals to modesty, she emphasized that Islam ordered sharing one's wealth with those who are less fortunate. She found her sisters to be too self-oriented and thereby lacking the kind of moral disposition that being a "beautiful Muslim" truly necessitated. Such an ethical orientation meant not only "giving away the bare minimum of one's money" but "carefully thinking if one needs another pair of shoes, a more expensive car, or has to organize an extravagant birthday party for a five-year-old," she told me.

In contrast to Ayşe and Mert, Emine also voluntarily brought up political issues in her conversations with me. For instance, unlike recent university graduates, Emine had been lucky to be appointed to a public teaching position shortly after finishing her degree. But even though she was employed, she continued to support her friends by participating in protests and attending their meetings. Youth unemployment is a pressing issue in Turkey, especially among white-collar professionals and university graduates. Referring to Erdoğan's July 2010 comment in which he said, "Not all university graduates are supposed to find employment," Emine told me: "He does not seem to care that young people want to work so that they can contribute to the well-being of our country." At the same time, however, she pointed out that unemployment was not a problem that was just created by the AKP, and explained: "These kinds of issues are the result of the powerful preying on those who are weak. But an Islamic life requires paying attention to issues of social justice. We need to protect those who cannot protect themselves." This understanding of faith as reconfiguring the relationship between the haves and the have-nots was quite significant for Emine. Although she never used terms such as class consciousness or economic inequality, she often emphasized that Islam was a religion of the "people." In fact, when I met her again after the 2013 Gezi Park protests, Emine told me that she had attended some of the meetings of the Anti-capitalist Muslims (Antikapitalist Müslümanlar) organization. When I asked her what attracted her to this group, she said: "Most of those people, like me, are against thinking of oneself as above another. We believe that Muslims need to stand up against oppression (zulüm), no matter who the perpetrator might be."

Emine's foregrounding of power and injustice, however, does not mean that she did not experience volunteer work at an affective level. Like Ayşe and Mert, Emine was also drawn to volunteerism as a venue to improve her own well-being. Accordingly, the dominant affective repertoire that defined Emine's orientation toward volunteering was disappointment and a sense of revolting against injustice. Her desire to overcome feelings of disappointment gave meaning to her faith, while volunteer work provided opportunities for expressing and resolving her feelings. In fact, she told me that she began to do volunteer work so that she could "calm down and stop feeling like she did not accomplish anything." In that sense, volunteer work operated as a refuge for Emine because it provided her with "an hour or two every weekend that was immune to all that worry."

For Emine, the ordinary world represented a sense of chaos exacerbated by economic and political injustice and exploitation. She found a sense of serenity and peacefulness through her encounters with poor women she met through a charity organization that was adjacent to a mosque in a lower-class neighborhood. Initially, she had visited this organization to donate children's clothes that her nieces and nephews had outgrown. Realizing that help was needed, she began to volunteer:

> I guess I felt drawn to this place, to these women. Of course, lots of people need help, they need money, food, and support. I do my best to donate what I can, I mobilize people that I know, my relatives, friends, and neighbors. I make sure that my sisters also do their share; I even make them come and volunteer their time during events so that they do not just send some worn clothes or old shoes, call it their sadaka, and move on with their lives. I also come to help, I want to feel useful; may Allah forgive me, I am not immune to feelings of grandeur. But I try my best to remain humble, I pray that Allah will use me as a conduit for delivering justice in this world.

Even though Emine first began to help during the assistance distribution days, an event that took place once a month, she soon realized that what these women needed "was not just food or coal, but someone to talk to." After talking to the NGO personnel, she started coming to the organization every weekend for a couple of hours to meet with women who sought her out. Over time, Emine began to develop a "close relationship" with these women by listening to their stories and giving them advice about their children's schooling and other familial matters. Soon, it became clear to her that most of these women were not aware of the social programs that were available to them. Even with the creation of the SOYBIS (see chapter 3) database, navigating the bureaucracy was an arduous task, especially for people who were illiterate and lacked computer skills. Thus, Emine began to listen to their needs and problems. She assessed their circumstances, looked up information online, identified potential services, and oversaw the application process. She downloaded, printed, and filled out paperwork, spending a great deal of time explaining which documents had to be taken to which government office, and sometimes providing guidance about civil society organizations as well. In doing all of this, Emine gave them the gift of information. In contrast to Ayşe, who found bureaucratic paperwork to be tedious and a "waste of time," Emine believed that assisting poor women in navigating the governmental red tape was one of the most effective ways to channel her philanthropic goodwill.

Most of these poor women already received assistance from the NGO, but Emine was not concerned with whether they were "doubling up." She said: "We know that they are in need, we know that they are mağdur (victims), then why would we expect them to survive with the minimum?" But, although Emine supported and encouraged women to seek in-kind and financial assistance from multiple locations, she never gave them money from her own pocket. For her, volunteerism was about forging egalitarian relationships. In addition to not giving them any money, Emine also hid her emotions from those she was trying to help. Sometimes, while listening to their stories, she felt embarrassment, pity, or fury. Most of these women suffered not only from material deprivation but were also victims of violence, and that made it even more difficult for her to keep her composure. I asked Emine why she tried to suppress her emotions, and she told me that it was to protect the aid recipients:

> I never would want it to be like those TV programs. The poor tell their story, they cry, the speaker cries, there is pity and pain, assistance is provided, but it is all a show. Of course, I feel sad. Often I go home afterward and tell my husband the stories I heard. But I do not burden them with my emotions. It is not because I am cold or that I do not care; the exact opposite—I care too much.

Emine did not want her volunteer work to turn into a spectacle of suffering, so she assumed a distant, objective demeanor while interacting with poor women, and she kept her emotions to herself. She also wanted to make sure that the aid recipients did not feel like they had to prove that they were in need. Withdrawing emotionally, Emine believed, freed the poor from putting on a performance. True intimacy, in this case, required a distant demeanor.

Emine's volunteer work, which accompanied her activism rather than replacing it, also illustrates that volunteerism may provide a sanctuary from the emotional volatility of the political domain. Whereas Emine often emphasized disappointment when she talked about the lack of justice in Turkish society, she also told me that she felt a sense of serenity after she spent her hours volunteering. For Emine, what mattered was to confront injustice, and often she felt disillusioned that ordinary people like her were not able to "make things better." When I asked her whether she thought her volunteer work creates the kind of change she desired, she answered thoughtfully: "It depends on one's perspective. Am I able to get rid of poverty? Probably not. But am I able to let the powerful know that the downtrodden have people that care for them? I believe so, and I mean well, and I hope that my work pleases Allah." Emine hoped to instigate long-lasting change via her political activism, but she was also attracted to volunteer work for its potential to generate a sense of solidarity among different groups.

While civic engagement and political activism may work in opposition, Emine saw them as complementary endeavors. The desire to make the world a better place was part of her Islamic devotion. Like Ayşe and Mert, Emine articulated her volunteer experience with reference to an emotional vocabulary. But, instead of referring to religious values of patience or humanitarian ideals of tolerance, Emine's affective repertoire oscillated between modes of anticipation and anguish, hope and desperation, and optimism and pragmatism. Although she desired structural change, because of the isolated nature of volunteer work, she could not realize her heart's desire. Despite her hesitation, however, she still found a way to align her goodwill with the spiritual sanctuary project.

Government of Intimacy

Attempts to cultivate self-care are on the rise in Turkey. This new concern, which spans journalistic, scientific, religious, psychological, and political fields, is promoted by bloggers, specialists, life coaches, social media influencers, and religious figures who give talks, teach courses, and organize retreats on wellness. Sam Binkley (2014) argues that this propensity toward governing one's psychological well-being transforms happiness into an enterprise, while making each individual responsible to live a life in which their spiritual potential is activated, and the emotional returns of their daily actions are maximized. Pious Muslims are also active participants in the happiness industry; a whole range of public figures now see Islam as a religion that ordains the careful administration of one's inner self as a way to get closer to Allah while also living a fulfilling and successful life.

In the past two decades, the Turkish state, often in partnership with Islamic NGOs, has introduced new programs designed to increase civic engagement and cultivate a spirit of volunteerism among citizens. The Muslim Social conceptualized Turkish citizens as autonomous individuals who had an overwhelming "need to help" (Malkki 2015) and incorporated these emotional sentiments into the governmental apparatus quite effectively. The social project of a spiritual sanctuary portrayed giving time to others as an indispensable element of a modern Muslim society. These volunteer programs, to a large extent, relied on the assumption that no one can be *against* helping poor families, street children, or the disabled. To question such an assumption would be to position oneself against the philanthropic spirit of such programs. To support and participate in such programs, on the other hand, was framed as common sense: a demonstration of compassion, of genuine investment in social harmony, and of the idea that deploying the emotional labor of volunteers was a more effective way of governing the Muslim Social.

Many retirees, unemployed young adults, housewives, and university students joined formal volunteer programs. They had wide-ranging motivations: some were bored, while others were going through a difficult personal time; some wanted to socialize, while others had to complete a "social project" to earn course credits. Just being a Muslim with a sense of responsibility to others was no longer the primary impetus for partaking in volunteer work. Those who wanted to do so had to fill out application forms; write essays; decide whether they cared more about poor children, the environment, or sports; and make sure that they got involved with the kind of project that provided the highest emotional dividends. The question was no longer simply "Does this person want to help others?" or "Do these people need help?" but also: "What is the specific cause or project that brings these two groups together?" "What kind of immediate, observable, calculable outcomes will these acts of helping produce?" A whole apparatus of mechanisms focused on attracting, retaining, and training volunteers thus surfaced. This machinery of social projects repackaged "being good" and "feeling good" as part of individual self-conduct. Religious obligations were still important, but so was self-care and self-fulfillment. The Muslim individual was not someone who just listened to religious sermons for moral guidance, but was also someone who could find answers to a wide range of questions through helping others who were less fortunate.

This chapter has examined these Islamic-neoliberal assemblages by paying particular attention to how individuals gave meaning to their volunteer experiences and encounters. Volunteers were drawn to these programs for a variety of reasons ranging from the personal to the political, from the mundane to the utopian, and from concerns about their own happiness to anxieties about the future of Turkey. Some, like Ayşe, longed to deepen their spiritual relationship with Allah. Others, like Mert, saw volunteer work as a conduit for generating personal satisfaction, whereas yet another group, like Emine, were moved by a desire to stand together with the needy and the weak. The portraits of these three individuals and their experiences contribute to our understanding of how volunteer work acquires meaning through affect. While Ayşe narrated her experience as a religious one through the emotive language of patience, Mert emphasized the happiness he felt when surrounded by an atmosphere of tolerance, and Emine stressed that volunteering was an inspirational form of worship when activism failed to bring social justice (*adalet*).

A last issue remains: Are these volunteer programs merely an instrument of depoliticization? Given that these programs operated as an alternative venue for associational life, youth mobilization, and even Islamist movements, it is difficult not to see them as such. Although this chapter has attended to the affective dimensions of volunteerism, it would be a mistake to assume that these volunteer programs lack a political dimension.

Rather, the relationship between the political and the personal is subject to interpretation; whereas, for Ayşe, volunteer work was an apolitical space, Mert considered giving time to those who were different as a way to rise above politics. In contrast, Emine experienced volunteer work as an opportunity for renewing her political energy and replenishing hope for a better future. These multiple narratives certainly suggest a more complicated portrait of neoliberal-Muslim subjectivity that prevents drawing easy distinctions between affective, technical, moral, and political registrars. Nevertheless, the volunteer experience still acquired meaning through the notion that Islamic "community" provided a spiritual sanctuary to disillusioned, isolated, and disenchanted individuals. By participating in these volunteer programs, Muslims are able to perform their piety while simultaneously contesting attempts to construct a uniform affective experience of belonging to the Muslim Social. Their religious experiences and encounters with the "Other" demonstrate an ethical complexity and emotive flexibility that destabilizes neoliberal expressions of individualism, but these social bonds are nevertheless forged between autonomous, free, and self-standing persons.

Conclusion

In 2022, the Association of Independent Industrialists and Businessmen (Müstakil Sanayici ve İşadamları Derneği, MÜSİAD) published a research report titled "Rethinking the Global Economy" (Dinç et al. 2021). Without directly mentioning the dire economic conditions in Turkey, the report stated that its objective was to provide specific recommendations so that Turkey would become one of the world's top ten economic powerhouses before 2050. One of the report's stated goals was the construction of a financial system that would not be "dependent on interest" and would thus be "just, redistributive, and sustainable" (40). The authors of the report argued that such an outcome was possible by seeking "Islamic finance solutions," one of which was the "incorporation of zakat funds into the financial system with the help of transparent technologies" (51). The emphasis on zakat fit into the report's overarching theme: the integration of Islamic socioeconomic conventions with the global financial infrastructure in an effective and seamless manner. The best way to "rethink the global economy," then, was by reimagining the role of Islam in facilitating both economic enterprise and societal well-being.

Far from being a recent development, the present book has argued that MÜSİAD's attempt to combine global-neoliberal elements with local-Islamic traditions has been ongoing since the early 2000s, and that, if implemented, these efforts to reconfigure the Turkish economy along Islamic lines would likely have unforeseen consequences. What I presented in this book are some of the many and diverse Islamic-neoliberal assemblages that emerged and circulated, shaping not only modalities of poverty governance but also pious subjectivities of middle-class Muslims in Turkey. My inquiry here suggests how an explicitly Islamic worldview negotiated and produced neoliberal elements such as commodification, individualization, privatization, and marketization, but also highlights that Islamic-neoliberal governmental assemblages unfold through contested visions of community.

Through the lens of Islamic charity, this book has explored the productive encounter between Islamic politics, dynamics of economic liberalization, and dwindling welfare developmentalism in Turkey. I traced how Islamic social projects combined communitarian values with neoliberal elements in a diverse, fragmented, and inconsistent manner, while paying careful attention to what these social imaginaries meant for pious Muslims in Turkey for whom governmental intervention was not just about alleviating poverty, but also a site for asserting a new kind of Turkish-Muslim identity. As Muslims imagined new ways to govern poverty, Islamic values and neoliberal elements came together in ways that transformed social service provision across public and private domains. These governmental assemblages, I contend, gave rise to a phenomenon that is underexamined in Turkey and elsewhere: the rise of the Muslim Social.

As a governmental apparatus, the Muslim Social was borne out of the interplay between multiple visions of Islamic community and neoliberal forms of governance. Assemblages of Islamic neoliberalism transformed practices of private charity and public welfare through the adoption of technical measures and the cultivation of public emotions. As a result, the Muslim Social was mainly understood through the prism of managerial expertise and emotional well-being and was no longer perceived via a political or moral framework. Informal, face-to-face, disorganized patterns of giving were gradually supplanted with technical logics of managerialism that privileged formal relations, benevolence toward distant strangers, and a careful orchestration of the aid experience. As neoliberal elements, practices, rationalities, and technologies became more widespread, these shifts were accompanied by changes in Islamic beliefs, traditions, and values; in other words, there was a mutually informing and co-productive relationship between neoliberalism and Islam, resulting in the formation of a new governmental apparatus.

In Turkey, Islamic social projects, which produced and enacted multiple visions of belonging, faith, and care, prompted the advent of the

Muslim Social, which in turn reconfigured the relationship between state, civil society, and citizenry. The AKP also played a fundamental role in promoting these social imaginaries: the government expressed neoliberal reforms in Islamic terms, sponsored the production of knowledge about how to revive faith-based traditions and practices, and disseminated new ideas about Muslim sociality through various channels. As religious values and market-oriented ethics became intertwined both at the institutional level and in everyday practice, Islamic neoliberalism assembled new concepts, practices, and subjectivities, thereby reconfiguring state–civil society relations, redesigning the administration of poverty relief programs, and redefining ideas about the proper way to give money and time. Religion and economy were not mutually exclusive categories; rather, they were reproduced in conjunction with diverse and fluid ideas about belonging, faith, individuality, and society.

While some scholars have found that neoliberalism leads to the spread of calculative ethics into religious practice (Rudnyckyj 2011, 20–21; Tuğal 2013, 144), my account has focused on the unique folding together of managerial measures and affective sensibilities. The assemblage of multiple and often contradictory notions of Islamic community and the varying and imperfect applications of those social imaginaries had an unintended political impact: the notion that social problems are best addressed through a combination of the *technical* and the *emotional*. Both private charity and public welfare assistance were reconfigured in ways that would make the collection, distribution, and organization of money, things, and people more streamlined and, thus, *governable*. The logic of technical expertise permeated welfare governance as Islamic NGOs and public SYD waqfs enthusiastically adopted managerial rationalities, such as audits, barcodes, documents, databases, forms, and filing systems. Accountability, expertise, and transparency became the governing parameters of state–civil society relations. At the same time, the language of moral obligations that hitherto saturated faith-based traditions of giving were supplanted with an increasing emphasis on the emotional well-being of both recipients and donors alike. Care, love, and self-healing became goals that were as important as, if not more than, religious duty and eternal salvation, as pious Muslims envisioned new ways to revive and restore Islamic charity.

While the shift from the political to the technical, and from the moral to the emotional, was not directly engineered by the AKP, the resultant governmental apparatus nevertheless benefited the power and authority of the state through the depoliticization of Islamic civil society.

In contrast to approaches that see religion as a reaction to neoliberalism, this book therefore concurs with a growing body of scholarship that examines the mutually productive linkages between faith, spirituality, and late modern capitalism (Hackworth 2012; Hoesterey 2015; Moodie 2021; Moreton 2010; Wilkinson 2016). Islamic neoliberalism is best understood as a diverse, fluid, and contested assemblage of discourses, interventions, and rationalities. While pious Muslims in Turkey neither totally rejected nor unreservedly embraced "global forms" (Ong and Collier 2008, 4), they were still actively involved in their articulation, negotiation, and production. Whereas in some instances, Islam was conceived as a religion that was inherently supportive of free enterprise, in other cases, Turkish Muslims saw Islam as an advocate for social justice (also see Zencirci 2020). By illustrating several ways in which neoliberal elements, dynamics, and logics, such as commodification, marketization, individualization, and privatization, transformed the conduct of social service provision across public institutions and nonstate actors, I argued for a recognition of the ways in which neoliberal elements were expressed in Islamic terms, and vice versa. Such a coexistence of market-enhancing and redistributive interpretations lays bare the fallacy of a monolithic notion of Islamic neoliberalism.

This multiplicity is partly due to the fact that Islamism has never been just a uniform religious ideology, a foreboding electoral strategy, or a fundamentalist scheme of moral refashioning, but rather a coalition of contingent, limited, and plural projects that interpret Islam in divergent ways. As I illustrated throughout the book, in Turkey, Islam was conceived as part of a civilizational heritage that harkens back to the Ottoman Empire (chapter 2) as a defining characteristic of the cultural essence of Turkish "people" (chapter 3), as a kind of faith-based solidarity with distant strangers (chapter 4), and as a personal sanctuary with the capacity to nourish the emotional needs of the modern individual (chapter 5). Each of these religious interpretations acquired meaning and substance in relation to ideas about nationalism, secularism, modernity, and capitalism that are specific to Turkey, and each of these social imaginaries was put into action by bureaucrats, civic actors, experts, politicians, laypersons, and volunteers, albeit in contested and imperfect ways. What gave Islam force for Turkish Muslims was neither deep-seated religious beliefs nor the persuasiveness of Islamist political propaganda, but the fact that Islam was open to interpretation and, hence, could offer guidance for believers who struggled, albeit in different ways, about how best to uphold their faith in a market society. Studying Islam through paying attention to these on-the-ground practices of meaning-making moves the focus away from the political propaganda or electoral strategies of Islamists, and instead calls for attending to the ways in which Islam resonates and "sticks" despite debate and disagreement. Such an approach also disavows claims about whether a certain act, belief, or practice could be considered "truly" Islamic. Instead of focusing on scriptural texts or theological assessments of how Muslims ought to live, I examined how Muslims themselves interpret, enact, and perform Islamic traditions of charity in their everyday lives. Privileging an anthropological notion of Islam in this manner allows recognizing faith as both a deeply held conviction and a creative meaning-making practice. It also forecloses normative assessments of what counts as a "truly" Islamic way of helping the poor.

Throughout the book, I combined an emphasis on the multiplicity of Islam with an approach to neoliberalism as a malleable, shifting, and context-based governmental assemblage. Across multiple sites of social service provision, neoliberal elements, technologies, practices, rationalities, and subjectivities blended—sometimes seamlessly but more often through friction—with Islamic beliefs, values, and traditions. I traced these assemblages as they emerged in various material objects such as advertisements, barcodes, databases, and filing systems, and as they surfaced in social interactions—be they between public employees and charity workers, volunteers and aid recipients, or middle-class Muslims and their imagined deserving others. Acknowledging this multiplicity both illustrates the power of neoliberal elements to capture the imagination of people and underscores the supremacy of local context over global forms.

In this concluding chapter, I turn to the broader implications of these findings for questions about the future of Turkish politics, specifically those concerning the democracy versus authoritarianism nexus, the methods of assessment appropriate for evaluating neoliberal welfare programs, and possibilities for resisting capitalism when any alternate undertakings seem to be quickly coopted, excluded, or silenced. While assemblage thinking often requires approaching conventional questions in a new light, doing so nevertheless opens a space of intellectual inquiry that can recognize the coexistence of political constraints *and* emancipatory possibilities.

Categorizing the Muslim Social?

In the early 2000s, the AKP presented itself as a moderate Islamic political party that resembled the Christian Democrats of Europe. The party's new platform, alongside its pro-secular and pro-EU outlook, brought the introduction of numerous reforms which improved Turkey's economic wealth and increased the chances of EU membership. In this post-9/11 international context, the idea that Turkey can act as a "model Muslim democracy" gained significant traction among academics and in policy circles.[1] Once considered a laboratory for the successful modernization of the Third World (see Adalet 2018), this time Turkey was endorsed as an exemplary democratic, secular, and pluralist political regime, and was promoted as one that can provide valuable lessons to the larger Muslim world.

But, after consolidating its power around 2009–10, the AKP's commitment to democracy, human rights, and multiculturalism wavered. The AKP's response to several of the key events that occurred after the 2010s serves to illustrate the shifting nature of the party's political commitments. In 2013, a small environmentalist group gathered to protest an urban development plan in Taksim that would demolish the Gezi Park and reconstruct Ottoman-era military barracks and a neo-Ottoman shopping mall. After the initial police crackdown, Turkish people from all walks of life joined the small assembly, thereby leading to one of the

---

1. I am compressing here into one sentence a broad range of scholarship that examines whether, and under what conditions, Turkey could act as a "model Muslim democracy" (among others, see Altunışık 2005; Mohapatra 2008; Secor 2011; Tepe 2005; Tol 2012; Uğur 2004).

largest antigovernment demonstrations in Turkey in the past decade. On the one hand, the Gezi Park protests demonstrated that the AKP's governing vision no longer resonated with Turkish citizens—pious and secular alike. On the other hand, these events also showed that the government was unwilling to acquiesce to the citizenry's democratic and participatory demands.

The AKP's power was further challenged and then strengthened as a result of the double parliamentary elections of 2015. The HDP initially crossed the 10% threshold on June 7, 2015, but was prevented from doing so in the rescheduled elections on November 1, 2015 (Grigoriadis 2016; Kalaycıoğlu 2018; Kaya and Whiting 2019; Yavuz and Özcan 2015). After establishing its electoral majority, the AKP began to reverse its policy on the Kurdish question, replacing its earlier discourse of Ottoman multiculturalism that recognized cultural rights with a majoritarian language of ethnic Turkish purity. The state resumed the war against the Kurdish population by using political strategies that ranged from cultural prohibition to political silencing, and from forced displacement to mass killings (Gürses 2020; Saeed 2019). Political leaders of Kurdish descent, including high-ranking officials of the HDP such as the cochairman Selahattin Demirtaş, were imprisoned. When, in January 2016, more than a thousand Turkish academics signed a petition calling for the state to cease its military operations and called for peace, the government responded with a witch-hunt, accusing signatories of treason and terrorism. Many academics were fired or forced to resign from their positions, others' property was confiscated, and some were falsely imprisoned or had to go into exile (Altınay 2019; Başer, Akgönül, and Öztürk 2017; Özdemir, Mutluer, and Özyürek 2019).

It was around the same time that the AKP's longstanding political coalition with the Gülen movement unraveled.[2] While the relationship between the AKP and the Gülen movement was already strained after the December 2013 corruption scandals, it was the coup attempt of July 15, 2016, that brought the split into public view. That night, President Erdoğan

---

2. See Taş (2017) for a history of Turkey's AKP–Gülen conflict.

addressed Turkey via Facetime and urged the "defenders of the nation" to take to the streets and protect the democratically elected government from the supporters of Fethullah Gülen. What followed was a violent confrontation between supporters of the regime and a small group of soldiers. Overnight, more than 250 people were killed, as uncertainty and fear about the country's political future ensued. Immediately afterward, a national state of emergency was declared on July 20, 2016. Since then, more than 40,000 people have been arrested and 150,000 people, including academics, civil servants, teachers, journalists, and political activists, have been fired or suspended in a series of mass purges that are often referred to as the "counter-coup" (Pandya, Oliden, and Anlı 2021). Disregarding criticisms of these wide-ranging crackdowns, the government has continued to claim that their only goal is to eliminate members and supporters of the Gülen movement, now considered to be a terrorist organization.

Each of these developments went against the earlier claim that Turkey could serve as a "model Muslim democracy" that successfully integrates capitalism, democracy, secularism, and Islam. Scholars of Turkish politics thus began to ask a new set of questions: Was the AKP's earlier commitment to democracy merely a façade? Was Turkey's recent turn toward authoritarianism the hidden goal of the AKP's Islamic ideology all along? And what political factors might explain the AKP's political endurance, despite growing internal criticism and shifting ideological alliances?

First, *The Muslim Social* asserts that the AKP benefits from Islamic-neoliberal governmental assemblages, but it also highlights the technical-emotional dimensions of the AKP's political hold, thereby questioning conventional arguments that attribute AKP's increasing authoritarianism either to its Islam-based political ideology or unwavering commitments to neoliberalism. Rather, this book suggests that one factor that may have contributed to the AKP's enduring political authority was the establishment of a preference for technical solutions to political problems. For example, the advent of the Muslim Social occurred alongside the cooptation of Islamic associational, civic, and philanthropic networks by the Turkish state. To curb the mobilizational power of Islamist grassroots networks, the AKP encouraged a focus on social service provision, systematically incorporating some groups while silencing and excluding others. Previously, especially during the 1990s, many of these Islam-based groups had played a crucial role in linking Islamic political society with the masses. But as Islamic civil society organizations concentrated on poverty alleviation, they experienced a form of mission drift: they spent less time and energy on mobilizing the poor and became preoccupied with delivering charity in an efficient manner. The reconfiguration of state–civil society relations during the AKP's reign, in other words, strengthened the state's control of the population rather than opening venues for democratic political participation. The resultant governmental assemblage replaced the political language of rights with an emphasis on technical managerialism, thereby curbing the oppositional power of Islamic civil society organizations.

Another element that fostered the AKP's political appeal was the emotionally laden language of Islamic community that, despite political claims to the contrary, was never truly inclusive of differences. In fact, the Islamic social projects that form the subject of this book were predicated upon different modes of exclusion: the marginalization of some civic groups from the realm of proper civil society, the classification of the poor into random categories of deservingness, the indifference toward the suffering of certain Muslim and non-Muslim populations, the construction of Turkish Muslims as "white saviors" of Muslim Others, and the positioning of radical Islamic activism outside the realm of permissible political activity. While the governmental concern about reviving, restoring, and replenishing Islamic community never came to fruition, the emotional languages which were deployed to manufacture such a yearning for community strengthened AKP's political appeal in the eyes of Turkish citizens.

While attending to the technical-emotional dimensions of governance provides fresh insights about Turkey's "authoritarian reversal," the findings of this book also suggest that the study of Islamic politics in Turkey cannot be reduced to the AKP's singular ideology or political dominance. Rather, this book has shown that the Muslim Social encompasses a heterogeneity of individual experiences, collective aspirations, and religious interpretations that are far more complicated than simplistic assumptions about party-voter linkages would have us believe. Although the AKP profited from the political synergy of faith-based social imaginaries, the linkages between party and society were neither uniform nor straightforward. Whereas charity work was a central component of the AKP's governmental vision (as it ties the self-motivated and entrepreneurial subject of the liberal imagination with the moral sensibilities of the Islamic faith), actors were drawn to this vision for diverse reasons. The nexus of symbolic discourses and material practices that comprise the Muslim Social in Turkey also highlight the agency of local actors.

Evaluating the Muslim Social?

Beyond its implications for questions of democracy in the Muslim world, the Turkish case also exemplifies a new phase in late capitalism, that of "social neoliberalism," a conjuncture marked by unfettered free markets *and* widespread social programs. This unlikely marriage between neoliberalism and the social has prompted a wide range of scholarly inquiry to understand whether these social programs improve or deepen economic inequality. Over the years, I was often asked similar questions by colleagues and friends: "Are you saying that these social programs actually benefit the poor?" they would inquire. While these policy-centric questions are significant, they do not fit within the analytical framework of this book. I am aware that some readers—depending on their own perspective—might nevertheless still find confirming evidence for their own assessments about these social programs.

What I want to emphasize is that the Muslim Social was not a governmental apparatus that responded to existing problems. As Miller and Rose (1988) suggest, "one needs to distinguish between programmatic aspirations and practical consequences, but also examine the ways in which they aid, hinder, compete or ally with one another, producing consequences which are not the realization of *any* programme" (172, emphasis in original). As such, it makes more sense to see the Muslim Social as a "will to improve" that problematized its own issues, identified its own goals, and determined its own criteria for success (Li 2007). But, while these social imaginaries, projects, and visions did not accomplish their intended goals, a systematic reality nonetheless emerged from these multifarious cultural, economic, and religious aspirations and governmental interventions. Even more, the Muslim Social constantly failed to deliver on its promises:

these "failures" were built into the governmental rationality. But it was the momentary possibility of realizing a vision of Islamic community, with all its difficulties and shortcomings, that motivated actors to get involved, even if the real point would never be reached.

Accordingly, this book has redirected the focus of attention from policy-centric metrics of success to the self-assessments of people who were involved in Islamic charity and social service provision in Turkey. This approach also highlights how the perceived "failures" of the governmental apparatus reinforced its logics, rationales, and techniques. If there was not enough data about the poor, then more information was to be sought. If the aid delivery experience was not dignified, freedom-enhancing, or respectful enough, then new technologies of distribution were to be introduced. If Turkish humanitarians did not feel connected to the beneficiaries of their generosity, then more striking images and effective slogans were to be designed. And if Muslim volunteers found themselves lonely or detached, more engaging informal get-togethers were to be organized. These interventions and innovations solved problems momentarily, and in doing so, they strengthened the force and legitimacy of the governmental apparatus by returning to the starting point: how to realize Islamic community in a market society?

At the same time, the Muslim Social's governmental "failures"—as seen by its own architects and visionaries—are quite apparent if we turn our focus to the experiences of the poor. As I discussed in the chapter on populist reform and social assistance (chapter 3), the will to respect the poor, enhance their freedom, and treat them as autonomous individuals coexisted with an administrative apparatus that transforms the poor into objects of surveillance and collects detailed information about their lives. Similarly, although governmental interventions were often justified with reference to what the poor truly need, face-to-face interactions regularly involved instances where aid recipients were mistreated, humiliated, and silenced.

One striking example of these interactions happened during an aid distribution day where poor women were waiting to receive aid at a small Islamic NGO's office in Ankara. Each recipient's name was called, and each woman received their box—a food package that contained mostly nonperishable goods such as beans, lentils, rice, and pasta. While package distribution continued, I was sitting on a bench and listening to a group of poor women who were chatting with one another. Topics included families, husbands, children, and children's teachers at school, as well as information about other organizations that provided aid. Suddenly, we all heard a commotion and turned around to find an older woman in her seventies pleading with one of the NGO's managers. She was telling him that she urgently needed a stove because hers was broken. The manager, disturbed by her insistent demeanor, yelled at her, saying that she was not eligible for receiving household appliance assistance yet—she had to wait another two months. Visibly upset, she came and sat next to me and said: "What am I supposed to do with food if I do not even have a stove?" For a while, we all tried to calm her and offered ideas about where she might be able to get some help. A little while later, the manager, to everyone's surprise, brought a small electric stove from one of the storage units at the back of the office. But, while handing it over, he firmly emphasized that she would not be eligible to receive any more appliances for the next year.

In another instance, this time at the social market of a public SYD waqf in Istanbul, I observed the interactions between civil servants and aid recipients during a clothing distribution day. A poor woman in her early thirties had come with her three children who were all around ten years old or younger. The children were excited to be picking out their own clothes, and were walking up and down the aisles, pulling skirts and pants from the hangers and showing these items to one another and their mother—their joy was palpable from their faces and voices. Disturbed by what she considered to be "unruly" behavior, one of the employees walked up to them, asked them to be silent, and directed them to a corner of the social market. Instead of letting the children or their mother pick their own clothes and shoes, the employee then picked out an outfit for each child and handed them over to their mother, explaining that these were the best options for them. By this point, the family had withdrawn: the children had lost their previous excitement and were looking around with sad faces—not entirely sure what they had done wrong.

In both cases, there is a discrepancy between the goal of governing poverty respectfully and compassionately and the ways in which the poor were treated by actors who were supposed to act in a professional and respectful manner. Although these interactions could occur in any poverty relief program, and hence can be cast off as once-in-a-while occurrences, I encountered similar situations and often learned about other instances of "failure": overseas humanitarian projects were abandoned, funds were misused, expired food items were distributed, and aid was given to people who did not fit the criteria of "deservingness."

Looking at these on-the-ground practices of poverty relief, it is difficult not to conclude that the Muslim Social was, at best, a limited attempt at addressing social problems and alleviating poverty. My point is not to contest the fact that these programs were perceived as inadequate, or to suggest that civil servants, employees, managers, and volunteers were unaware of these shortcomings. Quite the opposite; actors were mobilized with a renewed sense of determination to improve the provision of social assistance whenever governmental interventions did not achieve their intended goals. Discrepancies of these social programs were reconfigured by improving their technical design, by deepening their Islamic roots, or by refashioning the affective experiences of donors, recipients, or volunteers. As a result, these ongoing improvements enhanced, rather than undermined, the power and legitimacy of the governmental apparatus, and reinforced the idea that social problems are best addressed through a shifting assemblage of Islamic values, technical measures, and emotional sensibilities.

Delimiting the Muslim Social?

In 2009, I attended the Middle East Technical University Social Sciences Conference in Ankara. After examining the conference program, I decided to participate in a panel titled "Neoliberalism and Everyday Life in Turkey." But when I arrived at the room where the panel was being held, I realized that there was a small group of academics waiting outside to see if the conference organizers would move the panel to a larger space. After waiting for a couple of minutes, I left and instead listened to another panel on gender equality and democracy. Over the course of the conference, it became clear to me that panels on the topic of neoliberalism were generally receiving more attention than panels on other subjects.

During the same weekend, a newspaper article was addressing similar concerns. Titled "Where Is My Neoliberalism?" the author criticized the disproportional foci of the conference. He argued that most of the conference panels paired neoliberalism with a variety of political and economic issues, such as everyday life, education, and workers' rights, as well as the AKP. Such a narrow focus, the author argued, established and perpetuated a tendency to examine Turkish politics as an object of neoliberalism. He claimed that many scholars overlooked Turkey's "real" issues and debates, such as the ongoing conflict between the military establishment and the AKP, the Kurdish conflict, debates about the Armenian genocide, and challenges of democratization. This overemphasis reminded the author of an answer one of his friends provided to the question of "Who is a Turkish leftist?": "Someone who can connect each and every issue to neoliberalism, someone who can explain everything with reference to neoliberalism" (Kaya 2009).

This critique mirrors a longstanding problem in leftist scholarship that tends to treat capitalism as the only significant form of transformative power. Indeed, many scholars have argued that the concept of neoliberalism has been overextended beyond the point of being useful as an analytical explanatory tool, and they have rejected that there is a singular neoliberal logic that can illuminate the nature and existence of divergent social, political, and economic phenomena. These questions become even more pressing for studies such as this one that suggest neoliberalism not only coopts but also coexists alongside communitarian visions and mutual care arrangements. If every attempt at undermining market rule perpetuates neoliberalism, critiques argue, then how can we imagine a better political future?

In order to address these questions, we first need to acknowledge that governing through community is key to understanding neoliberalism in a variety of national contexts around the globe. The Chinese government has introduced the social credit system to govern individuals' everyday lives and their relations with others. Operating as a technology of power, the social credit system subjugates Chinese people to economizing logics while also cultivating a novel form of moral citizenship (Zhang 2020). In Egypt, urban planners mobilize discourses of local, particularistic, tightly knit communities in order to distort real estate markets in various neighborhoods. Governmental interventions such as the reversal of rent control, which ultimately disempower and marginalize poor Egyptians, are portrayed as efforts to foster social relations, and a way to resist the entrenchment of market power (El-Kazaz 2018).

In addition to the state, market actors are also preoccupied with the business of fostering communitarian values. Be it the rise of corporate social responsibility schemes or the financing of micro-credit initiatives, corporations—big and small—seek to cultivate new kinds of social relations and moral responsibilities among their consumers. Meanwhile, the global elite enthusiastically engages in philanthro-capitalism, a way of "doing good" that privileges rationalities and vocabularies of the business sector and applies them to developmental, humanitarian, and social change domains. As philanthropic organizations develop profitable business ventures, and as companies integrate charitable donations into the purchase of consumer goods, distinctions between monetary exchange and community care become muddled (McGoey 2014; Nickel and Eikenberry 2009; Villadsen 2011).

While these developments highlight the cooptation of languages of care and solidarity by neoliberal governments and corporations, social movements around the globe continue to challenge the substance, form, and promises of these multifaceted initiatives, as well as questioning the larger economic and political relations within which they operate. Instead of disregarding such invocations of solidarity as a futile attempt at resistance, Gibson-Graham (1996) invites us to "see this monolithic and homogenous Capitalism not as our 'reality' but as a fantasy of wholeness, one that operates to obscure diversity and disunity in the economy and society" (260). By examining the variegated interpretations of Islamic community and mapping the ways in which practices of mutual care were combined with neoliberal elements of commodification, individualization, marketization, and privatization by numerous actors and institutions in Turkey, I have demonstrated that community is neither entirely internal nor external to market-based ways of thinking and acting, but rather exists in a liminal space of political possibility.

Epilogue

On February 6, 2023, an earthquake measuring 7.8 on the Richter scale was followed by another one measuring 7.5. Both earthquakes hit near Kahramanmaraş, affecting southeastern Turkey and northern Syria. More than ten cities were severely impacted, including Adıyaman, Gaziantep, Malatya, Kahramanmaraş, and Hatay in Turkey and Aleppo, Latakia, and Idlib in Syria. The twin earthquakes resulted from the movement of the East Anatolian faultline. This was one of the deadliest earthquake sequences in the region, killing more than fifty thousand people in Turkey and Syria. Close to fifteen million people were impacted by the disaster, and approximately four million people were displaced. More than two hundred thousand buildings collapsed, and more than five hundred thousand buildings were so severely damaged that they became uninhabitable, leaving thousands of people homeless.

These statistics cannot capture the human suffering caused by the twin earthquakes. In fact, any kind of scholarly analysis feels disrespectful to lives lost and those people whose lives are forever changed. But in the face of this tragedy—caused by political failures as much as natural causes—silence also constitutes an intellectual offense, implying that we have forgotten or that our lives have gone back to normal. While I do not intend to provide a sense of closure, I wrote these pages because I believe that intellectual responsibility, at the very least, requires bearing witness.

Since the earthquake, politics of charity has been a frequent topic of public discussion, often brought up in relation to questions of organizational performance, proper methods for distributing aid in a respectful manner, and effective strategies for ensuring psychosocial healing among earthquake survivors. These issues, further, were often discussed in relation to concerns about the state's responsibility in the event of a humanitarian disaster. A cursory view of these contestations and disagreements may lead one to conclude that there is a fundamental contradiction at work between the claims put forth in this book about the Muslim Social, in which the Turkish state, with the support of a whole host of nongovernmental organizations, provided social services to the poor and needy through a governmental apparatus which combined emotional care and technical efficiency, and the lack of a systematic response to the 2023 earthquakes. However, a closer look at these controversies and disputes shows that the governmental logic—a unique combination of managerial efficiency and emotional well-being—which underpinned the biopolitical apparatus of the Muslim Social was not rejected, but instead deployed by a wide range of actors and institutions across the political spectrum. While many condemned the government for its inability to effectively respond to the earthquake, the yardstick used in these arguments, criticisms, and debates reflected the criteria established by the Muslim Social.

At first, watching the news from abroad, I was frustrated with my inability to do something to help those affected. At the same time, my friends, colleagues, and students kept asking me where they should donate money. They wanted to know which charity organizations were trustworthy and had the capacity to help. I silenced my own cynicism—what could any aid organization really do in the face of this devastation after all—and tried to put together lists that I could share with those eager to help. Troubled with similar concerns, Turks residing in Turkey as well as the Turkish diaspora were debating which organizations to support. When I asked their recommendations, many urban, middle-class contacts recommended the Friends Association (Ahbap Derneği)—a relatively new charity organization that had been founded by a famous Turkish rock singer, Haluk Levent, during the destructive summer wildfires of 2021. For individuals critical of the Turkish government, donating to the Turkish Red Cross (Kızılay) or to the Disaster and Emergency Management Ministry (AFAD) was seen as a grave mistake due to concerns over corruption and mismanagement. Other friends recommended giving to smaller, grassroots groups formed by people that were already on the ground. They did not trust any professional or transnational organizations, fearing that they would not be able provide adequate services. Some networks, desperate to bring the ethnic tensions in the region to the attention of the international community, circulated lists of alternative organizations which primarily focused on assisting the Kurdish minority as well as Syrian and Afghan refugees.

These disagreements about the best way to deliver emergency relief unfolded amid a harrowing realization that, with every passing minute, hundreds of people were dying under collapsed buildings while waiting to be rescued. The government failed to coordinate rescue efforts, instead resorting to a blatant form of necropolitics. During the first couple of days after the earthquake, most rescue efforts were organized by volunteers who had neither the training nor the equipment to save people. Although foreign rescue teams arrived swiftly, it seemed that governmental authorities were unable to, or uninterested in attempting to, coordinate their efforts. Many people argued that even AFAD, the governmental agency for disaster relief and management, arrived late to earthquake zones. Later it turned out that the AKP had dismantled the disaster-response infrastructure that was previously led by the Turkish Armed Forces, which explained the absence of military personnel and equipment from disaster zones. Frustrated with the lack of proper equipment and the insufficient number of teams to save their loved ones under collapsed buildings, survivors of the earthquake took to social media to ask: "Where is the state?" I remember watching one video of a middle-aged woman who declared: "I do not care if I am jailed, I demand answers! Where is our so-called glorious Ottoman state of five hundred years?" Similar sentiments of being abandoned by state agencies were expressed by many Turkish citizens who had the courage to voice their frustrations. The government crackdown on these critical voices mostly targeted social media accounts that collected various pleas for rescue posted by individuals, but the message was clear: any criticism of the government's disaster response was, according to Erdoğan, "dishonorable."

The lack of a proper emergency response was not the only reason behind the earthquakes' high human and economic costs. Another culprit was AKP's profit-oriented approach to the construction sector. Since coming to power, the AKP has encouraged largescale production of housing complexes. Special permits and zoning amnesties allowed many engineers and architects to continue their construction projects without complying with building codes and regulations. The corruption and mismanagement of the construction sector led to the death of thousands of people who could have been alive if only government-sponsored housing complexes had been built according to code.

While criticisms over the coordination of aid efforts and the corrupt construction sector exposed the cracks of AKP's governmental apparatus, the state's authority was reinforced through necropolitics as the government made decisions about who should be left to die and who should live. This was the case concerning the issue of decaying bodies under rubble, when the government did not hesitate to act, in this instance, by pouring cement so that the smell of corpses did not disturb the living, but also so that attention could be redirected to problems that could potentially be solved. The political will to transform the earthquake into something governable—instead of the unwieldy chaos that brought with it a surge of condemnation—manifested itself when the Turkish government, approximately a week after the earthquake hit, asked foreign rescue teams to halt their operations and leave the country immediately.

Despite the lack of an organized response, the underlying logic of the Muslim Social gradually became apparent as the government ramped up its efforts to aid survivors and rebuild cities. These political efforts to bring the earthquake into the realm of the governable emphasized familiar themes of patriotic philanthropy, managerial efficiency, and emotional well-being.

On February 16, 2023, the government partnered with major television channels to organize an aid campaign. The goal was to cultivate a spirit of social generosity and encourage monetary donations, especially from large corporations. The "Turkey One Heart" (Türkiye Tek Yürek) campaign continued the venerable tradition of the Turkish state organizing humanitarian efforts with the help of private donations. At the same time, the tradition of state-mediated social solidarity was amplified through the media-charity nexus. In fact, the campaign mimicked the philanthropic logic of high-profile fundraising telethons often organized

by American and European television channels. The television program—
which lasted more than seven hours—showcased famous actors and
singers pleading with the audience. Corporate donors—which received
tax relief in exchange for their donations—were portrayed as patriotic-
philanthropic heroes. Emotional appeals were combined with assurances
that government-affiliated organizations such as AFAD and Kızılay were
not only trustworthy but also capable of organizing relief efforts and
assisting survivors. In addition to emphasizing that the state was the main
agent of humanitarian relief, this campaign also sought to replace crush-
ing images of disaster and the occasional miraculous rescue with an atmosphere of social solidarity.

The AKP's political focus on recovery and rebuilding was expressed
in a few ways. For instance, the government introduced a database to iden-
tify earthquake victims, categorize their material and sociopsychological
needs, and organize the distribution of aid and assistance. Earthquake victims were to be registered at specific governmental bureaus. Once registered, survivors became eligible to receive monetary aid (*deprem yardımı*).
In addition, state agencies were tasked with determining the terms of displaced peoples' resettlement. Some were provided with tents and others
were given container houses, whereas other groups were relocated to various cities. The hurried registration of survivors allowed the government
to collect extensive information about citizens, thereby folding these individuals into a governable population with identifiable needs and social
rights. Such population-level interventions cast thousands of people under
the surveillance of the state.

Another way in which the AKP tried to depict itself in a positive
light was by directing the public's attention toward governmental plans
for urban recovery. Just a month after the earthquake, it was announced
that the government's main goal was to build more than seventy thousand
houses in the earthquake-struck region, and to complete these housing
projects in less than a year. This televised event included a simultaneous
"breaking ground" ceremony in ten cities most impacted by the earthquake, thereby enabling the government to sign new contracts with eager
construction companies. In this Turkish version of disaster capitalism, the
construction of new public housing complexes by private companies was

portrayed as the most efficient way of rebuilding after the catastrophe, instead of being acknowledged as one of the main factors that contributed to the disaster in the first place.

In addition, Muslim Social's technologies of aid provision were promptly reimagined with earthquake survivors in mind. First, grass-roots organizations began collecting donations of basic provisions, and organized them into aid packages so that they could be delivered to earthquake survivors. Questions about what was urgently needed and what was appropriate to give marked these initial efforts. Then, new public-private partnerships between supermarket chains, government institutions, and Islamic NGOs were formed to coordinate, fund, and deliver aid packages to disaster zones. Other NGOs, critical of the package system, instead focused on creating "aid supermarkets" in urban centers which received high numbers of migrants. Those who were lucky enough to secure housing needed a whole host of material things, ranging from clothing to furniture, from kitchen utensils to school materials. Being able to freely choose what they need instead of being given a package was claimed to be a way to protect the autonomy and dignity of earthquake survivors. Images on social media were scrutinized according to similar criteria of autonomy and dignity. Volunteers in earthquake zones posted images of donated goods that they deemed inappropriate or deficient, such as broken toys or worn-out clothes, thereby questioning whether donors truly cared about the people they were supposedly helping.

Qualms about respecting the honor of earthquake survivors also came up in relation to the issue of governmental authorities' trips to the earthquake region. These visits and speeches were not only criticized for being merely staged photo-ops but also for their failure to treat survivors with dignity and respect. One circulating video showed a group of bureaucrats walking through muddy streets with child survivors of the earthquake—while all adults wore sturdy rain boots, the children only had flimsy slippers on. Another newsclip displayed one of Erdoğan's aides scolding children for their "misbehavior" during the president's speech. Manufactured images of earthquake survivors—and in some cases, victims—became so prevalent in Turkish media that, as a response, some grassroots groups purposefully refrained from posting photographs of aid recipients, tent residents, or visitors to emergency clinics and soup kitchens. The ways in which earthquake survivors were photographed (or not) became a way to discuss whether they were treated well by those who rushed to help.

Approximately a month after the earthquake, billboards depicting Erdoğan were put up in urban centers around the country. In these images, Erdoğan was depicted as visiting earthquake zones, providing solace to earthquake victims, or talking with children. These compassionate encounters and heartfelt conversations took place against a visual background of disaster, but the tragedy and chaos of the past couple of weeks was eclipsed by the compassionate interaction between Erdoğan and citizens. These images communicated that the state was available to address not only the material but also the emotional needs of citizens.

In addition to these visual representations, Erdoğan also mixed emotional appeals with religious themes each time he addressed earthquake survivors. One of the most controversial speeches he gave was in Adıyaman, where he asked for forgiveness due to the later arrival of governmental authorities to the region. In contrast to his usual self-righteous stance, with this speech Erdoğan admitted to a level of wrongdoing but attributed the state's relative absence to natural causes such as damages to highways and unfavorable weather conditions. The word he used for asking forgiveness—*helallık istemek*— has a strong religious connotation and refers to a sense of clemency that extends to the afterlife. While this call may have resonated with some Turkish citizens, many were distraught and found such a request for forgiveness offensive. Demonstrators in Hatay—one of the cities with the highest death toll—for instance, used "we will not forgive" (*hakkımızı helal etmiyoruz*) as the main slogan for their antigovernment protests. This phrase was also popular as a hashtag on social media for those who wished to express their frustration with the government's call for emotional healing. Turkish citizens did not want the government to manage their emotional response to the earthquake; they also did not want to be told how to feel or whether to forgive. But, even so, they did not dispute the norm of an emotional framework as the path to recovery.

As the state attempted to administer the afterlives of the earthquake by deploying technologies, rationalities, and practices of the Muslim Social, the experience of the earthquake also showed that "community" was not only in the purview of the state. On the one hand, the politicized nature of the Muslim Social prevented the provision of material aid and emotional support by ordinary people. On the other hand, even in such an oppressive political atmosphere, government-through-community manifested itself through grassroots organizations, NGOs, and various civic formations, as well as through amateur groups. Interestingly, even those who criticized the government's relief and rebuilding efforts referred to managerial principles and affective criteria, demanding the proficient organization of aid delivery efforts or promoting alternative modes of emotional connection to foster collective healing. While not everyone agreed with the parameters of the Muslim Social, even marginal networks of care upheld the fundamental logics of this governmental apparatus.

In short, while the Muslim Social may have failed to respond to the earthquake effectively, the earthquake laid bare that the underlying assumptions of this governmental apparatus were now taken for granted by Turkish citizens. Given the results of the 2023 presidential election, it is likely that the established parameters of the Muslim Social will continue to wield power across public imaginaries, ethical practices, and political technologies.

Glossary

Bibliography

Index

Glossary

The definitions reflect the main usage in this book.

Dernek: civic association
Hayır: benevolence
Hayırseverlik: philanthropy
İbadet: worship
İftar: dinner that concludes the fasting day during Ramadan
İnfak: individual giving; giving from one's own self
İyilik: goodness toward others
Külliye: a waqf complex; Islamic architectural style
Mağdur: the oppressed; victims of war or national disaster
Mazlum: the innocent, often referring to the powerless
Muhtaç: the needy, deserving poor
Ramazan, Ramadan: the ninth month of the Muslim calendar; the month of fasting
Sadaka, sadaqa: voluntary almsgiving
Ümmet, ummah: the global community of Muslim believers
Vakfiye: waqf deed
Vakıf, waqf: religious endowments
Zekat, zakat: compulsory almsgiving

Bibliography

The bibliography is alphabetized following the Turkish alphabet.

Acar, Feride, and Gülbanu Altunok. 2013. "The 'Politics of Intimate' at the Intersection of Neo-Liberalism and Neo-Conservatism in Contemporary Turkey." *Women's Studies International Forum* 41: 14–23.

Acharya, Amitav. 2020. "The Myth of the 'Civilization State': Rising Powers and the Cultural Challenge to World Order." *Ethics and International Affairs* 34, no. 2: 139–56. https://doi.org/10.1017/S0892679420000192.

Açıkel, Fethi. 2016. "AKP İslamcılığının Üç Ideolojik ve Üç Jeopolitik Dönüşümü: İslami Liberalizm, Pan-İslamist Popülizm ve İslamcı Ulusalcılık." *Birikim* 332: 10–40.

Adak Turan, Sevgi. 2004. "Formation of Authoritarian Secularism in Turkey: Ramadans in the Early Republican Era (1923–1938)." MA thesis, Sabanci University. http://research.sabanciuniv.edu/8230/1/turansevgiadak.pdf.

Adalet, Begüm. 2018. *Hotels and Highways: The Construction of Modernization Theory in Cold War Turkey.* Stanford, CA: Stanford Univ. Press.

Adaman, Fikret, and Bengi Akbulut. 2021. "Erdoğan's Three-Pillared Neoliberalism: Authoritarianism, Populism and Developmentalism." *Geoforum* 124: 279–89. http://doi.org/10.1016/j.geoforum.2019.12.013.

Adaman, Fikret, and Oya Pınar Ardıç. 2008. "Social Exclusion in the Slum Areas of Large Cities in Turkey." *New Perspectives on Turkey* 38: 29–60. https://doi.org/10.1017/S089663460000491X.

Adaş, Emin Baki. 2006. "The Making of Entrepreneurial Islam and the Islamic Spirit of Capitalism." *Journal for Cultural Research* 10, no. 2: 113–37. https://doi.org/10.1080/14797580600624745.

Ağartan, Tuba. 2012. "Marketization and Universalism: Crafting the Right Balance in the Turkish Healthcare System." *Current Sociology* 60, no. 4: 456–71. https://doi.org/10.1177/0011392112438331.

233

234 Bibliography

Ağartan, Tuba, and Ellen Kuhlmann. 2019. "New Public Management, Physicians and Populism: Turkey's Experience with Health Reforms." *Sociology of Health and Illness* 41, no. 7: 1410–25. https://doi.org/10.1111/1467-9566.12956.

Ağırakça, Ahmet. 2018. "Musibet ve Sıkıntılar Bir İmtihandır." *Fikriyat*, January 5, 2018. https://www.fikriyat.com/yazarlar/ahmet-agirakca/2018/01/05/musibet-ve-sikintilar-bir-imtihandir.

Ahmet Yesevi Derneği (@ahmetyesevider). 2018. "'Çocuklar Üşümesin' HAY-DER'den Suriye'ye Büyük Kış Yardımı! Gıda, barınma, ısınma ve hijyen malzemelerinden oluşan büyük kış yardım konvoyu için hazırlıklara başlandı. #ÇocuklarÜşümesin." Twitter post, October 31, 2018. https://twitter.com/ahmetyesevider/status/1057595348963725312.

Ainslie, Mary J. 2021. "Chinese Philosemitism and Historical Statecraft: Incorporating Jews and Israel into Contemporary Chinese Civilizationism." *The China Quarterly* 245 (March): 208–26. https://doi.org/10.1017/S0305741020000302.

Akboğa, Sema. 2017. "The Current State of Volunteering in Turkey." In *Perspectives on Volunteering: Voices from the South*, edited by Jacqueline Butcher and Christopher J. Einolf, 245–61. Cham, Switzerland: Springer International Publishing.

Akça, İsmet, Ahmet Bekmen, and Barış Alp Özden, eds. 2014. *Turkey Reframed: Constituting Neoliberal Hegemony*. London: Pluto Press.

Akçalı, Emel, and Umut Korkut. 2015. "Urban Transformation in Istanbul and Budapest: Neoliberal Governmentality in the EU's Semi-Periphery and Its Limits." *Political Geography* 46: 76–88. https://doi.org/10.1016/j.polgeo.2014.12.004.

Akçalı, Emel, Lerna Yanık, and Ho-Fung Hung. 2015. "Inter-Asian (Post-) Neoliberalism: Adoption, Disjuncture and Transgression." *Asian Journal of Social Science* 43, no. 1–2: 5–21. https://doi.org/10.1163/15685314-04301002.

Akıncı, Uğur. 1999. "The Welfare Party's Municipal Track Record: Evaluating Islamist Municipal Activism in Turkey." *Middle East Journal* 53, no. 1: 75–94.

Akkan, Başak. 2018. "Politics of Care in Turkey: Sacred Familialism in a Changing Political Context." *Social Politics: International Studies in Gender, State and Society* 25, no. 1: 72–91.

Akten, Ayşenur Aydoğdu. 2017. "Müslüman Depresyona Girer Mi?" *Genç Yorum Dergisi*, August 12, 2017. https://www.gencyorumdergisi.com/2017/12/musluman-depresyona-girer-mi/.

Akyıldız, Ali. 2003. "Vakıfların Kamu Hizmetlerine Yönlendirilmesi ve Vakıflar Genel Müdürlüğünün Rölü." In *Vakıf Medeniyeti Sempozyumu Kitabı*, 105–18. Ankara: Vakıflar Genel Müdürlüğü Yayınları.

Akyovalı, Hatice Merhem. 2018. "Depresyon Mübarek Bir Hastalıktır." *TV 111*, May 28, 2018. http://www.tv111.com.tr/haberler/depresyon-mubarek-bir -hastaliktir-1096.html.

"Albüm—Atatürk Ortaokulu." TC Milli Eğitim Bakanlığı Samsun/Ayvacık Atatürk Ortaokulu. accessed July 17, 2018. http://ayvacikataturkoo.meb.k12.tr /tema/dosyadetay.php?KATEGORINO=368834&git=19.

Alemdaroğlu, Ayça. 2005. "Politics of the Body and Eugenic Discourse in Early Republican Turkey." *Body and Society* 11, no. 3: 61–76. https://doi.org/10.1177 %2F1357034X05056191.

Alemdaroğlu, Ayça. 2021. "Governing Youth in Times of Dissent: Essay Competitions, Politics of History, and Emotions." *Turkish Studies* 22, no. 2: 222–41. https://doi.org/10.1080/14683849.2020.1868299.

Alkan-Zeybek, Hilal. 2012. "Ethics of Care, Politics of Solidarity: Islamic Charitable Organisations in Turkey." In *Ethnographies of Islam: Ritual Performances and Everyday Practices*, edited by Bauduouin Dupret, Thomas Pierret, Paulo G. Pinto, and Kathryn Spellman-Poots, 144–52. Edinburgh: Edinburgh Univ. Press.

Altınay, Ayşe Gül. 2019. "Undoing Academic Cultures of Militarism: Turkey and Beyond." *Current Anthropology* 60 (S19): S15–25. https://doi.org/10.1086 /700182.

Altunışık, Meliha Benli. 2005. "The Turkish Model and Democratization in the Middle East." *Arab Studies Quarterly* 27 (1–2): 45–63.

Altunok, Gülbanu. 2016. "Neo-Conservatism, Sovereign Power and Bio-Power: Female Subjectivity in Contemporary Turkey." *Research and Policy on Turkey* 1, no. 2: 132–46. https://doi.org/10.1080/23760818.2016.1201244.

Alvarez, Sonia. 1998. "Latin American Feminisms "Go Global": Trends of the 1990s and Challenges for the New Millennium." In *Cultures of Politics, Politics of Culture: Re-Visioning Latin American Social Movements*, edited by Sonia Alvarez, Evelino Dagnino, and Arturo Escobar, 293–324. Boulder, CO: Westview Press.

Alvarez, Sonia. 2017. "Beyond the Civil Society Agenda? Participation and Practices of Governance, Governability and Governmentality in Latin America." In *Beyond Civil Society: Activism, Participation, and Protest in Latin*

America, edited by Sonia Alvarez, Jeffrey Rubin, Gianpaolo Baiocchi, Agustin Lao-Montes, and Millie Thayer, 316–30. Durham, NC: Duke Univ. Press.

Anadolu Ajansı. 2017. "TİKA'nın Gönüllü Elçileri Nijer'de saz ev yaptı." August 27, 2017. https://www.aa.com.tr/tr/dunya/tikanin-gonullu-elcileri-nijerde-saz -ev-yapti-/894884.

Analiese, Richard, and Daromir Rudnyckyj. 2009. "Economies of Affect." *Journal of the Royal Anthropological Institute* 15, no. 1: 57–77. https://doi.org /10.1111/j.1467-9655.2008.01530.x.

1987. "Anavatan İktidarının Yüzakı İcraatlerinden Biri: Sosyal Yardımlaşmayı ve Dayanışmayı Teşvik Fonu: Hayırlı Fon." Ankara: Anavatan Partisi Yayınları.

Anders, Gerhard. 2009. *In the Shadow of Good Governance: An Ethnography of Civil Service Reform in Africa*. Leiden and Boston: Brill.

Anderson, Ben, Matthew Kearnes, Colin McFarlane, and Dan Swanton. 2012. "On Assemblages and Geography." *Dialogues in Human Geography* 2, no. 2: 171–89. https://doi.org/10.1177%2F2043820612449261.

Andrews, Matt. 2008. "The Good Governance Agenda: Beyond Indicators without Theory." *Oxford Development Studies* 36, no. 4: 379–407. https://doi.org /10.1080/13600810802455120.

Angell, Elizabeth, Timur Hammond, and Danielle van Dobben Schoon. 2011. "Assembling Istanbul: Buildings and Bodies in a World City: Introduction." *City* 18, no. 6: 644–54. https://doi.org/10.1080/13604813.2014.962882.

Apaydın, Fulya. 2015. "Financialization and the Push for Non-State Social Service Provision: Philanthropic Activities of Islamic and Conventional Banks in Turkey." *Forum for Development Studies* 42, no. 3: 441–65. https://doi.org /10.1080/08039410.2015.1033453.

Appe, Susan. 2016. "NGO Networks, the Diffusion and Adaptation of NGO Managerialism, and NGO Legitimacy in Latin America." *Voluntas* 27: 187–208.

Aral, Hasan. 2000. "Toplumsal Barışın Teminatı Zekat." *Diyanet Dergisi* 110: 60–66.

Aras, Bülent, and Pınar Akpınar. 2015. "The Role of Humanitarian NGOs in Turkey's Peacebuilding." *International Peacekeeping* 22, no. 3: 230–47. https:// doi.org/10.1080/13533312.2015.1033374.

Arat-Koç, Sedef. 2018. "Culturalizing Politics, Hyper-Politicizing 'Culture': 'White' vs. 'Black Turks' and the Making of Authoritarian Populism in Turkey." *Dialectical Anthropology* 14, no.4: 1–18. https://doi.org/10.1007/s10624 -018-9500-2.

Arıcanlı, Tosun, and Dani Rodrik. 1990. *The Political Economy of Turkey: Debt, Adjustment and Sustainability*. London: Palgrave Macmillan.

Arnold, Caroline E. 2012. "In the Service of Industrialization: Etatism, Social Services and the Construction of Industrial Labour Forces in Turkey (1930–50)." *Middle Eastern Studies* 48, no. 3: 363–85. https://doi.org/10.1080/0026 3206.2012.661720.

Arslanalp, Mert. 2018. "Coalitional Politics of Housing Policy in AKP's Turkey." In *POMEPS Studies 31: Social Policy in the Middle East North Africa* (Project on Middle East Political Science), 25–33.

Aslan, Senem. 2021. "Public Tears: Populism and the Politics of Emotion in AKP's Turkey." *International Journal of Middle East Studies* 53, no. 1: 1–17. https://doi.org/10.1017/S0020743820000859.

Aslanidis, Paris. 2016. "Is Populism an Ideology? A Refutation and a New Perspective." *Political Studies* 64: 88–104. https://doi.org/10.1111/1467-9248.12224.

Atalay, Zeynep. 2017. "Partners in Patriarchy: Faith-Based Organizations and Neoliberalism in Turkey." *Critical Sociology* 45, no. 3: 431–45. https://doi.org/10.1177%2F0896920517711488.

Atasoy, Yıldız. 2009. *Islam's Marriage with Neoliberalism: State Transformation in Turkey*. London and New York: Palgrave Macmillan.

Atia, Mona. 2013. *Building a House in Heaven: Pious Neoliberalism and Islamic Charity in Egypt*. Minneapolis: Univ. of Minnesota Press.

Aybars, Ayşe Idil, and Dimitris Tsarouhas. 2010. "Straddling Two Continents: Social Policy and Welfare Politics in Turkey." *Social Policy and Administration* 44, no. 6: 746–63. http://dx.doi.org/10.1111/j.1467-9515.2010.00741.x.

Ayça, Emine. 2014. "Parayla Saadet Olur." *Her Nefes* 55: 24–26.

Aydın, Cemil. 2017. *The Idea of the Muslim World: A Global Intellectual History*. Cambridge and London: Harvard Univ. Press.

Aydıntaşbaş, Aslı. 2014. "Beyoğlu'nda Para Geçmeyen Market!" *Milliyet*, February 28, 2014. https://www.milliyet.com.tr/gundem/beyoglu-nda-para-gecmeyen -market-1843862.

Ayhan, Berkay. 2019. "Constituting Financialized Subjectivities: Cultural Political Economy of Financial Literacy in Turkey." *Turkish Studies* 20, no. 5: 680–707. https://doi.org/10.1080/14683849.2018.1520103.

Aykaç, Pınar. 2019. "Musealisation as a Strategy for the Reconstruction of an Idealized Ottoman Past: Istanbul's Sultanahmet District as 'Museum-Quarter.'" *International Journal of Heritage Studies* 25, no. 2: 160–77. https://doi.org/10 .1080/13527258.2018.1475407.

Baban, Feyzi, Suzan Ilcan, and Kim Rygiel. 2016. "Syrian Refugees in Turkey: Pathways to Precarity, Differential Inclusion, and Negotiated Citizenship

Rights." *Journal of Ethnic and Migration Studies* 43, no. 1: 41–57. https://doi.org/10.1080/1369183X.2016.1192996.

Bakırezer, Güven, and Yücel Demirer. 2009. "Ak Parti'nin Sosyal Siyaseti." In *AKP Kitabı: Bir Dönüşümün Bilançosu*, edited by İlhan Uzgel and Bülent Duru, 153–78. Ankara: Phoenix.

Bal, Ihsan, and Sedat Laçiner. 2001. "The Challenge of Revolutionary Terrorism to Turkish Democracy 1960–80." *Terrorism and Political Violence* 13, no. 4: 90–115. https://doi.org/10.1080/09546550109609701.

Barnett, Michael, and Thomas Weiss. 2008. *Humanitarianism in Question: Politics, Power, and Ethics.* New York: Cornell Univ. Press.

Baron, Beth. 2014. *The Orphan Scandal: Christian Missionaries and the Rise of the Muslim Brotherhood.* Stanford, CA: Stanford Univ. Press.

Başaran, Betül. 2014. *Selim III, Social Control and Policing in Istanbul at the End of the Eighteenth Century: Between Crisis and Order.* Leiden and Boston: Brill.

"Başbakan Sadaka Kültürü Diye Eleştirilen Yardımlar Hakkında Konuştu." *ATV Ana Haber*, January 27, 2010.

Başer, Bahar, Samim Akgönül, and Ahmet Erdi Öztürk. 2017. "'Academics for Peace' in Turkey: A Case of Criminalising Dissent and Critical Thought via Counterterrorism Policy." *Critical Studies on Terrorism* 10 (2): 274–96.

Bayancuk, Halis. 2019. "Psikolojik Rahatsızlık İtikad Zayıflığı Mıdır?" *Tevhid Dergisi* 81. https://tevhiddergisi.org/psikolojik-rahatsizlik-i-tikad-zayifligi-midir/.

Bayar, Ali. 1996. "The Developmental State and Economic Policy in Turkey." *Third World Quarterly* 17, no. 4: 773–85. https://doi.org/10.1080/01436599615371.

Bayat, Asef. 2002. "Activism and Social Development in the Middle East." *International Journal of Middle East Studies* 34, no. 1: 1–28. https://doi.org/10.1017/S0020743802001010.

Bayat, Asef. 2007. *Making Islam Democratic: Social Movements and the Post-Islamist Turn.* Stanford, CA: Stanford Univ. Press.

Bayraktar, Ulaş, and Çağla Tansung. 2016. "Local Service Delivery in Turkey." In *Public and Social Services in Europe: From Public and Municipal to Private Sector Provision*, edited by Hellmut Wollmann, Ivan Kopric, and Gerard Marcou, 217–32. London: Palgrave Macmillan.

Bedirhanoğlu, Pınar. 2021. "Cronyism through Financialization: Turkey's Neoliberal Transformation from Özal to Erdoğan." *Social Research: An International Quarterly* 88, no. 2: 359–79.

Bee, Cristiano, and Ayhan Kaya. 2017. "Youth and Active Citizenship in Turkey: Engagement, Participation and Emancipation." *Southeast European and Black Sea Studies* 17, no. 1: 129–43. https://doi.org/10.1080/14683857.2016.1 232893.

Benthall, Jonathan. 1999. "Financial Worship: The Quranic Injunction to Almsgiving." *Journal of the Royal Anthropological Institute* 5, no. 1: 27–42. https://doi.org/10.2307/2660961.

Benthall, Jonathan. 2011. "Islamic Humanitarianism in Adversarial Context." In *Forces of Compassion: Humanitarianism between Ethics and Politics*, edited by Erica Bornstein and Peter Redfield, 99–121. Santa Fe, NM: School for Advanced Research Press.

Benthall, Jonathan, and Jerome Bellion-Jourdan. 2003. *The Charitable Crescent: Politics of Aid in the Muslim World*. London: I. B. Taurus.

Berlant, Lauren. 2004. *Compassion: The Culture and Politics of an Emotion*. London: Routledge.

Berlant, Lauren. 2011. *Cruel Optimism*. Durham, NC: Duke Univ. Press.

Bevir, Mark, and Rod A. W. Rhodes. 2010. *The State as Cultural Practice*. Oxford: Oxford Univ. Press.

"Beyoğlu Belediyesi Ramazanda Yoksullara Kucak Açıyor." 2015. *İhlas Haber Ajansı*, June 12, 2015. https://www.iha.com.tr/haber-beyoglu-belediyesi-ramazanda-yoksullara-kucak-aciyor-470530/.

"Beyoğlu Sosyal Market Açıldı." n.d. *Beyoğlu Belediyesi Sosyal Yardım İşleri Müdürlüğü*, accessed June 12, 2011, http://www.beyoglusosyalyardim.com/hizmetler/detay.aspx?SectionId=1744. Site inactive on July 20, 2023.

Biehl, João, and Ramah McKay. 2012. "Ethnography as Political Critique." *Anthropological Quarterly* 85, no. 4: 1209–27. https://doi.org/10.1353/anq.2012.0057.

Binkley, Sam. 2014. *Happiness as Enterprise: An Essay on Neoliberal Life*. Albany: State Univ. of New York Press.

Birtek, Faruk. 1985. "The Rise and Fall of Etatism in Turkey, 1932–1950: The Uncertain Road in the Restructuring of a Semiperipheral Economy." *Review (Fernand Braudel Center)* 8, no. 3: 407–38.

Bloom, Leslie Rebecca, and Deborah Kilgore. 2003. "The Volunteer Citizen after Welfare Reform in the United States: An Ethnographic Study of Volunteerism in Action." *VOLUNTAS: International Journal of Voluntary and Nonprofit Organizations* 14, no. 4: 431–54. https://doi.org/10.1023/B:VOLU.0000007468.54144.df.

Bolat, Özkan. 2016. "Sosyal Yardım İstihdam Bağlantısı Kapsamında Ülke Uy-gulamalarının İncelenmesi ve İşkur İçin Öneriler." *Uzmanlık Tezi*. Ankara: Çalışma ve Sosyal Güvenlik Bakanlığı, Türkiye İş Kurumu Genel Müdür-lüğü. https://media.iskur.gov.tr/15681/ozkan-bolat.pdf.

Boltanski, Luc. 1999. *Distant Suffering: Morality, Media and Politics*. Translated by Graham Burchell. Cambridge: Cambridge Univ. Press.

Bonner, Michael, Mine Ener, and Amy Singer, eds. 2003. *Poverty and Charity in Middle Eastern Contexts*. Albany: State Univ. of New York Press.

Boratav, Korkut, and Metin Özuğurlu. 2006. "Social Policies and Distributional Dynamics in Turkey: 1923–2002." In *Social Policy in the Middle East: Economic, Political and Gender Dynamics*, edited by Massoud Karshenas and Valentine Moghadam, 156–89. Basingstoke, UK: Palgrave Macmillan.

Borchgrevink, Kaja. 2020. "NGOization of Islamic Charity: Claiming Legitimacy in Changing Institutional Contexts." *VOLUNTAS: International Journal of Voluntary and Nonprofit Organizations* 31: 1049–62.

Bornstein, Erica. 2011. "The Value of Orphans." In *Forces of Compassion: Humanitarianism between Ethics and Politics*, edited by Erica Bornstein and Peter Redfield, 123–48. Santa Fe, NM: School for Advanced Research Press.

Bornstein, Erica. 2012. *Disquieting Gifts: Humanitarianism in New Delhi*. Stanford, CA: Stanford Univ. Press.

Bornstein, Erica, and Peter Redfield, eds. 2011. *Forces of Compassion: Humanitarianism between Ethics and Politics*. Santa Fe, NM: School for Advanced Research Press.

Bourdieu, Pierre. 2003. *Firing Back: Against the Tyranny of the Market 2*. London: Verso Books.

Boyraz, Cemil. 2018. "Neoliberal Populism and Governmentality in Turkey: The Foundation of Communication Centers during the AKP Era." *Philosophy and Social Criticism* 44, no. 4: 437–52. https://doi.org/10.1177/0191453718755205.

Bozdoğan, Sibel, and Reşat Kasaba. 1997. *Rethinking Modernity and National Identity in Turkey*. Seattle: Univ. of Washington Press.

Bozkurt, Umut. 2013. "Neoliberalism with a Human Face: Making Sense of the Justice and Development Party's Neoliberal Populism in Turkey." *Science and Society* 77, no. 3: 372–96. https://doi.org/10.1521/siso.2013.77.3.372.

Bozoğlu, Gönül. 2019. "'A Great Bliss to Keep the Sensation of Conquest Alive!': The Emotional Politics of the Panorama 1453 Museum in Istanbul." In *European Memory in Populism: Representations of Self and Other*, edited by Chiara de Cesari and Ayhan Kaya, 91–111. London and New York: Routledge.

Börzel, Tanja, Yasemin Pamuk, and Andreas Stahn. 2008. "Good Governance in the European Union." Berlin Working Paper on European Integration No. 7. Freie Universitat Berlin. https://refubium.fu-berlin.de/bitstream/handle/fub188/19026/2008-7_Boerzel_Pamuk_Stahn.pdf?sequence=1.

Brady, Michelle. 2014. "Ethnographies of Neoliberal Governmentalities: From the Neoliberal Apparatus to Neoliberalism and Governmental Assemblages." *Foucault Studies* 18: 11–33. https://doi.org/10.22439/fs.v0i18.4649.

Brady, Michelle, and Randy K. Lippert. 2016. *Governing Practices: Neoliberalism, Governmentality, and the Ethnographic Imaginary*. Toronto: Univ. of Toronto Press.

Brankamp, Hanno. 2020. "Refugees in Uniform: Community Policing as a Technology of Government in Kakuma Refugee Camp, Kenya." *Journal of Eastern African Studies* 14, no. 2: 270–90. https://doi.org/10.1080/17531055.202.1725318.

Breman, Jan, Kevan Harris, Ching Kwan Lee, and Marcel van der Linden, eds. 2019. *The Social Question in the Twenty-First Century: A Global View*. Berkeley: Univ. of California Press.

Brenner, Neil, David J. Madden, and David Wachsmuth. 2011. "Assemblage Urbanism and the Challenges of Critical Urban Theory." *City* 15, no. 2: 225–40. https://doi.org/10.1080/13604813.2011.568717.

Brenner, Neil, Jamie Peck, and Nik Theodore. 2010. "Variegated Neoliberalization: Geographies, Modalities, Pathways." *Global Networks* 10, no. 2: 182–222. https://doi.org/10.1111/j.1471-0374.2009.00277.x.

Briggs, Laura. 2003. "Mother, Child, Race, Nation: The Visual Iconography of Rescue and the Politics of Transnational and Transracial Adoption." *Gender and History* 15, no. 2: 179–200. http://dx.doi.org/10.1111/1468-0424.00298.

Brinkerhoff, Derick, and Arthur Goldsmith. 2005. "Institutional Dualism and International Development: A Revisionist Interpretation of Good Governance." *Administration and Society* 37, no. 2: 199–224.

Brooke, Steven. 2019. *Winning Hearts and Votes: Social Services and the Islamist Political Advantage*. Ithaca, NY: Cornell Univ. Press.

Brown, Wendy. 2015. *Undoing the Demos: Neoliberalism's Stealth Revolution*. Cambridge, MA: MIT Press.

Brubaker, Rogers. 2017a. "Between Nationalism and Civilizationism: The European Populist Moment in Comparative Perspective." *Ethnic and Racial Studies* 40, no. 8: 1191–1226.

Brubaker, Rogers. 2017b. "Why Populism?" *Theory and Society* 46: 357–85. https://doi.org/10.1007/s11186-017-9301-7.

Buğra, Ayşe. 2003. "The Place of the Economy in Turkish Society." *South Atlantic Quarterly* 102, no. 2: 453–70. http://dx.doi.org/10.1215/00382876-102-2-3 -453.

Buğra, Ayşe. 2007. "Poverty and Citizenship: An Overview of the Social-Policy Environment in Republican Turkey." *International Journal of Middle East Studies* 39, no. 1: 33–52. http://dx.doi.org/10.1017/S0020743807212528.

Buğra, Ayşe. 2008. *Kapitalizm, Yoksulluk ve Türkiye'de Sosyal Politika.* Istanbul: İletişim Yayınları.

Buğra, Ayşe. 2014. "Türkiye'de Sosyal Yardım Uygulamaları: Vatandaşlık Hakkı Mı Sadaka Mı?" *Al Jazeera Turkey,* September 19, 2014. http://www.aljazeera .com.tr/gorus/turkiyede-sosyal-yardim-uygulamalari-vatandaslik-hakki-mi -sadaka-mi.

Buğra, Ayşe, and Sinem Adar. 2007. *Türkiye'nin Kamu Sosyal Koruma Harcamalarının Karşılaştırmalı Bir Analizi.* Istanbul: Sosyal Politika Forumu.

Buğra, Ayşe, and Ayşen Candaş. 2011. "Change and Continuity under an Eclectic Social Security Regime: The Case of Turkey." *Middle Eastern Studies* 47, no. 3: 515–28. https://doi.org/10.1080/00263206.2011.565145.

Buğra, Ayşe, and Cağlar Keyder. 2006. "The Turkish Welfare Regime in Transformation." *Journal of European Social Policy* 16, no. 3: 169–92. https://doi .org/10.1177%2F0958928706065593.

Buğra, Ayşe, and Osman Savaşkan. 2014. *New Capitalism in Turkey: The Relationship between Politics, Religion and Business.* Cheltenham, UK, and Northampton, MA: Edward Elgar.

Burchell, Graham, Colin Gordon, and Peter Miller, eds. 1991. *The Foucault Effect: Studies in Governmentality.* Chicago: Univ. of Chicago Press.

Burr, Millard, and Robert Collins. 2006. *Alms for Jihad: Charity and Terrorism in the Islamic World.* Cambridge: Cambridge Univ. Press.

Busemeyer, Marius R., Caroline de la Porte, Julian L. Garritzmann, and Emmanuele Pavolini. 2018. "The Future of the Social Investment State: Politics, Policies, and Outcomes." *Journal of European Public Policy* 25, no. 6: 801–9. https://doi.org/10.1080/13501763.2017.1402944.

"Bütünleşik Sosyal Yardım Hizmetleri Projesi Çalıştay Toplantısı Yapıldı." 2008. *Dayanışma Dergisi* 1: 11–12.

Büyükçıngıl, Banu. 2015. "Vermenin Bereketi." *Her Nefes* 67: 18–19.

Cammett, Melani, and Pauline Jones Luong. 2014. "Is There an Islamist Political Advantage?" *Annual Review of Political Science* 17: 187–206. https://doi .org/10.1146/annurev-polisci-071112-221207.

Campbell, David A., and Ali Çarkoğlu. 2019. "Informal Giving in Turkey." *VOL-UNTAS: International Journal of Voluntary and Nonprofit Organizations* 30, no. 4: 738–53. https://doi.org/10.1007/s11266-019-00095-7.

Can, Yasemin İpek. 2013. "Securing 'Security' Amid Neoliberal Restructuring: Civil Society and Volunteerism in Post-1990 Turkey." In *Rhetorics of Insecurity: Belonging and Violence in the Neoliberal Era*, edited by Zeynep Gambetti and Marcial Godoy-Anativia, 93–124. New York: NYU Press.

Canefe, Nergis. 2016. "Management of Irregular Migration: Syrians in Turkey as Paradigm Shifters for Forced Migration Studies." *New Perspectives on Turkey* 54: 9–32. http://dx.doi.org/10.1017/npt.2016.6.

Carney, Josh. 2014. "Re-Creating History and Recreating Publics: The Success and Failure of Recent Ottoman Costume Dramas in Turkish Media." *European Journal of Turkish Studies*, no. 19. http://ejts.revues.orgwwwq.ejts.revues.org/5050.

Carney, Josh. 2019. "ResurReaction: Competing Visions of Turkey's (Proto) Ottoman Past in Magnificent Century and Resurrection Ertuğrul." *Middle East Critique* 28, no. 2: 101–20. https://doi.org/10.1080/19436149.2019.1599534.

Cemalettin, Çoğurcu. 2010. "Sosyal Yardımlaşma ve Dayanışma Genel Müdürlüğü'nün Stratejik Plan ve Proje Çalışmaları." *Dayanışma Dergisi* 10: 78–81.

Cengiz, Kurtuluş, Önder Küçükural, and Hande Gür. 2021. *Türkiye'de Spiritüel Arayışlar: Deizm, Yoga, Budizm, Meditasyon, Reiki Vb.* Istanbul: İletişim Yayınları.

Cheney, Kristen E., and Karen Smith Rotabi. 2017. "How the Global Orphan Industrial Complex Jeopardizes Local Child Protection Systems." In *Conflict, Violence and Peace. Geographies of Children and Young People*, edited by Christopher Harker, Kathrin Horschelmann, and Tracey Skelton, Vol. 11, 89–109. Singapore: Springer.

Choudry, Aziz, and Dip Kapoor. 2013. *NGOization: Complicity, Contradictions, and Prospects*. New York: Zed Books.

Chouliaraki, Lilie. 2010. "Post-Humanitarianism: Humanitarian Communication beyond a Politics of Pity." *International Journal of Cultural Studies* 13, no. 2: 107–26. https://doi.org/10.1177%2F1367877909356720.

Chouliaraki, Lilie. 2013a. "Cosmopolitanism as Irony: A Critique of Post-Humanitarianism." In *After Cosmopolitanism*, edited by Rosi Braidotti, Patrick Hanafin, and Bolette Blaagaard, 77–96. New York: Routledge.

Chouliaraki, Lilie. 2013b. *The Ironic Spectator: Solidarity in the Age of Post-Humanitarianism*. Cambridge: Polity.

"CHP'li İBB Başkanı Ekrem İmamoğlu'ndan Gıda Paketine 'Fırsatçı' Tarifesi." 2020. *Takvim*, March 30, 2020. https://www.takvim.com.tr/guncel/2020/03/30/chpli-ibb-baskani-ekrem-imamoglundan-gida-paketine-firsatci-tarifesi.

"CHP'li İzmir Büyükşehir Belediyesi, AK Partili İlçe Başkanına da Ramazan Yardımı Gönderdi." 2008. haberler.com, September 25, 2008. https://www.haberler.com/chp-li-izmir-buyuksehir-belediyesi-ak-partili-ilce-haberi/.

Christofis, Nikos. 2018. "The AKP's 'Yeni Turkiye': Challenging the Kemalist Narrative?" *Mediterranean Quarterly* 29, no. 3: 11–32.

Çelik, Nihat, and Emre İşeri. 2016. "Islamically Oriented Humanitarian NGOs in Turkey: AKP Foreign Policy Parallelism." *Turkish Studies* 17, no. 3: 429–48. https://doi.org/10.1080/14683849.2016.1204917.

Cindoğlu, Dilek, and Didem Ünal. 2017. "Gender and Sexuality in Authoritarian Discursive Strategies of 'New Turkey.'" *European Journal of Women's Studies* 24, no. 1: 39–54. https://doi.org/10.1177%2F1350506816679003.

Cindoğlu, Dilek, and Gizem Zencirci. 2008. "The Headscarf in Turkey in the Public and State Spheres." *Middle Eastern Studies* 44, no. 5: 791–806. https://doi.org/10.1080/00263200802285187.

Cizre-Sakallıoğlu, Ümit. 1997. "The Anatomy of Turkish Military's Political Autonomy." *Comparative Politics* 29, no. 2: 151–66. https://doi.org/10.2307/422077.

Cizre-Sakallıoğlu, Ümit, and Menderes Çınar. 2003. "Turkey (2002): Kemalism, Islamism and Politics in the Light of the February 28 Process." *South Atlantic Quarterly* 102, no. 2: 309–32. https://doi.org/10.1215/00382876-102-2-3-309.

Collett, Elizabeth. 2016. "The Paradox of the EU–Turkey Refugee Deal." Migration Policy Institute, March 2016. https://www.migrationpolicy.org/news/paradox-eu-turkey-refugee-deal.

Collier, Stephen. 2012a. "Neoliberalism as Big Leviathan, or . . . ? A Response to Wacquant and Hilgers." *Social Anthropology* 20, no. 2: 186–95.

Collier, Stephen. 2012b. *Post-Soviet Social: Neoliberalism, Social Modernity, and Biopolitics.* Princeton, NJ: Princeton Univ. Press.

Cooper, Glenda. 2018. *Reporting Humanitarian Disasters in a Social Media Age.* New York: Routledge. https://doi.org/10.4324/9781351054546.

Coşar, Simten, and Metin Yeğenoğlu. 2009. "The Neoliberal Restructuring of Turkey's Social Security System." *Monthly Review* 60 (11): 36–49. http://dx.doi.org/10.14452/MR-060-11-2009-04_3.

Coşkun, Selim, and Samet Güneş. 2009. "Ülkemizdeki Sosyal Yardımları İyileştirme Çalışmalarının Değerlendirilmesi." *Dayanışma Dergisi* 2: 76–82.

Cottle, Simon, and David Nolan. 2007. "Global Humanitarianism and the Changing Aid-Media Field." *Journalism Studies* 8, no. 6: 862–78. https://doi .org/10.1080/14616700701556104.

Cruikshank, Barbara. 1999. *The Will to Empower.* Ithaca, NY: Cornell Univ. Press.

Çağlan, Kevser, and Gülüşan Göcen. 2020. "Psikolojik Yardım Almanın Dini/ Manevi Açıdan Damgalanması ve Bu Süreci Yaşayanların Manevi Danış-manlık Hizmetlerinden Beklentileri." *Değerler Eğitimi Dergisi* 18, no. 39: 137–72.

Çakmaklı, Didem. 2015. "Active Citizenship in Turkey: Learning Citizenship in Civil Society Organizations." *Citizenship Studies* 9, no. 3–4: 421–35. https:// doi.org/10.1080/13621025.2015.1006174.

Çetinsaya, Gökhan. 1999. "Rethinking Nationalism and Islam: Some Prelimi-nary Notes on the Roots of 'Turkish-Islamic Synthesis' in Modern Turkish Political Thought." *The Muslim World* 89, no. 3–4: 350–76. https://doi.org /10.1111/j.1478-1913.1999.tb02753.x.

Çevik, Neslihan. 2016. *Muslimism in Turkey and Beyond: Religion in the Modern World.* New York: Palgrave Macmillan.

Çınar, Alev. 2001. "National History as a Contested Site: The Conquest of Istan-bul and Islamist Negotiations of the Nation." *Comparative Studies in Society and History* 43, no. 2: 364–91. https://doi.org/10.1017/S0010417501003528.

Çınar, Alev. 2005. *Modernity, Islam, and Secularism in Turkey: Bodies, Places and Time.* Minneapolis: Univ. of Minnesota Press.

Çınar, Alev. 2008. "Subversion and Subjugation in the Public Sphere: Secularism and the Islamic Headscarf." *Signs: Journal of Women in Culture and Society* 33, no. 4: 891–913. https://doi.org/10.1086/528850.

Çınar, Alev. 2019. "İslamcı Dergilerde Siyasal Düşüncenin Üretimi: Siyasi Kuram-İslami Düşünce İlişkisi." In *1980 Sonrası İslamcı Dergilerde Meseleler, Kav-ramlar ve İsimler,* edited by Lütfi Sunar, 183–211. Konya, Turkey: Konya Bü-yükşehir Belediyesi.

Çınar, Menderes. 2018. "Turkey's 'Western' or 'Muslim' Identity and the AKP's Civilizational Discourse." *Turkish Studies* 19, no. 2: 176–97. https://doi.org /10.1080/14683849.2017.1411199.

Çızakça, Murat. 2000. *A History of Philanthropic Foundations: The Islamic World from the Seventh Century to the Present.* Istanbul: Boğaziçi Univ. Press.

Çızakça, Murat. 2011. *Islamic Capitalism and Finance: Origins, Evolution and the Future.* Cheltenham, UK, and Northampton, MA: Edward Elgar.

Çolak, Yılmaz. 2006. "Ottomanism vs. Kemalism: Collective Memory and Cultural Pluralism in 1990s Turkey." *Middle Eastern Studies* 42 (4): 587–602. https://doi.org/10.1080/00263200600642274.

Çomak, İhsan. 2011. "Türkiye'nin Afrika Politikası ve Sağlık Sektöründe Çalışan Türk STK'ların TİKA'nın Desteğinde Afrika'da Yürüttüğü Faaliyetlerin Bu Politikaya Etkisi." *Avrasya Etüdleri* 40, no. 2: 201–22.

D'Aoust, Anne-Marie. 2014. "Ties that Bind? Engaging Emotions, Governmentality and Neoliberalism: Introduction to the Special Issue." *Global Society* 28, no. 3: 267–76. https://doi.org/10.1080/13600826.2014.900743.

Dalacoura, Katerina. 2017. "'East' and 'West' in Contemporary Turkey: Threads of a New Universalism." *Third World Quarterly* 38, no. 9: 2066–81. https://doi.org/10.1080/01436597.2017.1315301.

Daley, Patricia. 2013. "Rescuing African Bodies: Celebrities, Consumerism and Neoliberal Humanitarianism." *Review of African Political Economy* 40, no. 137: 375–93. https://doi.org/10.1080/03056244.2013.816944.

Danforth, Nicholas. 2015. "The Menderes Metaphor." *Turkish Policy Quarterly* 13, no. 4: 99–105.

Darke, Paul Anthony. 2004. "The Changing Face of Representations of Disability in the Media." In *Disabling Barriers, Enabling Environments*, 2nd ed., edited by John Swain, Sally French, Colin Barnes, and Carol Thomas, 100–106. London: Sage Publications.

Davies, Jonathan S. 2007. "Against 'Partnership': Toward a Local Challenge to Global Neoliberalism." In *Governing Cities in a Global Era: Urban Innovation, Competition, and Democratic Reform*, edited by Robin Hambleton and Jill Simone Gross, 199–210. New York: Palgrave Macmillan. https://doi.org/10.1057/9780230608795_15.

Davutoğlu, Ahmet. 2013. "Turkey's Humanitarian Diplomacy: Objectives, Challenges and Prospects." *Nationalities Papers* 41, no. 6: 865–70. https://doi.org/10.1080/00905992.2013.857299.

"Dayanışma Evine Sosyal Market Açılıyor." 2011. *Dayanışma Dergisi* 12: 44–45.

Dean, Jon. 2015. "Volunteering, the Market, and Neoliberalism." *People, Place and Policy* 9, no. 2: 139–48. https://doi.org/10.3351/ppp.0009.0002.0005.

Dean, Mitchell. 2010. *Governmentality: Power and Rule in Modern Society*, 2nd ed. London: Sage Publications.

Dean, Mitchell. 2017. "The Secret Life of Neoliberal Subjectivity." In *Rethinking Neoliberalism: Resisting the Disciplinary Regime*, edited by Sanford F. Schram and Marianna Pavlovskaya, 23–41. New York: Routledge.

Deeb, Lara. 2006. *An Enchanted Modern: Gender and Public Piety in Shi'i Lebanon*. Princeton, NJ: Princeton Univ. Press.

Deleuze, Gilles, and Felix Guattari. 2003. *A Thousand Plateaus*, 10th ed. Minneapolis: Univ. of Minnesota Press.

Dellepiane-Avellaneda, Sebastian. 2010. "Review Article: Good Governance, Institutions and Economic Development: Beyond the Conventional Wisdom." *British Journal of Political Science* 40, no. 1: 195–224. https://doi.org/10.1017/S0007123409990287.

Demiralp, Seda. 2009. "The Rise of Islamic Capital and the Decline of Islamic Radicalism in Turkey." *Comparative Politics* 41, no. 3: 315–35. https://doi.org/10.5129/001041509X12911362972278.

Demiralp, Seda. 2018. "Making Winners: Urban Transformation and Neoliberal Populism in Turkey." *Middle East Journal* 72, no. 1: 89–108. https://doi.org/10.3751/72.1.15.

Demireşik, Halime. 2015. "Müslüman Depresyona Girer Mi?" *Şebnem*, 126 (August). https://www.sebnemdergisi.com/musluman-depresyona-girer-mi.html.

Demirkaya, Yüksel, ed. 2016. *New Public Management in Turkey: Local Government Reform*. New York: Routledge.

Dencik, Lina, and Anne Kaun. 2020. "Datafication and the Welfare State." *Global Perspectives* 1, no. 1: 12912. https://doi.org/10.1525/gp.2020.12912.

Deniz Feneri Derneği. 2006. "Personelimize Depo Yönetimi Eğitimi." November 11, 2006. https://www.denizfeneri.org.tr/haberlerarsiv/personelimize-depo-yonetimi-egitimi_1511/.

Deniz Feneri Derneği. 2012. "Yardım Et, Depresyonu Yen." July 9, 2012. http://www.denizfeneri.org.tr/icerik.Aspx?kod=yardim-et-depresyonu-yen. Site inactive on July 20, 2023.

Deniz Feneri Derneği. 2016. "Deniz Feneri'nden Nijer'e Sağlık Yardımı." January 26, 2016. https://www.denizfeneri.org.tr/haberler/deniz-fenerinden-nijer-e-saglik-yardimi_4140/.

Deniz Feneri Derneği. n.d. "Bin Şehit Bin Su Kuyusu." Deniz Feneri Derneği. https://www.denizfeneri.org.tr/bagis/bin-sehit-bin-su-kuyusu_2355/.

2018. *Deniz Feneri Derneği Faaliyet Raporu 2017*. Istanbul: Deniz Feneri Yayınları.

2002. *Deniz Feneri Sosyal Yardımlaşma ve Dayanışma Derneği Yıllık Raporu*. Istanbul: Deniz Feneri Yayınları.

Deniz Feneri Yayınları. 2010. *Bir İnsanlık Destanı: Yüzyılın İyilik Harekatı*. Istanbul: Deniz Feneri Yayınları.

2010. "Denizli SYD Vakfı Çalışanlarına Eğitim Sertifikası." *Dayanışma Dergisi* 8: 14–15.

Denli, Özlem, Armağan Öztürk, and Ayhan Bilgin. 2017. "Hosting the Nation: Populist Themes in Erdoğan's Muhtar Meetings." In *The Transformation of Public Sphere: An Interdisciplinary Debate about the Recent Development of Publicity in Turkey*, edited by Armağan Öztürk and Ayhan Bilgin, 135–48. Baden-Baden, Germany: Nomos. https://doi.org/10.5771/9783845286303-135.

Derbal, Nora. 2022. *Charity in Saudi Arabia: Civil Society Under Authoritarianism*. Cambridge: Cambridge Univ. Press.

Deringil, Selim. 2003. "'They Live in a State of Nomadism and Savagery': The Late Ottoman Empire and the Post-Colonial Debate." *Comparative Studies in Society and History* 45, no. 2: 311–42. http://dx.doi.org/10.1017/S001041750300015X.

Desai, Karishma. 2019. "Letting Girls Learn, Letting Girls Rise: Commodifying Girlhoods in Humanitarian Campaigns." In *Disadvantaged Childhoods and Humanitarian Intervention: Processes of Affective Commodification and Objectification*, edited by Kristen Cheney and Aviva Sinervo, 63–85. Cham, Switzerland: Palgrave Macmillan. https://doi.org/10.1007/978-3-030-01623-4_3.

"Devlet Bakanımız Hayati Yazıcı 'Sosyal Yardım Sadaka Değildir.'" 2010. *Dayanışma Dergisi* 6: 12–16.

Dinç, Yusuf, Servet Bayındır, Mehmet Saraç, and İbrahim Güran Yumuşak. 2021. "Küresel Ekonomiyi Yeniden Düşünme: 2022 Türkiye Ekonomisi Raporu." *MÜSİAD Ekonomik Araştırmalar*. Istanbul: Müstakil İşadamları ve Sanayiciler Derneği.

Dodurka, Berra Zeynep. 2014. *Türkiye'de Merkezi Devlet Eliyle Yapılan Sosyal Yardımlar*. Boğaziçi University, Social Policy Forum, December 2014.

Dogra, Nandita. 2013. *Representations of Global Poverty: Aid, Development and International NGOs*. London: Bloomsbury.

Doğan, Erkan. 2010. "Parliamentary Experience of the Turkish Labor Party: 1965–1969." *Turkish Studies* 11, no. 3: 313–28. http://dx.doi.org/10.1080/14683849.2010.506722.

Doğramacı, Ayşe. 2017. "İnsan ve Depresyon." *Ribat Dergisi* 417 (September). http://www.ribatdergisi.com.tr/yazilar/165/Insan-ve-Depresyon.html.

Donzelot, Jacques. 1979. *The Policing of Families*. New York: Pantheon Books.

Dorlach, Tim. 2015. "The Prospects of Egalitarian Capitalism in the Global South: Turkish Social Neoliberalism in Global Perspective." *Economy and Society* 44, no. 4: 519–44. https://doi.org/10.1080/03085147.2015.1090736.

Dorlach, Tim. 2016. "The AKP between Populism and Neoliberalism: Lessons from Pharmaceutical Policy." *New Perspectives on Turkey* 55: 55–83. https://doi.org/10.1017/npt.2016.23.

Dost Eli Derneği. 2021. "Nijer'e Giden Dost Eli Yardım Ekibi Konya'ya Döndü." Dost Eli Derneği, December 25, 2021. https://dosteli.org.tr/haber-NIJERE-GIDEN-DOST-ELI-YARDIM-EKIBI-KONYAYA-DONDU_235.

Doumani, Beshara. 2017. *Family Life in the Ottoman Mediterranean: A Social History*. Cambridge: Cambridge Univ. Press.

Douglas, Mary, and Baron Isherwood. 1979. *The World of Goods*. London: Routledge.

Duckett, Jane. 2020. "Neoliberalism, Authoritarian Politics and Social Policy in China." *Development and Change* 51, no. 2: 523–39.

Duru, Muhittin Celal. 1939. *Sosyal Yardım: Prensipleri ve Tatbikleri*. Istanbul: Ebüzziya.

Dülger, Kenan. 2017. "Etkinliği Giderek Artan Yeni Bir Kavram Olarak İnsani Diplomasi ve Bu Alanda Örnek Teşkil Eden Türkiye'nin İnsani Diplomasi Anlayışı." *International Journal of Political Studies* 3, no. 2: 1–20.

Eagleton-Pierce, Matthew. 2019. "The Rise of Managerialism in International NGOs." *Review of International Political Economy* 27, no. 2: 970–94.

Ebrahim, Alnoor. 2005. "Accountability Myopia: Losing Sight of Organizational Learning." *Nonprofit and Voluntary Sector Quarterly* 34, no. 1: 56–87.

Eder, Mine. 2010. "Retreating State? Political Economy of Welfare Regime Change in Turkey." *Middle East Law and Governance* 2, no. 2: 152–84. http://dx.doi.org/10.1163/187633710X500739.

Eder, Mine, and Derya Özkul. 2016. "Editor's Introduction: Precarious Lives and Syrian Refugees in Turkey." *New Perspectives on Turkey* 54: 1–8. http://dx.doi.org/10.1017/npt.2016.5.

Ege, Aslı. 2022. "Foreign Policy as a Means of the AKP's Struggle with Kemalism in Relation to Domestic Variables." *Turkish Studies* 23, no. 4: 554–75.

Ege, Remziye. 2011. "Gönüllülük, Din ve Din Eğitimi." *Dini Araştırmalar* 14, no. 38: 12–13.

Eggen, Oyvind. 2012. "Performing Good Governance: The Aesthetics of Bureaucratic Practice in Malawi." *Ethnos* 77, no. 1 (March 1, 2012): 1–23. https://doi.org/10.1080/00141844.2011.580357.

El-Gamal, Mahmoud A. 2006. *Islamic Finance: Law, Economics, and Practice*. Cambridge: Cambridge Univ. Press.

El-Kazaz, Sarah. 2018. "Building 'Community' and Markets in Contemporary Cairo." *Comparative Studies in Society and History* 60, no. 2: 476–505. https://doi.org/10.1017/S0010417518000129.

Eliasoph, Nina. 2011. *Making Volunteers: Civic Life after Welfare's End.* Princeton, NJ: Princeton Univ. Press.

Elveren, Adem. 2008. "Social Security Reform in Turkey: A Critical Perspective." *Review of Radical Political Economics* 40, no. 2: 212–32. http://dx.doi.org/10.1177/0486613407310561.

Emiroğlu, İslam. 2009. "SYD Vakıfları ve Sosyal Devlet." *Dayanışma Dergisi* 2: 572–76.

Ener, Mine. 2005. "Religious Prerogatives and Policing the Poor in Two Ottoman Contexts." *Journal of Interdisciplinary History* 35, no. 3: 501–11. https://doi.org/10.1162/0022195052564306.

Enson Haber. 2014. "Ak Parti İstanbul'dan Suriye'liler İçin Kampanya." December 25, 2014. https://www.ensonhaber.com/ic-haber/ak-partiden-suriyeli-siginmacilar-icin-kampanya-2014-12-25.

Erdem, Chien Yang. 2017. "Ottomentality: Neoliberal Governance of Culture and Neo-Ottoman Management of Diversity." *Turkish Studies* 18, no. 4: 710–28. https://doi.org/10.1080/14683849.2017.1354702.

Erdoğan, Mehmet. 2013. "İslam'ın Köprüsü Zekat ve Sadakanın Sosyal Paylaşım Açısından Önemi." *Din ve Hayat* 18: 48–52.

Erdoğan, Murat. 2015. *Türkiye'deki Suriyeliler: Toplumsal Kabul ve Uyum.* Istanbul: Bilgi Üniversitesi Yayınları.

Erdoğan, Necmi. 2007. *Yoksulluk Halleri.* Istanbul: İletişim Yayınları.

Ergut, Ferdan. 2002. "Policing the Poor in the Late Ottoman Empire." *Middle Eastern Studies* 38, no. 2: 149–64. https://doi.org/10.1080/714004457.

Erkmen, T. Deniz. 2021. "Flexible Selves in Flexible Times? Yoga and Neoliberal Subjectivities in Istanbul." *Sociology* 55, no. 5: 1035–52. https://doi.org/10.1177/0038038521998930.

"Erzurum'da Suriye Kış Yardımı-Erzurum Müftülüğü-Türkiye Diyanet Vakfı." 2022. *Müftülük Haberler,* January 27, 2022. https://www.muftulukhaberler.com/erzurum-da-suriye-kis-yardimi/19953/.

Evered, Emine Ö., and Kyle T. Evered. 2013. "'Protecting the National Body': Regulating the Practice and the Place of Prostitution in Early Republican Turkey." *Gender, Place and Culture: A Journal of Feminist Geography* 20, no. 7: 839–57. http://dx.doi.org/10.1080/0966369X.2012.753584.

Evered, Kyle T., and Emine Ö. Evered. 2012. "State, Peasant, Mosquito: The Biopolitics of Public Health Education and Malaria in Early Republican Turkey." *Political Geography* 31, no. 5: 311–23. http://dx.doi.org/10.1016/j.polgeo.2012.05.002.

Exertzoglou, Haris. 2010. "Medicine, Philanthropy and the Construction of Poverty in Istanbul in the Nineteenth and Early Twentieth Centuries." In *Economy and Society on Both Shores of the Aegean*, edited by Vangelis Kechriotis and Lorans Tanatar Baruh, 249–76. Athens: AlphaPolitismos.

"Fakirlere Müjde." 1986. *Milliyet*. May 17, 1986.

Farías, Ignacio, and Thomas Bender. 2012. *Urban Assemblages: How Actor-Network Theory Changes Urban Studies*. London and New York: Routledge.

Fassin, Didier. 2007. "Humanitarianism as a Politics of Life." *Public Culture* 19, no. 3: 499–520. http://dx.doi.org/10.1215/08992363-2007-007.

Fassin, Didier. 2011. *Humanitarian Reason: A Moral History of the Present*. Oakland: Univ. of California Press.

Featherstone, David. 2011. "On Assemblage and Articulation." *Area* 43, no. 2: 139–42. https://doi.org/10.1111/j.1475-4762.2011.01007.x.

Fehrenbach, Heide, and Davide Rodogno. 2015. "'A Horrific Photo of a Drowned Syrian Child': Humanitarian Photography and NGO Media Strategies in Historical Perspective." *International Review of the Red Cross* 97, no. 900: 1121–55. https://doi.org/10.1017/S1816383116000369.

Ferguson, James. 1994a. "The Anti-Politics Machine 'Development' and Bureaucratic Power in Lesotho." *The Ecologist* 24, no. 5: 177–81.

Ferguson, James. 1994b. *The Anti-Politics Machine: "Development," Depoliticization and Bureaucratic Power in Lesotho*. Minneapolis: Univ. of Minnesota Press.

Ferguson, James. 2007. "Formalities of Poverty: Thinking about Social Assistance in Neoliberal South Africa." *African Studies Review* 50, no. 2: 71–86.

Ferguson, James. 2015. *Give a Man a Fish: Reflections on the New Politics of Distribution*. Durham, NC: Duke Univ. Press.

Fisher Onar, Nora. 2009. "Echoes of a Universalism Lost: Rival Representations of the Ottomans in Today's Turkey." *Middle Eastern Studies* 45, no. 2: 229–41. https://doi.org/10.1080/00263200802697290.

"5871 Sayılı Yardım Toplama Kanunu." 1983. https://www.mevzuat.gov.tr/MevzuatMetin/1.5.2860.pdf.

Fleischer, Friederike. 2011. "Technology of Self, Technology of Power. Volunteering as Encounter in Guangzhou, China." *Ethnos: A Journal of Anthropology* 76, no. 3: 300–325. http://dx.doi.org/10.1080/00141844.2011.565126.

Foucault, Michel. 1980. *Power/Knowledge: Selected Interviews and Other Writings, 1972–1977.* Edited by Colin Gordon. New York: Pantheon.

Foucault, Michel. 1991. "Governmentality." In *The Foucault Effect: Studies in Governmentality,* edited by Graham Burchell, Colin Gordon, and Peter Miller, 87–105. London: Harvester Wheatshaft.

Foucault, Michel. 2012. *Discipline and Punish: The Birth of the Prison.* New York: Vintage Books.

Frewer, Tim. 2013. "Doing NGO Work: The Politics of Being 'Civil Society' and Promoting 'Good Governance' in Cambodia." *Australian Geographer* 44, no. 1: 97–114. https://doi.org/10.1080/00049182.2013.765350.

Ganesh, Shiv, and Kirstie Mcallum. 2009. "Discourses of Volunteerism." *Annals of the International Communication Association* 33, no. 1: 343–83. http://dx.doi.org/10.1080/23808985.2009.11679091.

Gans-Morse, Jordan, Mariana Borges, Alexay Makarin, Theresa Mannah-Blankson, Andre Nickow, and Dong Zhang. 2018. "Reducing Bureaucratic Corruption: Interdisciplinary Perspectives on What Works." *World Development* 105: 171–88.

Garay, Candelaria. 2016. *Social Policy Expansion in Latin America.* Cambridge: Cambridge Univ. Press.

Geertz, Clifford. 1973. *The Interpretation of Cultures.* New York: Basic Books.

"Genç Gönüllüler: Bir Gençlik Projesi." Genç Gönüllüler, accessed October 18, 2018, http://gencgonulluler.gov.tr/Hakkimizda. Site inactive on July 20, 2023.

Gibson-Graham, J. K. 1996. *"The" End of Capitalism (as We Knew It): A Feminist Critique of Political Economy.* Minneapolis: Univ. of Minnesota Press.

Ginio, Eyal. 2003. "Living on the Margins of Charity: Coping with Poverty in an Ottoman Provincial City." In *Poverty and Charity in Middle Eastern Contexts,* edited by Amy Singer, Michael Bonner, and Mine Ener, 165–84. New York: State Univ. of New York Press.

Girei, Emanuela. 2016. "NGOs, Management and Development: Harnessing Counter-Hegemonic Possibilities." *Organization Studies* 37, no. 2: 193–212.

Gisselquist, Rachel M. 2012. "Good Governance as a Concept, and Why This Matters for Development Policy." WIDER Working Paper. https://www.econstor.eu/handle/10419/81039.

Gledhill, John. 2018. "Governance Issues in Development." In *The International Encyclopedia of Anthropology,* edited by Hilary Callan and Simon Coleman. https://onlinelibrary.wiley.com/doi/abs/10.1002/9781118924396.wbiea1529.

Gontijo, Lorenzo C. B., and Roberson S. Barbosa. 2020. "Erdoğan's Pragmatism and the Ascension of AKP in Turkey: Islam and Neo-Ottomanism." *Digest of Middle East Studies* 29, no. 1: 76–91. https://doi.org/10.1111/dome.12205.

Goodlad, Lauren. 2001. "'Making the Working Man Like Me': Charity, Pastorship, and Middle-Class Identity in Nineteenth-Century Britain; Thomas Chalmers and Dr. James Phillips Kay." *Victorian Studies* 43, no. 4: 591–617. https://www.jstor.org/stable/3830065.

Göçmen, İpek. 2014. "Religion, Politics and Social Assistance in Turkey: The Rise of Religiously Motivated Associations." *Journal of European Social Policy* 24, no. 1: 92–103. https://doi.org/10.1177%2F0958928713511278.

Göçmen, İpek. 2018. "Non-Public Welfare in Turkey: New and Old Forms of Religiously Motivated Associations." *Research and Policy on Turkey* 3, no. 2: 187–200.

Gökarıksel, Banu, and Anna Secor. 2012. "'Even I Was Tempted': The Moral Ambivalence and Ethical Practice of Veiling-Fashion in Turkey." *Annals of the Association of American Geographers* 102, no. 4: 847–62. https://doi.org/10.1080/00045608.2011.601221.

Göle, Nilüfer. 1994. "Toward an Autonomization of Politics and Civil Society in Turkey." In *Politics in the Third Turkish Republic*, edited by Metin Heper and Ahmet Evin, 213–22. Boulder, CO: Westview Press.

Göle, Nilüfer. 2017. "Turkey Is Undergoing a Radical Shift, from Pluralism to Islamic Populism." *New Perspectives Quarterly* 34, no. 4: 45–49.

"Gönül Elçileri." Turkiye Cumhuriyeti Aile, Çalışma ve Sosyal Hizmetler Bakanlığı Gönül Elçileri Projesi. Accessed October 18, 2018. https://gonulelcileri.aile.g Gönül Elçileri ov.tr/gonul-elcileri.

"Gönüllü Yüreklerin Kardeşlik Köprüsü." 2018. Star, October 7, 2018.

Görmüş, Evrim. 2018. "Food Banks and Food Insecurity: Cases of Brazil and Turkey." *Forum for Development Studies* 46, no. 1: 67–81. https://doi.org/10.1080/08039410.2018.1450288.

Gran, Peter. 1979. *Islamic Roots of Capitalism: Egypt, 1760–1840.* Syracuse: Syracuse Univ. Press.

Griffiths, Mark. 2015. "I've Got Goose Bumps Just Talking about It!: Affective Life on Neoliberalized Volunteering Programs." *Tourist Studies* 15, no. 2: 205–21. https://doi.org/10.1177%2F1468797614563437.

Grigoriadis, Ioannis. 2016. "The Peoples' Democratic Party (HDP) and the 2015 Elections." *Turkish Studies* 17, no. 1: 39–46.

Grindle, Merille. 2012. "Good Governance: The Inflation of an Idea." In *Planning Ideas That Matter: Livability, Territoriality, Governance, and Reflective Practice*, edited by Bishwapriya Sanyal, Lawrence J. Vale, and Christina D. Rosan, 259–82. Cambridge, MA: MIT Press.

Grütjen, Daniel. 2008. "The Turkish Welfare Regime: An Example of the Southern European Model? The Role of the State, Market, and Family in Welfare Provision." *Turkish Policy Quarterly* 7, no. 1: 111–29.

Gunter, Michael. 1989. "Political Instability in Turkey during the 1970s." *Journal of Conflict Studies* 9, no. 1: 63–77.

Gülalp, Haldun. 1999. "Political Islam in Turkey: The Rise and Fall of the Refah Party." *The Muslim World* 89, no. 1: 22–41. http://dx.doi.org/10.1111/j.1478-1913.1999.tb03667.x.

Gülalp, Haldun. 2001. "Globalization and Political Islam: The Social Basis of Turkey's Welfare Party." *International Journal of Middle East Studies* 33, no. 3: 433–48.

Gülmez, Mesut. 2007. "Sosyal Politika Biliminin Öncüsü Prof. Dr. Cahit Talas." *Çalışma ve Toplum* 1: 23–26.

Gümüşcü, Şebnem, and Deniz Sert. 2009. "The Power of the Devout Bourgeoisie: The Case of the Justice and Development Party in Turkey." *Middle Eastern Studies* 45, no. 6: 953–68. https://doi.org/10.1080/00263200903268710.

Güner, Ezgi. 2021. "Rethinking Whiteness in Turkey through the AKP's Foreign Policy in Africa South of the Sahara." *Middle East Report* 299 (Summer). https://merip.org/2021/08/rethinking-whiteness-in-turkey-through-the-akps-foreign-policy-in-africa-south-of-the-sahara/.

Güner, Osman. 2004. "Yoksulluk, Din ve Sivil Toplum." *Köprü Dergisi*, 88: 37–42. https://www.koprudergisi.com/guz-2004/yoksulluk-din-ve-sivil-toplum/.

Güneş, Hasan Hüseyin, and Şevket Ercan Kızılay. 2011. "Osmanlı Vakıf Geleneği, Toplumsal Alan ve Yoksullar: Ayasofya Nahiyesi Örneği." *OPUS* 1: 160–87.

Gürbilek, Nurdan. 1992. *Vitrinde Yaşamak: 1980'lerin Kültürel İklimi.* Istanbul: Metis Yayınları.

Gürboğa, Nurşen. 2009. "Compulsory Mine Work: The Single-Party Regime and the Zonguldak Coalfield as a Site of Contention, 1940–1947." *International Review of Social History* 54, no. 17: 115–42. https://doi.org/10.1017/S0020859009990265.

Gürbüz, Mustafa. 2014. *The Long Winter: Turkish Politics after the Corruption Scandal.* New York: Rethink Institute.

Gürel, Burak. 2011. "Agrarian Change and Labour Supply in Turkey, 1950–1980." *Journal of Agrarian Change* 11, no. 2: 195–219. https://doi.org/10.1111/j.1471 -0366.2010.00299.x.

Gürel, Burak, Bermal Küçük, and Sercan Taş. 2019. "The Rural Roots of the Rise of the Justice and Development Party in Turkey." *Journal of Peasant Studies* 46, no. 3: 457–79.

Gürses, Mehmet. 2020. "The Evolving Kurdish Question in Turkey." *Middle East Critique* 29, no. 3: 307–18.

Güvenç-Salgırlı, Sanem. 2011. "Eugenics for the Doctors: Medicine and Social Control in 1930s Turkey." *Journal of the History of Medicine and Allied Sciences* 66, no. 3: 281–312.

Güvenç-Salgırlı, Sanem, and Bahar Aykan. 2018. "Circuits of Security: Debating the Political Rationality of Neoliberal Governmentality in Contemporary Turkey." *Comparative Studies of South Asia, Africa and the Middle East* 38, no. 1: 73–88. https://doi.org/10.1215/1089201x-4389991.

Hackworth, Jason. 2012. *Faith Based: Religious Neoliberalism and the Politics of Welfare in the United States*. Athens: Univ. of Georgia Press.

Hafez, Melis. 2021. *Inventing Laziness: The Culture of Productivity in Late Ottoman Society*. Cambridge: Cambridge Univ. Press.

Hale, William. 2005. "Christian Democracy and the AKP: Parallels and Contrasts." *Turkish Studies* 6, no. 2: 293–310. https://doi.org/10.1080/146838405 00119601.

Hammond, Timur. 2014. "Matters of the Mosque: Changing Configurations of Buildings and Belief in an Istanbul District." *City* 18, no. 6: 679–90.

Harrison, Elizabeth. 2006. "Unpacking the Anti-Corruption Agenda: Dilemmas for Anthropologists." *Oxford Development Studies* 34, no. 1: 15–29.

Hattam, Jennifer. 2020. "The Forgotten Stones that Still Inspire Turks to Help Their Neighbors." *Atlas Obscura*. August 24, 2020. https://www.atlasobscura .com/articles/history-charity-stones-turkey.

Hemment, Julie. 2012. "Redefining Need, Reconfiguring Expectations: The Rise of State-Run Youth Voluntarism Programs in Russia." *Anthropological Quarterly* 85, no. 2: 519–54. http://dx.doi.org/10.1353/anq.2012.0034.

Herrold, Catherine E. 2020. *Delta Democracy: Pathways to Incremental Civic Revolution in Egypt and Beyond*. Oxford: Oxford Univ. Press.

Heynemann, Stephen. 2004. *Islam and Social Policy*. Nashville, TN: Vanderbilt Univ. Press.

Higgins, Vaughan, and Wendy Larner, eds. 2017. *Assembling Neoliberalism: Expertise, Practices, Subjects.* New York: Palgrave Macmillan.

Hilgers, Mathieu. 2013. "Embodying Neoliberalism: Thoughts and Responses to Critics." *Social Anthropology* 21, no. 1: 75–89. https://doi.org/10.1111/1469-8676.12010.

Hirschkind, Charles. 2006. *The Ethical Soundscape: Cassette Sermons and Islamic Counterpublics.* New York: Columbia Univ. Press.

Hoesterey, James Bourk. 2015. *Rebranding Islam: Piety, Prosperity, and a Self-Help Guru.* Stanford, CA: Stanford Univ. Press.

Hoexter, Miriam. 1998. "Waqf Studies in the Twentieth Century: The State of the Art." *Journal of the Economic and Social History of the Orient* 41: 474–95.

Hoggarth, Davinia. 2016. "The Rise of Islamic Finance: Post-Colonial Market-Building in Central Asia and Russia." *International Affairs* 92, no. 1: 115–36. https://doi.org/10.1111/1468-2346.12508.

Houston, Christopher. 2001. "The Brewing of Islamist Modernity: Tea Gardens and Public Space in Istanbul." *Theory, Culture, and Society* 18, no. 6: 77–97. https://doi.org/10.1177%2F02632760122052057.

Hout, Will. 2012. *EU Strategies on Governance Reform Between Development and State-Building.* London: Routledge.

Hull, Matthew S. 2012. *The Government of Paper: The Materiality of Bureaucracy in Urban Pakistan.* Berkeley: Univ. of California Press.

Hvenmark, John. 2016. "Ideology, Practice, and Process? A Review of the Concept of Managerialism in Civil Society Studies." *Voluntas* 27: 2833–59.

Hyatt, Susan. 2001. "From Citizen to Volunteer: Neoliberal Governance and the Erasure of Poverty." In *The New Poverty Studies: The Ethnography of Power, Politics, and Impoverished People in the United States,* edited by Judith Goode and Jeff Maskovsky, 435–69. New York and London: New York Univ. Press.

Ilcan, Suzan, and Tanya Basok. 2004. "Community Government: Voluntary Agencies, Social Justice, and the Responsibilization of Citizens." *Citizenship Studies* 8, no. 2: 129–44. https://doi.org/10.1080/1362102042000214714.

Inglehart, Ronald F., and Pippa Norris. 2016. "Trump, Brexit and the Rise of Populism: Economic Have-Nots and Cultural Backlash." Harvard Kennedy School Faculty Research Working Paper Series, August.

IHH. 2015b. "Her Sınıfın Bir Yetim Kardeşi Var 'Kelebek Etkisi.'" YouTube, October 19, 2015. https://www.youtube.com/watch?time_continue=116&v=HRXf3n6R01I.

IHH. 2017. "Her Sınıfın Bir Yetim Kardeşi Var ‖ Tanıtım Filmi – 2017." YouTube, October 24, 2017. https://www.youtube.com/watch?v=XlMaK2aCln4.

IHH. 2018. "Suriye'ye Acil Un Yardımı Çağrısı," August 15, 2018. https://ihh.org.tr/haber/suriyeye-acil-un-yardimi-cagrisi.

IHH. n.d.-a. "Her Sınıfın Bir Yetim Kardeşi Var." https://www.ihh.org.tr/her-sinifin-bir-yetim-kardesi-var.

IHH. n.d.-b. "Yetim." https://www.ihh.org.tr/yetim.

Işık, Damla. 2012. "The Specter and Reality of Corruption in State and Civil Society: Privatizing and Auditing Poor Relief in Turkey." *Comparative Studies of South Asia, Africa, and the Middle East* 32, no. 1: 57–69. http://dx.doi.org/10.1215/1089201X-1545363.

Işık, Damla. 2014. "Vakıf as Intent and Practice: Charity and Poor Relief in Turkey." *International Journal of Middle East Studies* 46, no. 2: 307–27. https://doi.org/10.1017/S0020743814000129.

Işık, Damla. 2021. "Engineering Self and Civil Society: The Promise of Charity in Turkey." *Religion* 51, no. 1: 58–73. https://doi.org/10.1080/0048721X.2020.1792052.

İçduygu, Ahmet. 2015. *Syrian Refugees in Turkey: The Long Road Ahead.* Washington, DC: Transatlantic Council on Migration, Migration Policy Institute.

"İhtiyaç Sahipleri İçin Alışveriş Kartı Çıkarttı." 2011. haberler.com, July 30, 2011. https://www.haberler.com/ihtiyac-sahipleri-icin-alisveris-karti-cikartti-2901506-haberi/.

"İmamoğlu Bak Ne Paketler Var." 2020. *Haber Vitrini*, April 7, 2020. http://www.habervitrini.com/imamoglu-bak-ne-paketler-var/1003410.

İnsani Yardım Vakfı (IHH). 2015a. "Vakit Ramazan 'Nijer.'" YouTube, July 6, 2015. https://www.youtube.com/watch?v=XE5K9vhpNsU.

İnsel, Ahmet. 2003. "The AKP and Normalizing Democracy in Turkey." *South Atlantic Quarterly* 102, no. 2: 293–308. http://dx.doi.org/10.1215/00382876-102-2-3-293.

"İzmir Büyükşehir'den 'İncitmeyen' Yardım." 2014. *İhlas Haber Ajansı*, May 27, 2014. https://www.iha.com.tr/kayseri-haberleri/izmir-buyuksehirden-incitmeyen-yardim-772522/.

Jassal, Smita Tewari. 2014. "The Sohbet: Talking Islam in Turkey." *Sociology of Islam* 1, no. 3–4: 188–208.

Jawad, Rana. 2009. *Social Welfare and Religion in the Middle East: A Lebanese Perspective.* Bristol, UK: Policy Press.

Jones, Branwen Gruffydd. 2013. "'Good Governance' and 'State Failure': Genealogies of Imperial Discourse." *Cambridge Review of International Affairs* 26, no. 1 (March): 49–70. https://doi.org/10.1080/09557571.2012.734785.

Jung, Dietrich, Marie Juul Petersen, and Sara Lei Sparre. 2014. *Politics of Modern Muslim Subjectivities: Islam, Youth, and Social Activism in the Middle East.* New York: Palgrave Macmillan.

Kadıoğlu, Ayşe. 1998. "Republican Epistemology and Islamic Discourses in Turkey in the 1990s." *The Muslim World* 88, no. 1: 1–21.

Kadıoğlu, Ayşe. 2005. "Civil Society, Islam, and Democracy in Turkey: A Study of Three Islamic Non-Governmental Organizations." *The Muslim World* 95, no. 1: 23–41.

Kalaycıoğlu, Ersin. 2002. "The Motherland Party: The Challenge of Institutionalization in a Charismatic Leader Party." *Turkish Studies* 3, no. 1: 41–61.

Kalaycıoğlu, Ersin. 2018. "Two Elections and a Political Regime in Crisis: Turkish Politics at the Crossroads." *Southeast European and Black Sea Studies* 18, no. 1: 21–51. https://doi.org/10.1080/14683857.2017.1379148.

Kamat, Sangeeta. 2004. "The Privatization of Public Interest: Theorizing NGO Discourse in a Neoliberal Era." *Review of International Political Economy* 11, no. 1: 155–76. https://doi.org/10.1080/0969229042000179794.

Kamrava, Mehran. 1998. "Pseudo-Democratic Politics and Populist Possibilities: The Rise and Demise of Turkey's Refah Party." *British Journal of Middle Eastern Studies* 25, no. 2: 275–301. https://doi.org/10.1080/13530199808705669.

Kapoor, Ilan. 2012. *Celebrity Humanitarianism: The Ideology of Global Charity.* London and New York: Routledge.

Kaptan, Senem. 2020. "'No Virus Is Stronger than Our Unity': Shifting Forms of Governmental Intimacies during COVID-19." *Anthropology in Action* 27, no. 3 (Winter): 31–34.

Karabağlı, Hülya. 2015. "CHP'li Ilhan Cihaner'den IHH Sorusu." *T24 Bağımsız İnternet Gazetesi*, December 19, 2015. http://t24.com.tr/haber/chpli-ilhan-cihanerden-ihh-sorusu,320983.

Karaman, Ozan. 2013. "Urban Neoliberalism with Islamic Characteristics." *Urban Studies* 50, no. 16: 3412–27. https://doi.org/10.1177/0042098013482505.

Karaömerlioğlu, M. Asım. 1998. "The People's Houses and the Cult of the Peasant in Turkey." *Middle Eastern Studies* 34, no. 4: 67–91.

Karim, Wazir Jahan. 2010. "The Economic Crisis, Capitalism and Islam: The Making of a New Economic Order?" *Globalizations* 7, no. 1–2: 105–25. https://doi.org/10.1080/14747731003593315.

Karpat, Kemal. 1963. "The People's Houses in Turkey: Establishment and Growth." *Middle East Journal* 17, no. 1–2: 55–67.

Karshenas, Massoud, and Valentine Moghadam. 2009. "Bringing Social Policy Back in: A Look at the Middle East and North Africa." *International Journal of Social Welfare* 18, no. s1: 52–61. https://doi.org/10.1111/j.1468-2397.2009.00628.x.

Kartal, Mehmet Abidin. 2019. "Osmanlı'nın Hayırmatikleri: Sadaka Taşları." *Risalehaber*, June 6, 2019. https://www.risalehaber.com/osmanlinin-hayirmatikleri-sadaka-taslari-21144yy.htm.

Kavaklı, Kerim Can. 2018. "Domestic Politics and the Motives of Emerging Donors: Evidence from Turkish Foreign Aid." *Political Research Quarterly* 71, no. 3: 614–27. https://dx.doi.org/10.1177/1065912917750783.

Kaya, Akyıldız. 2009. "Nerde benim Neoliberalizmim?" *Radikal* 2, December 20, 2009.

Kaya, Ayhan. 2015. "Islamisation of Turkey under the AKP Rule: Empowering Family, Faith and Charity." *South European Society and Politics* 20, no. 1: 47–69. https://doi.org/10.1080/13608746.2014.979031.

Kaya, Zeynep N., and Matthew Whiting. 2019. "The HDP, the AKP and the Battle for Turkish Democracy." *Ethnopolitics* 18, no. 1: 92–106. https://doi.org/10.1080/17449057.2018.1525168.

Kayaalp, Ebru. 2014. *Remaking Politics, Markets, and Citizens in Turkey: Governing Through Smoke*. London: Bloomsbury Academic.

"Kayapınar Belediyesinden 3 Bin Kişiye Gıda Yardımı Yapıldı." 2017. *Milliyet*, June 14, 2017. https://www.milliyet.com.tr/yerel-haberler/diyarbakir/kayapinar-belediyesinden-3-bin-kisiye-gida-yardimi-12107787.

"Kayseri'de İhtiyaç Sahiplerine Ücretsiz 'Market.'" 2015. haberler.com, July 1, 2015. https://www.haberler.com/kayseri-de-ihtiyac-sahiplerine-ucretsiz-market-7467316-haberi/.

Kazıcı, Ziya. 2003. *Osmanlı Vakıf Medeniyeti*. Istanbul: Bilge Yayıncılık.

Kesin Karar. 2022. "Müftülük ve TDV'den Yardım Kampanyası," January 22, 2022. https://www.kesinkarar.com/muftuluk-ve-tdvden-yardim-kampanyasi/. Site inactive on July 20, 2023.

Keyman, E. Fuat, and Ahmet İçduygu. 2003. "Globalization, Civil Society, and Citizenship in Turkey: Actors, Boundaries, and Discourses." *Citizenship Studies* 7, no. 2: 219–34.

Keyman, E. Fuat, and Ahmet İçduygu. 2013. "Introduction: Citizenship, Identity, and the Question of Democracy in Turkey." In *Citizenship in a Global World:*

European Questions and Turkish Experiences, edited by Ahmet İçduygu and Fuat Keyman, 1–29. London: Routledge.

Kezer, Zeynep. 2009. "An Imaginable Community: The Material Culture of Nation-Building in Early Republican Turkey." *Environment and Planning D: Society and Space* 27, no. 3: 508–30. https://doi.org/10.1068%2Fd10907.

Kılıç, Azer. 2008. "The Gender Dimension of Social Policy Reform in Turkey: Towards Equal Citizenship." *Social Policy and Administration* 42, no. 5: 487–503.

Kısa, Adnan, and Mustafa Z. Younis. 2006. "Financing Health Care for The Poor in Turkey: Is a Temporary Solution Becoming a Permanent Scheme?" *Public Health Reports* 121, no. 6: 764–68. https://doi.org/10.1177/00333549061 2100617.

"Kış İyilik Koleksiyonu." 2020. Sadaka Taşı Derneği, December 1, 2020. https://www.sadakatasi.org.tr//page/2020-2021-kis-iyilik-koleksiyonu/389.

"Kızılcahamam Toplantısı Gerçekleştirildi." 2010. *Dayanışma Dergisi* 7: 20–22.

Kiely, Ray. 1998. "Neoliberalism Revised? A Critical Account of World Bank Conceptions of Good Governance and Market Friendly Intervention." *International Journal of Health Services* 28, no. 4: 683–702.

"Kimse Yok Mu Derneği'nin Gönüllü Bayan Üyeleri Yeni Gönüllüler Kazanıyor." 2011. *SonDakika.com*, February 24, 2011. https://www.sondakika.com/haber/haber-kimse-yok-mu-dernegi-nin-gonullu-bayan-uyeleri-2555881/.

Kimya, Fırat. 2019. "Political Economy of Corruption in Turkey: Declining Petty Corruption, Rise of Cronyism?" *Turkish Studies* 20, no. 3 (May): 351–76. https://doi.org/10.1080/14683849.2018.1531352.

Kingfisher, Catherine, and Jeff Maskovsky. 2008. "Introduction: The Limits of Neoliberalism." *Critique of Anthropology* 28, no. 2: 115–26. https://doi.org/10.1177/0308275X08090544.

Kipnis, Andrew. 2007. "Neoliberalism Redefined: Suzhi Discourse and Tropes of Neoliberalism in the People's Republic of China." *Journal of the Royal Anthropological Institute* 13: 396.

Knafo, Samuel. 2020. "Neoliberalism and the Origins of Public Management." *Review of International Political Economy* 27, no. 4 (July): 780–801. https://doi.org/10.1080/09692290.2019.1625425.

Kochuyt, Thierry. 2009. "God, Gifts and Poor People: On Charity in Islam." *Social Compass* 56, no. 1: 98–116. http://dx.doi.org/10.1177/0037768608100345.

Koç, Mustafa. 2014. "Food Banking in Turkey: Conservative Politics in a Neo-Liberal State." In *First World Hunger Revisited: Food Charity or the Right to Food?*, edited by Graham Riches and Tiina Silvasti, 146–59. London: Palgrave Macmillan.

Koffman, Ofra, Shani Orgad, and Rosalind Gill. 2015. "Girl Power and 'Selfie Humanitarianism.'" *Continuum: Journal of Media and Cultural Studies* 29, no. 2: 157–68.

"Konya'da İhtiyaçlar 'Sosyal Kart' Ile Alışveriş Merkezlerinden Karşılanacak." 2010. haberler.com, August 12, 2010. https://www.haberler.com/konya-da -ihtiyaclar-sosyal-kart-ile-alisveris-2189270-haberi/.

Korkut, Umut, and Hande Eslen-Ziya. 2016. "The Discursive Governance of Population Politics: The Evolution of a Pro-Birth Regime in Turkey." *Social Politics* 23, no. 4: 555–75. http://dx.doi.org/10.1093/sp/jxw003.

Köseoğlu, Talha. 2019. "Islamists and the State: Changing Discourses on the State, Civil Society and Democracy in Turkey." *Turkish Studies* 20, no. 3: 323–50.

Kraidy, Marwan, and Omar Al-Ghazzi. 2013. "Neo-Ottoman Cool: Turkish Popular Culture in the Arab Public Sphere." *Popular Communication* 11: 17–29. https://doi.org/10.1080/15405702.2013.747940.

Kroessin, Mohammed R., and Abdulfatah S. Mohamed. 2008. "Saudi Arabian NGOs in Somalia: 'Wahabi' Da'wah or Humanitarian Aid?" In *Development, Civil Society and Faith-Based Organizations: Bridging the Sacred and the Secular*, edited by Gerard Clarke and Michael Jennings, 187–213. London: Palgrave Macmillan.

Kuran, Timur. 2001. "The Provision of Public Goods under Islamic Law: Origins, Impact and Limitations of the Waqf System." *Law and Society Review* 35, no. 4: 841–98.

Kuş, Mehmet. 2007. "Röportaj: Psikiyatr Doç. Dr. Kemal Sayar: Muthaç Olana Yardım Eden İnsan, Dünyanın En Mutlu İnsanı Olur." *Kimse Yok Mu Derneği Dergisi* 2: 33–37.

Kutlu, Denizcan. 2015. *Türkiye'de Sosyal Yardım Rejiminin Oluşumu: Birikim Denetim Disiplin.* Istanbul: Nota Bene.

Kuzey Haber Ajansı. 2013. "Türkiye'den Nijer'e Yardım Eli-Nijer Başbakanı İle Söyleşi, TRT Dünya Gündemi." YouTube, November 1, 2013. https://www .youtube.com/watch?v=mQaFkay-alA.

Kuzmanovic, Daniella. 2008. "Civilization and EU–Turkey relations." In *Religion, Politics, and Turkey's EU Accession*, edited by Dietrich Jung and Catharina Raudvere, 41–63. New York: Palgrave Macmillan.

Kuzmanovic, Daniella. 2012. *Refractions of Civil Society.* New York: Palgrave Macmillan.

"Kültürümüzde Sadaka Var." 2009. *Vatan*, January 1, 2009. http://www.gazete vatan.com/-kulturumuzde-*sadaqa*-var--216263-siyaset/.

Laclau, Ernesto. 2005. *On Populist Reason*. London: Verso.

Lamprou, Alexandros. 2015. *Nation-Building in Modern Turkey: The "People's Houses," the State and the Citizen*. London and New York: Bloomsbury Publishing.

Lapsley, Irvine. 2009. "New Public Management: The Cruelest Invention of the Human Spirit?" *Abacus* 45, no. 1: 1–21. https://doi.org/10.1111/j.1467-6281 .2009.00275.x.

Latief, Hilman. 2013. "The Politics of Benevolence: Political Patronage of Party-Based Charitable Organizations in Contemporary Indonesian Islam." *Al-Jami'ah: Journal of Islamic Studies* 51, no. 2: 337–63.

Lazarev, Egor, and Kanaal Sharma. 2017. "Brother or Burden: An Experiment on Reducing Prejudice toward Syrian Refugees in Turkey." *Political Science Research and Methods* 5, no. 2: 201–19. http://dx.doi.org/10.1017/psrm.2015.57.

Le Zotte, Jennifer. 2013. "'Not Charity, but a Chance': Philanthropic Capitalism and the Rise of American Thrift Stores, 1894–1930." *New England Quarterly* 86, no. 2: 169–95. https://doi.org/10.1162/TNEQ_a_00275.

LeBlanc, Marie Nathalie. 2020. "Charity, NGO-ization and Emergent Ethics of Volunteerism: The Case of Islamic NGOs in Côte d'Ivoire." In *Muslim Faith-Based Organizations and Social Welfare in Africa*, edited by Holger Weiss, 85–117. Cham, Switzerland: Springer International Publishing. https://doi .org/10.1007/978-3-030-38308-4_4.

Leisering, Lutz, ed. 2021. *One Hundred Years of Social Protection: The Changing Social Question in Brazil, India, China, and South Africa*. Cham, Switzerland: Palgrave Macmillan.

Levitt, Matthew. 2006. *Hamas: Politics, Charity and Terrorism in the Service of Jihad*. New Haven, CT: Yale Univ. Press.

Li, Tania Murray. 2007. *The Will to Improve: Governmentality, Development and the Practice of Politics*. Durham, NC: Duke Univ. Press.

Libal, Kathryn. 2000. "The Children's Protection Society: Nationalizing Child Welfare in Early Republican Turkey." *New Perspectives on Turkey* 23: 53–78. http://dx.doi.org/10.1017/S0896634600003381.

Linde, Fabian. 2016. "The Civilizational Turn in Russian Political Discourse: From Pan-Europeanism to Civilizational Distinctiveness." *Russian Review* 75, no. 4: 604–25.

Lombardi, Ben. 1997. "Turkey-The Return of the Reluctant Generals?" *Political Science Quarterly* 112, no. 2: 191–215. https://doi.org/10.2307/2657938.

Lüküslü, Demet. 2016. "Creating a Pious Generation: Youth and Education Policies of the AKP in Turkey." *Southeast European and Black Sea Studies* 16, no. 4: 637–49. http://dx.doi.org/10.1080/14683857.2016.1243332.

Lüküslü, Demet, and Şakir Dinçşahin. 2013. "Shaping Bodies Shaping Minds: Selim Sırrı Tarcan and the Origins of Modern Physical Education in Turkey." *International Journal of the History of Sport* 30, no. 3: 195–209. http://dx.doi.org/10.1080/09523367.2012.742067.

Madi-Şişman, Özlem. 2017. *Muslims, Money, and Democracy in Turkey: Reluctant Capitalists*. New York: Palgrave Macmillan.

Mahmood, Saba. 2005. *Politics of Piety: The Islamic Revival and the Feminist Subject*. Princeton, NJ: Princeton Univ. Press.

Makal, Ahmet. 1999. *Türkiye'de Tek Partili Dönemde Çalışma İlişkileri: 1920–1946*. Ankara: İmge Kitabevi.

Maksudyan, Nazan. 2014. *Orphans and Destitute Children in the Late Ottoman Empire*. Syracuse, NY: Syracuse Univ. Press.

Malkki, Liisa. 2015. *The Need to Help: The Domestic Arts of International Humanitarianism*. Durham, NC: Duke Univ. Press.

Manzo, Kate. 2008. "Imaging Humanitarianism: NGO Identity and the Iconography of Childhood." *Antipode: A Radical Journal of Geography* 40, no. 4: 632–57. https://doi.org/10.1111/j.1467-8330.2008.00627.x.

Mauss, Marcel. 1967. *The Gift: Forms and Functions of Exchange in Archaic Societies*. New York and London: W. W. Norton and Company.

McFarlane, Colin. 2011a. "On Context: Assemblage, Political Economy and Structure." *City* 15, no. 3–4 (August): 375–88. https://doi.org/10.1080/1360 4813.2011.595111.

McFarlane, Colin. 2011b. "The City as Assemblage: Dwelling and Urban Space." *Environment and Planning D: Society and Space* 29: 649–71. https://doi.org /10.1068%2Fd4710.

McGoey, Linsey. 2014. "The Philanthropic State: Market–State Hybrids in the Philanthrocapitalist Turn." *Third World Quarterly* 35: 109–25.

McGuigan, Jim. 2016. *Neoliberal Culture*. Basingstoke, UK: Palgrave Macmillan.

McLean, Fiona. 2006. "Introduction: Heritage and Identity." *International Journal of Heritage Studies* 12, no. 1: 3–7. https://doi.org/10.1080/135272505003 84431.

Mello, Brian. 2010. "Communists and Compromisers: Explaining Divergences within Turkish Labor Activism, 1960–1980." *European Journal of Turkish Studies*, 11. https://doi.org/10.4000/ejts.4343.

Miller, Peter, and Nikolas Rose. 1988. "The Tavistock Programme: The Government of Subjectivity and Social Life." *Sociology* 22, no. 2: 171–92. https://doi.org/10.1177%2F0038038588022002002.

Mills, Amy. 2011. "The Ottoman Legacy: Urban Geographies, National Imaginaries, and Global Discourses of Tolerance." *Comparative Studies of South Asia, Africa and the Middle East* 31, no. 1: 183–95. https://doi.org/10.1215/1089201X-2010-066.

Mills, Amy. 2014. "Cultures of Assemblage, Resituating Urban Theory: A Response to the Papers on 'Assembling Istanbul.'" *City* 18, no. 6 (November): 693. https://doi.org/10.1080/13604813.2014.962884.

Ministry of National Education. n.d. "İstanbul/Başakşehir—Başakşehir Kız Anadolu İmam Hatip Lisesi, İHH Yetim Projesi." TC Milli Eğitim Bakanlığı, 3. http://bkaihl.meb.k12.tr/meb_iys_dosyalar/34/36/758723/fotograf_galerisi_1183385.html.

Mitchell, Katharyne. 2016. "Celebrity Humanitarianism, Transnational Emotion and the Rise of Neoliberal Citizenship." *Global Networks* 16, no. 3: 288–306. https://doi.org/10.1111/glob.12114.

Mitchell, Katharyne. 2017. "'Factivism': A New Configuration of Humanitarian Reason." *Geopolitics* 22, no. 1: 110–28. https://doi.org/10.1080/14650045.2016.1185606.

Mitchell, Timothy. 1991. "The Limits of the State: Beyond Statist Approaches and Their Critics." *American Political Science Review* 85, no. 1: 77–96.

Mitchell, Timothy. 2002. *Rule of Experts: Egypt, Techno-Politics, Modernity.* Berkeley: Univ. of California Press.

Mittermaier, Amira. 2013. "Trading With God: Islam, Calculation, Excess." In *A Companion to the Anthropology of Religion*, edited by Janice Boddy and Michael Lambek, 274–300. London: Wiley-Blackwell.

Mittermaier, Amira. 2014. "Beyond Compassion: Islamic Voluntarism in Egypt." *American Ethnologist* 41, no. 3: 518–31. https://doi.org/10.1111/amet.12092.

Mittermaier, Amira. 2019. *Giving to God: Islamic Charity in Revolutionary Times.* Oakland: Univ. of California Press.

Mkandawire, Thandika. 2005. "Targeting and Universalism in Poverty Reduction." *United Nations Research Institute for Social Development*, no.

23 (December). https://www.eprionline.com/wp-content/uploads/2011/03/Mkandawire2005TargetingUniversalism.pdf.

Mohamad, Maznah. 2020. *The Divine Bureaucracy and Disenchantment of Social Life: A Study of Bureaucratic Islam in Malaysia*. Singapore: Springer.

Mohapatra, Aswini K. 2008. "Democratization in the Arab World: Relevance of the Turkish Model." *International Studies* 45, no. 4: 271–94.

Molyneux, Maxine. 2006. "Mothers at the Service of the New Poverty Agenda: Progresa/Oportunidades, Mexico's Conditional Transfer Programme." *Social Policy and Administration* 40, no. 4: 425–49. http://dx.doi.org/10.1111/j.1467-9515.2006.00497.x.

Moodie, Deonnie. 2021. "Retail Religion: Hinduism for a Neoliberal Age." *Journal of the American Academy of Religion* 89, no. 3: 863–84.

Moreton, Bethany. 2009. *To Serve God and Wal-Mart: The Making of Christian Free Enterprise*. Cambridge, MA: Harvard Univ. Press.

Morvaridi, Behrooz. 2013. "The Politics of Philanthropy and Welfare Governance: The Case of Turkey." *European Journal of Development Research* 25, no. 2: 305–21. http://dx.doi.org/10.1057/ejdr.2012.54.

Mostafanezhad, Mary. 2014. *Volunteer Tourism: Popular Humanitarianism in Neoliberal Times*. London: Routledge.

Moudouros, Nikos. 2014. "The 'Harmonization' of Islam with the Neoliberal Transformation: The Case of Turkey." *Globalizations* 11, no. 6: 843–57. https://doi.org/10.1080/14747731.2014.904157.

Moumtaz, Nada. 2018. "Theme Issue: A Third Wave of Waqf Studies." *Islamic Law and Society* 25, no. 1–2: 1–10. https://doi.org/10.1163/15685195-02512P01.

Moumtaz, Nada. 2021. *God's Property: Islam, Charity, and the Modern State*. Berkeley, CA: Univ. of California Press. https://doi.org/10.1525/luminos.100.

Muehlebach, Andrea. 2009. "Complexio Oppositorum: Notes on the Left in Neoliberal Italy." *Public Culture* 21, no. 3: 498. https://doi.org/10.1215/08992363-2009-005.

Muehlebach, Andrea. 2012. *The Moral Neoliberal: Welfare and Citizenship in Italy*. Chicago: Univ. of Chicago Press.

Mungiu-Pippidi, Alina. 2015. *The Quest for Good Governance: How Societies Develop Control of Corruption*. Cambridge: Cambridge Univ. Press.

Murinson, Alexander. 2006. "The Strategic Depth Doctrine of Turkish Foreign Policy." *Middle Eastern Studies* 42, no. 6: 945–64. http://dx.doi.org/10.1080/00263200600923526.

Musa, Eşref, Burak Karacaoğlu, and Levent Tok. 2019. "Türk Gönüllülerden Nijer'de Binlerce Kişiye Kurban Eti." *Anadolu Ajansı*, August 14, 2019. https://www.aa.com.tr/tr/dunya/turk-gonullulerden-nijerde-binlerce-kisiye -kurban-eti/1556660.

Müller, Dominik M. 2018. "Bureaucratic Islam Compared: Classificatory Power and State-ified Religious Meaning-Making in Brunei and Singapore." *Journal of Law and Religion* 33, no. 2: 212–47. https://doi.org/10.1017/jlr.2018.29.

Müller, Jan-Werner. 2016. *What Is Populism?* London: Penguin.

Mürsel, Safa. "Toplumsal Kalkınma Zekatla Olur." *Nur Dergi*, accessed March 2, 2019, http://www.nurdergi.com/ilahiyat/2056-toplumsal-kalkinma-zekatla -olur.html. Site inactive on July 20, 2023.

"Müslüman Depresyona Girer Mi?" 2012. *İslami Hayat.* http://islamihayatdergisi .com/konular/detay/mslman-depresyona-girer-mi. Site inactive on July 20, 2023.

"Müslümanlar da Depresyona Girer." 2021. *Camia Haber*, February 5, 2021. https://camiahaber.com/2021/02/05/muslumanlar-da-depresyona-girer/.

Nacar, Can. 2009. "'Our Lives Were Not as Valuable as an Animal': Workers in State-Run Industries in World-War-II Turkey." *International Review of Social History* 54, no. 17: 143–66. https://doi.org/10.1017/S0020859009990277.

Nanda, Ved P. 2006. "The 'Good Governance' Concept Revisited." *ANNALS of the American Academy of Political and Social Science* 603, no. 1: 269–83. https://doi.org/10.1177/0002716205282847.

Narince, Mehmet. 2004. *Cumhuriyet'in 80. Yılında Uluslararası Vakıf Sempozyumu Kitabı: 15–17 Aralık 2003*. Ankara: Vakıflar Genel Müdürlüğü Yayınları.

Narlı, Nilüfer. 1999. "The Rise of the Islamist Movement in Turkey." *Middle East Review of International Affairs* 3, no. 3: 38–48.

Nasr, Vali. 2009. *The Rise of Islamic Capitalism: Why the New Muslim Middle Class Is the Key to Defeating Extremism*. New York: Free Press.

Navaro-Yashin, Yael. 1998. "Uses and Abuses of 'State and Civil Society' in Contemporary Turkey." *New Perspectives on Turkey* 18, no. 2: 1–22.

Navaro-Yashin, Yael. 2000. "'Evde Taylorizm': Türkiye Cumhuriyeti'nin İlk Yıllarında Evişinin Rasyonelleşmesi." *Toplum ve Bilim* 84: 53–74.

Navaro-Yashin, Yael. 2002. *Faces of the State: Secularism and Public Life in Turkey*. Princeton, NJ: Princeton Univ. Press.

Nickel, Patricia Mooney, and Angela M. Eikenberry. 2009. "A Critique of the Discourse of Marketized Philanthropy." *American Behavioral Scientist* 52, no. 7: 974–89.

"Nijer'e Cansuyu." 2013. *Cansuyu Derneği*, February 1, 2013. https://cansuyu.org.tr/nijere-cansuyu-tr-2153.html.

Oberauer, Norbert. 2008. "'Fantastic Charities': The Transformation of Waqf Practice in Colonial Zanzibar." *Islamic Law and Society* 15: 315–70. http://dx.doi.org/10.1163/156851908X366156.

Ong, Aihwa, and Stephen J. Collier. 2004. *Global Assemblages: Technology, Politics, and Ethics as Anthropological Problems*. London: Blackwell Publishers.

Ongur, Hakan Övünç. 2015. "Identifying Ottomanisms: The Discursive Evolution of Ottoman Pasts in the Turkish Presents." *Middle Eastern Studies* 51, no. 3: 416–32. https://doi.org/10.1080/00263206.2014.976622.

Oomen, Wouter, Emiel Martens, and Anna Piccoli. 2021. "The Neoliberal Workings of the Family Meal Campaign: Unfortunate Others, European Citizens, and the Branding of the EU." *European Journal of Cultural Studies*, 24, no. 1: 295–313. https://doi.org/10.1177/1367549420919851.

Orgad, Shani. 2013. "Visualizers of Solidarity: Organizational Politics in Humanitarian and International Development NGOs." *Visual Communication* 12, no. 3: 295–314. https://doi.org/10.1177/1470357213483057.

Orgad, Shani, and Bruna Irene Seu. 2014. "'Intimacy at a distance' in Humanitarian Communication." *Media, Culture and Society* 36, no. 7: 916-934

Oruç, Emine. 2010. "Tüketim Toplumu Mu Tüketen Toplumu Mu?" (Ankara, *Bir Damla Sosyal Yardımlaşma ve Dayanışma Derneği Faaliyet Bülteni*).

Osella, Filippo, and Caroline Osella. 2009. "Muslim Entrepreneurs in Public Life between India and the Gulf: Making Good and Doing Good." *Journal of the Royal Anthropological Institute* 15, no. 1: 202–21. http://dx.doi.org/10.1111/j.1467-9655.2009.01550.x.

Öktem, Kerem, and Cansu Erdoğan. 2019. "Between Welfare State and (State-Organised) Charity: How Turkey's Social Assistance Regime Blends Two Competing Policy Paradigms." *International Journal of Sociology and Social Policy* 40, no. 3–4: 205–19. https://doi.org/10.1108/IJSSP-11-2018-0217.

Öncü, Ayşe. 2010. "Narratives of Istanbul's Ottoman Heritage." In *Spatial Conceptions of the Nation: Modernizing Geographies in Greece and Turkey*, edited by Nikiforos Diamandourus, Thalia Dragonas, and Çağlar Keyder, 205–271. London and New York: I. B. Tauris.

Önder, Nilgün. 1998. "Integrating with the Global Market: The State and the Crisis of Political Representation Turkey in the 1980s and 1990s." *International Journal of Political Economy* 28, no. 2: 44–84. https://doi.org/10.1080/08911916.1998.11643965.

Öniş, Ziya. 1997. "The Political Economy of Islamic Resurgence in Turkey: The Rise of the Welfare Party in Perspective." *Third World Quarterly* 18, no.4: 743–66. https://doi.org/10.1080/01436599714740.

Öniş, Ziya. 2001. "Political Islam at the Crossroads: From Hegemony to Co-Existence." *Contemporary Politics* 7, no. 4: 281–98. https://doi.org/10.1080 /13569770120106435.

Öniş, Ziya. 2004. "Turgut Özal and His Economic Legacy: Turkish Neo-Liberalism in Critical Perspective." *Middle Eastern Studies* 40, no. 4: 113–34. http://dx .doi.org/10.1080/00263200410001700338.

"Özal: Sosyal Dayanışma Bizde Batıdan Farklı." 1986. *Hürriyet*, June 2, 1986.

Özaral, Başak. 2012. "Islam and the Moral Economy." In *The Sociology of Islam: Secularism, Economy, and Politics*, edited by Tugrul Keskin, 21–45. New York: Ithaca Press.

Özbay, Cenk, Maral Erol, Z. Umut Türem, and Ayşecan Terzioğlu. 2016. *The Making of Neoliberal Turkey*. New York: Routledge.

Özbek, Müge. 2010. "The Regulation of Prostitution in Beyoğlu (1875–1915)." *Middle Eastern Studies* 46, no. 4: 555–68. http://dx.doi.org/10.1080/002632 06.2010.492991.

Özbek, Nadir. 1999. "The Politics of Poor Relief in the Late Ottoman Empire, 1876–1914." *New Perspectives on Turkey* 21: 1–33.

Özbek, Nadir. 2003. "Imperial Gifts and Sultanic Legitimation during the Late Ottoman Empire, 1876–1909." In *Poverty and Charity in Middle Eastern Contexts*, edited by Michael Bonner, Mine Ener, and Amy Singer, 203–23. Albany: State Univ. of New York Press.

Özbek, Nadir. 2006. *Social Security and Social Policy in Republican Turkey*. Istanbul: Tarih Vakfı Yayınları.

Özbek, Nadir. 2009. "'Beggars' and 'Vagrants' in Ottoman State Policy and Public Discourse, 1876–1914." *Middle Eastern Studies* 45, no. 5: 783–801. https:// doi.org/10.1080/00263200903135570.

Özbudun, Ergun. 2006. "From Political Islam to Conservative Democracy: The Case of the Justice and Development Party in Turkey." *South European Society and Politics* 11, no. 3–4: 543–57. https://doi.org/10.1080/13608740600856561.

Özcan, Emrah. 2017. "Unutulan Gelenek 'Sadaka Taşı.'" August 25, 2017. https:// evrenseldegerler.org.tr/unutulan-gelenek-sadaka-tasi/.

Özcan, Serpil. 2014. "Fıtır ve Sadaka Taşları." *Kadın ve Aile* 19. https://www .kadinveaile.com/fitir-ve-sadaka-taslari/.

Özdemir, Seçkin Sertdemir, Nil Mutluer, and Esra Özyürek. 2019. "Exile and Plurality in Neoliberal Times: Turkey's Academics for Peace." *Public Culture* 31, no. 2: 235–59. https://doi.org/10.1215/08992363-7286801.

Özdemir, Yonca. 2020. "AKP's Neoliberal Populism and Contradictions of New Social Policies in Turkey." *Contemporary Politics* 26, no. 3: 245–67.

Özel, Işık, and Kerem Yıldırım. 2019. "Political Consequences of Welfare Regimes: Social Assistance and Support for Presidentialism in Turkey." *South European Society and Politics* 24, no. 4: 485–511.

Özkan, Behlül. 2014. "Turkey, Davutoğlu and the Idea of Pan-Islamism." *Survival: Global Politics and Strategy* 56, no. 4: 119–40. https://doi.org/10.1080/00396338.2014.941570.

Özkan, Mehmet. 2012. "A New Actor or Passer-By? The Political Economy of Turkey's Engagement with Africa." *Journal of Balkan and Near Eastern Studies* 14, no. 1: 113–33. https://doi.org/10.1080/19448953.2012.656968.

Özpek, Burak Bilgehan, and Nebahat Tanrıverdi Yaşar. 2018. "Populism and Foreign Policy in Turkey under the AKP Rule." *Turkish Studies* 19, no. 2: 198–216. https://doi.org/10.1080/14683849.2017.1400912.

Öztürk, Nazif. 2005. "İslam ve Türk Kültüründe Vakıflar." *Vakıflar Dergisi* 29: 7–20.

Pak Lei Chong, Gladys. 2011. "Volunteers as the 'New' Model Citizens: Governing Citizens through Soft Power." *China Information* 25, no. 1: 33–59. https://doi.org/10.1177/0920203X10393212.

Paker, Hande. 2005. "Particularistic Interactions: State (In)Capacity, Civil Society, and Disaster Management." In *Environmentalism in Turkey: Between Democracy and Development*, edited by Fikret Adaman and Murat Arsel, 291–306. New York: Ashgate Publishing.

Paker, Hande. 2017. "The 'Politics of Serving' and Neoliberal Developmentalism: The Megaprojects of the AKP as Tools of Hegemony Building." In *Neoliberal Turkey and Its Discontents: Economic Policy and the Environment under Erdogan*, edited by Fikret Adaman, Bengi Akbulut, and Murat Arsel, 103–19. London and New York: I. B. Tauris and Co.

Pamuk, Şevket. 1981. "Political economy of industrialization in Turkey." *MERIP Reports* 93: 26–32. https://doi.org/10.2307/3011660.

Pamuk, Şevket. 2000. "Turkey's Response to the Great Depression in Comparative Perspective, 1929–1939." Working Paper 21. European University Institute. https://cadmus.eui.eu//handle/1814/1661.

Pandya, Sophia, Brenda Oliden, and Ibrahim Aytaç Anlı. 2021. "Shunned and Purged: Turkey's Crackdown on the Hizmet (Gülen) Movement." In *Human Rights in Turkey: Assaults on Human Dignity*, edited by Hasan Aydın and Winston Langley, 199–225. Cham, Switzerland: Springer International Publishing. https://doi.org/10.1007/978-3-030-57476-5_10.

Parry, Jonathan. 2000. "The 'Crisis of Corruption' and 'The Idea of India': A Worm's Eye View." In *Morals of Legitimacy: Between Agency and System*, edited by Italo Pardo, 27–55. New York: Berghahn Books.

Patton, Marcie J. 2009. "The Synergy between Neoliberalism and Communitarianism: 'Erdoğan's Third Way.'" *Comparative Studies of South Asia, Africa, and the Middle East* 29, no. 3: 438–49. http://dx.doi.org/10.1215/1089201X-2009-030.

Peck, Jaime. 2013. "Explaining (with) Neoliberalism." *Territory, Politics, Governance* 1, no. 2: 132–57. https://doi.org/10.1080/21622671.2013.785365.

Peri, Oded. 1992. "Waqf and Ottoman Welfare Policy." *Journal of the Economic and Social History of the Orient* 35, no. 2: 167–86. https://doi.org/10.1163/156852092X00093.

Petersen, Marie Juul. 2015. *For Humanity or for the Umma? Aid and Islam in Transnational Muslim NGOs*. Oxford: Oxford Univ. Press.

Petras, James. 1997. "Imperialism and NGOs in Latin America." *Monthly Review* 49, no. 7: 10–27. https://doi.org/10.14452/MR-049-07-1997-11_2.

Pianciola, Niccolo, and Paolo Sartori. 2007. "Waqf in Turkestan: The Colonial Legacy and the Fate of an Islamic Institution in Early Soviet Central Asia, 1917–1924." *Central Asian Survey* 26, no. 4: 475–98. http://dx.doi.org/10.1080/02634930802017929.

Pioppi, Daniela. 2004. "From Religious Charity to the Welfare State and Back: The Case of Islamic Endowments (Waqfs) Revival in Egypt." Working Paper 34. European University Institute.

Piotukh, Volha. 2015. *Biopolitics, Governmentality and Humanitarianism: 'Caring' for the Population in Afghanistan and Belarus*. London and New York: Routledge.

Pollard, Jane, and Michael Samers. 2007. "Islamic Banking and Finance: Postcolonial Political Economy and the Decentring of Economic Geography." *Transactions of the Institute of British Geographers* 32, no. 3: 313–30. http://dx.doi.org/10.1111/j.1475-5661.2007.00255.x.

Powell, Martin, and Erdem Yörük. 2017. "Straddling Two Continents and beyond Three Worlds? The Case of Turkey's Welfare Regime." *New Perspectives on Turkey* 57: 85–114.

Powers, David. 1989. "Orientalism, Colonialism, and Legal History: The At-tack on Muslim Family Endowments in Algeria and India." *Comparative Studies in Society and History* 31, no. 3: 535–71. https://doi.org/10.1017/S00 10417500016030.

Procacci, Giovanna. 1991. "Social Economy and the Government of Poverty." In *The Foucault Effect: Studies in Governmentality*, edited by Graham Burchell, Colin Gordon, and Peter Miller, 151–68. Chicago: Univ. of Chicago Press.

Rabinow, Paul. 1989. *French Modern: Norms and Forms of the Social Environment*. Chicago: Univ. of Chicago Press.

Razavi, Shahra. 2007. "The Return to Social Policy and the Persistent Neglect of Unpaid Care." *Development and Change* 38, no. 3: 377–400. http://dx.doi .org/10.1111/j.1467-7660.2007.00416.x.

Reid-Henry, Simon M. 2014. "Humanitarianism as Liberal Diagnostic: Humanitarian Reason and the Political Rationalities of the Liberal Will-to-Care." *Transactions of the Institute of British Geographers* 39, no. 3: 418–31. http:// dx.doi.org/10.1111/tran.12029.

Rethel, Lena. 2011. "Whose Legitimacy? Islamic Finance and the Global Financial Order." *Review of International Political Economy* 18, no. 1: 75–98. https://doi.org/10.1080/09692290902983999.

Romano, Yalkın, and Mehmet Penpecioğlu. 2009. "Yoksulluktan Yeni Yoksulluğa: Türkiye'de Kent Yoksulluğunun Değişen Dinamikleri Üzerine Bir İnceleme." *Toplum ve Demokrasi* 3, no. 5: 135–150.

Rose, Nikolas. 1990. *Governing the Soul: The Shaping of the Private Self*. Florence: Routledge.

Rose, Nikolas. 1996. "The Death of the Social? Refiguring the Territory of Government." *Economy and Society* 25, no. 3: 327–56. https://doi.org/10.1080/03 085149600000018.

Rosol, Marit. 2012. "Community Volunteering as Neoliberal Strategy? Green Space Production in Berlin." *Antipode* 44, no. 1: 239–57. http://dx.doi.org /10.1111/j.1467-8330.2011.00861.x.

Roy, Ananya. 2010. *Poverty Capital: Microfinance and the Making of Development*. New York and London: Routledge.

Roy, Sara. 2011. *Hamas and Civil Society in Gaza: Engaging the Islamist Social Sector*. Princeton, NJ: Princeton Univ. Press.

Rozakou, Katerina. 2016. "Crafting the Volunteer: Voluntary Associations and the Reformation of Sociality." *Journal of Modern Greek Studies* 34, no. 1: 79–102. https://doi.org/10.1353/mgs.2016.0014.

Ruckert, Arne, Laura Macdonald, and Kristina R. Proulx. 2017. "Post-Neoliberalism in Latin America: A Conceptual Review." *Third World Quarterly* 38, no. 7: 1583–1602. https://doi.org/10.1080/01436597.2016.1259558.

Rudnyckyj, Daromir. 2010. *Spiritual Economies: Islam, Globalization, and the Afterlife of Development*. Ithaca, NY: Cornell Univ. Press.

Rudnyckyj, Daromir. 2011. "Circulating Tears and Managing Hearts: Governing through Affect in an Indonesian Steel Factory." *Anthropological Quarterly* 11, no. 1: 63–87. http://dx.doi.org/10.1177/1463499610395444.

Sabra, Adam. 2000. *Poverty and Charity in Medieval Islam: Mamluk Egypt, 1250–1517*. Cambridge: Cambridge Univ. Press.

Saeed, Seevan. 2019. "The Dilemma of the Kurdish Struggle in Turkey." *Journal of Balkan and Near Eastern Studies* 21, no. 3: 274–85. https://doi.org/10.1080/19448953.2018.1497752.

Sayan-Cengiz, Feyda. 2020. "Gender in Turkey's Islamic Oriented Self-Help Literature: Constructing Self-Regulating Female Subjectivity." *International Journal of Communication* 14: 5499–5517.

Sayarı, Sabri. 2010. "Political Violence and Terrorism in Turkey, 1976–80: A Retrospective Analysis." *Terrorism and Political Violence* 22, no. 2: 198–215. https://doi.org/10.1080/09546550903574438.

Scharff, Christina. 2016. "The Psychic Life of Neoliberalism: Mapping the Contours of Entrepreneurial Subjectivity." *Theory, Culture and Society* 33, no. 6: 107–22.

Scherz, China. 2013. "Let Us Make God Our Banker: Ethics, Temporality, and Agency in a Ugandan Charity Home." *American Ethnologist* 40, no. 4: 624–36. https://doi.org/10.1111/amet.12043.

Schielke, Samuli. 2009. "Being Good in Ramadan: Ambivalence, Fragmentation, and the Moral Self in the Lives of Young Egyptians." *Journal of the Royal Anthropological Institute* 15, no. 1: 24–40. http://dx.doi.org/10.1111/j.1467-9655.2009.01540.x.

Secor, Anna. 2011. "Turkey's Democracy: A Model for the Troubled Middle East?" *Eurasian Geography and Economics* 52, no. 2: 157–72.

Selçuk, Orçun. 2016. "Strong Presidents and Weak Institutions: Populism in Turkey, Venezuela and Ecuador." *Southeast European and Black Sea Studies* 16, no. 4: 571–89. https://doi.org/10.1080/14683857.2016.1242893.

Seu, Irene Bruna, and Shani Orgad. 2017. *Caring in Crisis? Humanitarianism, the Public and NGOs*. London: Palgrave Macmillan.

Sevim, Nidayı. 2010. *Medeniyetimizde Toplumsal Dayanışma ve Sadaka Taşları.* Istanbul: Kitap Dostu.

Sevim, Nidayi. 2014. "Sadaka Taşları." Antoloji.com, November 20, 2014. https://www.antoloji.com/sadaka-taslari-siiri/.

Shamir, Ronen. 2008. "The Age of Responsibilization: On Market-Embedded Morality." *Economy and Society* 37, no. 1: 1–19. https://doi.org/10.1080/0308 5140701760833.

Shefer, Miri. 2003. "Charity and Hospitality: Hospitals in the Ottoman Empire in the Early Modern Period." In *Poverty and Charity in Middle Eastern Contexts,* edited by Amy Singer, Michael Bonner, and Mine Ener, 121–43. Albany: State Univ. of New York Press.

Shivji, Issa G. 2007. *Silences in NGO Discourse: The Role and Future of NGOs in Africa.* Oxford: Fahamu Books.

Shue, Vivienne. 2011. "The Political Economy of Compassion: China's 'Charity Supermarket' Saga." *Journal of Contemporary China* 20, no. 72: 751–72. https://doi.org/10.1080/10670564.2011.604493.

Simon, Gregory. 2009. "The Soul Freed of Cares? Islamic Prayer, Subjectivity, and the Contradictions of Moral Selfhood in Minangkabau, Indonesia." *American Ethnologist* 36, no. 2: 258–75. https://doi.org/10.1111/j.1548-1425 .2009.01134.x.

Simpson, Kate. 2005. "Dropping out or Signing Up? The Professionalization of Youth Travel." *Antipode* 37, no. 3: 447–69. https://doi.org/10.1111/j.0066-4812 .2005.00506.x.

"Sincan'da Sosyal Market Açıldı." 2010. *Dayanışma Dergisi* 8: 9–12.

Singer, Amy. 2006. "Soup and Sadaqa: Charity in Islamic Societies." *Historical Research* 79, no. 205: 306–24. http://dx.doi.org/10.1111/j.1468-2281.2006.00 363.x.

Singer, Amy. 2008. *Charity in Islamic Societies.* Cambridge: Cambridge Univ. Press.

Singer, Amy. 2011. "The Persistence of Philanthropy." *Comparative Studies of South Asia, Africa, and the Middle East* 31, no. 3: 557–68. https://doi.org/10 .1215/1089201X-1426737.

Singer, Amy. 2012. *Constructing Ottoman Beneficence: An Imperial Soup Kitchen in Jerusalem.* Albany: State Univ. of New York Press.

Singer, Amy. 2018. "Replace Stasis with Motion to Fathom the Persistence of Waqf: The Complex Histories and Legacies of a Muslim Institution." *The Muslim World* 108, no. 4: 702–16. https://doi.org/10.1111/muwo.12270.

Sloane-White, Patricia. 2017. *Corporate Islam: Sharia and the Modern Workplace*. Cambridge: Cambridge Univ. Press.

Somers, Margaret. 2008. *Genealogies of Citizenship: Markets, Statelessness, and the Right to Have Rights*. Cambridge: Cambridge Univ. Press.

"Sosyal Inceleme Formu." *Deniz Feneri Sosyal Yardımlaşma ve Dayanışma Derneği*, accessed January 18, 2017. http://sisnet.denizfeneri.org.tr/_docs/form.pdf. Site inactive on July 20, 2023.

"Sosyal Koruma ve Gelir Dağılımı Göstergeleri." 2018. *Türkiye Cumhuriyeti Cumhurbaşkanlığı*, accessed January 11, 2021. https://www.sbb.gov.tr/sosyal-koruma-ve-gelir-dagilimi-gostergeleri/.

"Sosyal Medyayı Karıştıran Fotoğraf: Şov Gibi Yardım Yapılır Mı!" 2015. *Hürriyet*, July 14, 2015. https://www.hurriyet.com.tr/gundem/sosyal-medyayi-karistiran-fotograf-sov-gibi-yardim-yapilir-mi-29547760.

"Sosyal Yardım Kartı Yardımı." n.d. *Sakarya Belediyesi*. https://sgm.sakarya.bel.tr/Hizmetler/HizmetDetay/29/4.

"Sosyal Yardım Sistemi Değişiyor." 2012. CNNTURK, January 18, 2012. http://www.cnnturk.com/2012/turkiye/01/18/sosyal.yardim.sistemi.degisiyor/645415.0/. Site inactive on July 20, 2023.

"Sosyal Yardımlaşma ve Dayanışma Vakıfları." Aile, Çalışma ve Sosyal Hizmetler Bakanlığı, accessed September 29, 2020. https://www.ailevecalisma.gov.tr/sygm/genel-mudurluk/sosyal-yardimlasma-ve-dayanisma-vakiflari/. Site inactive on July 20, 2023.

"Sosyal Yardımlaşma ve Dayanışma Vakıfları Personel Eğitimi Başladı." 2009. *Dayanışma Dergisi* 2: 8–11.

Sözer, Hande. 2020. "Humanitarianism with a Neo-Liberal Face: Vulnerability Intervention as Vulnerability Redistribution." *Journal of Ethnic and Migration Studies* 46, no. 11: 2163–80. https://doi.org/10.1080/1369183X.2019.1573661.

Steinmetz, George. 1993. *Regulating the Social: The Welfare State and Local Politics in Imperial Germany*. Princeton, NJ: Princeton Univ. Press.

Stewart, Kathleen. 2007. *Ordinary Affects*. Durham, NC: Duke Univ. Press.

Strathern, Marilyn. 2000. *Audit Cultures: Anthropological Studies in Accountability, Ethics, and the Academy*. New York: Routledge.

Sunar, Lütfi. 2018. "Türkiye'de İslami STK'ların Kurumsal Yapı ve Faaliyetlerinin Değişimi." Kurumsal Yönetim Akademisi Araştırma Raporları:1. Istanbul: İlke Yayınları.

"Suriye'ye Kış Yardım Kampanyası." 2019. *Medeniyet Vakfı*, January 8, 2019. http://www.medeniyetvakfi.org/vakif/ana-sayfa/guencel-haberler/suriye -ye-kis-yardim-kampanyasi.

Swynegedouw, Erik. 2005. "Governance Innovation and the Citizen: The Janus Face of Governance-beyond-the-State." *Urban Studies* 11: 1991–2006.

"SYD Vakıfları Sivil Toplum Kuruluşlarının Ufkunu Açıyor." 2010. *Dayanışma Dergisi* 9: 69–74.

Szekely, Ora. 2015. "Doing Well by Doing Good: Understanding Hamas's Social Services as Political Advertising." *Studies in Conflict and Terrorism* 38, no. 4: 275–92.

"Şahinbey'de Fakirin Bayramlığı Sosyal Market'ten." 2014. *Son Dakika*, July 25, 2014. https://www.sondakika.com/haber/haber-sahinbey-de-fakirin-bayramligi -sosyal-marketten-6302871/.

Şehlikoğlu, Sertaç. 2021. *Working Out Desire: Women, Sport and Self-Making in Istanbul.* Syracuse, NY: Syracuse Univ. Press.

Şimşek, Sefa. 2004. "The Transformation of Civil Society in Turkey: From Quantity to Quality." *Turkish Studies* 5, no. 3: 46–74. https://doi.org/10.1080/1468 384042000270326.

Tabakoğlu, Ahmet. 2006. "Osmanlı Sosyal Devlet Anlayışı." *Sosyal Politikalar Dergisi* 1: 76–82.

Tachau, Frank, and Metin Heper. 1983. "The State, Politics and the Military in Turkey." *Comparative Politics* 16, no. 1: 17–33. https://doi.org/10.2307 /421593.

Tan, Evrim. 2020. "Quo Vadis? The Local Government in Turkey after Public Management Reforms." *International Review of Administrative Sciences* 86, no. 1: 115–33. https://doi.org/10.1177%2F0020852317752268.

Tarhan, Nevzat. 2007. "İyilik Yap, Huzur Bul." *Diyalog Avrasya Platformu DA Dergisi* 27: 28–33.

Taş, Hakkı. 2017. "A History of Turkey's AKP-Gülen Conflict." *Mediterranean Politics* 23, no. 3: 395–402. https://doi.org/10.1080/13629395.2017.1328766.

Taş, Hakkı. 2020. "The Chronopolitics of National Populism." *Identities: Global Studies in Culture and Power* 18, no. 1: 1–19. https://doi.org/10.1080/10702 89X.2020.1735160.

Taşcı, Faruk. 2014. "A Psycho-Social Solution to Problems Related to Social Assistance Recipients: 'Sadaqa Stones Modeling.'" *İktisat Fakültesi Mecmuası* 64, no. 2: 89–108.

Taşcı, Faruk. 2017. *Türkiye'de Sosyal Politika ve Dönüşüm: Zihniyet, Aktörler, Uygulamalar.* Istanbul: SETA Siyaset, Ekonomi ve Toplum Araştırmaları Vakfı Yayınları.

Taşgetiren, Ahmet. 2009. "Evrensel Sorumluluk Şuuru." *Altınoluk Dergisi* 284: 6.

Taylor, Christopher. 2018. "Receipts and Other Forms of Islamic Charity: Accounting for Piety in Modern North India." *Modern Asian Studies* 52, no. 1: 266–96. https://doi.org/10.1017/S0026749X17000221.

Taylor, Ian. 2004. "Hegemony, Neoliberal 'Good Governance' and the International Monetary Fund: A Gramscian Perspective." In *Global Institutions and Development: Framing the World?*, edited by Morten Boas and Desmond McNeill, 124–136. London and New York: Routledge.

"10 Bin Kişiye Sosyal Kart." 2010. *Konya Yenigün Gazetesi*, August 11, 2010. http://www.konyayenigun.com/bolge/10-bin-kisiye-sosyal-kart-h17273.html.

Tepe, Sultan. 2005. "Turkey's AKP: A Model 'Muslim-Democratic' Party?" *Journal of Democracy* 16, no. 3: 69–82.

Ticktin, Miriam. 2011. *Casualties of Care: Immigration and the Politics of Humanitarianism in France.* Berkeley: Univ. of California Press.

Tobin, Sarah A. 2016. *Everyday Piety: Islam and Economy in Jordan.* Ithaca, NY: Cornell Univ. Press.

Tokdoğan, Nagehan. 2020. "Reading Politics through Emotions: Ontological Ressentiment as the Emotional Basis of Current Politics in Turkey." *Nations and Nationalism* 26, no. 2: 388–406. https://doi.org/10.1111/nana.12546.

Tol, Gönül. 2012. "The 'Turkish Model' in the Middle East." *Current History* 111, no. 749: 350–5.

Topbaş, Osman Nuri. 2008. *Medeniyetimizin Fazilet Zirvelerinden: Vakıf, İnfak, Hizmet.* Istanbul: Erkam Yayınları.

Topkara, Selma. n.d. "İyilik Yapma Psikolojisi." *Deniz Feneri Sosyal Yardımlaşma ve Dayanışma Derneği.* http://www.denizfeneri.org.tr/kurumsal/iyilik-yapma-psikolojisi_78/.

Tsing, Anna. 2005. *Friction: An Ethnography of Global Connection.* Princeton Univ. Press.

Tuğal, Cihan. 2009. *Passive Revolution: Absorbing the Islamic Challenge to Capitalism.* Stanford, CA: Stanford Univ. Press.

Tuğal, Cihan. 2013. "Contesting Benevolence: Market Orientations among Muslim Aid Providers in Egypt." *Qualitative Sociology* 36, no. 2: 141–59. https://doi.org/10.1007/s11133-013-9248-6.

Tuğal, Cihan. 2017a. *Caring for the Poor: Islamic and Christian Benevolence in a Liberal World*. London and New York: Routledge.

Tuğal, Cihan. 2017b. "The Uneven Neoliberalization of Good Works: Islamic Charitable Fields and Their Impact on Diffusion." *American Journal of Sociology* 123, no. 2: 426–64. https://doi.org/10.1086/692706.

Tunç, Tanfer Emin, and Gökhan Tunç. 2021. "Wonderland Eurasia: Theme Parks and Neo-Ottoman Identity Politics in Ankara, Turkey." *Popular Entertainment Studies* 11, no. 1–2: 93–113.

Turner, Lewis. 2020. "'#Refugees Can Be Entrepreneurs Too!' Humanitarianism, Race, and the Marketing of Syrian Refugees." *Review of International Studies* 46, no. 1: 137–55. https://doi.org/10.1017/S0260210519000342.

"2 Milyon Yoksula Özel Kart." 2013. *Hürriyet*, July 3, 2013. https://www.hurriyet.com.tr/ekonomi/2-milyon-yoksula-ozel-kart-23639761.

"2006 Vakıf Medeniyeti Yılı." 2006. *İstanbul Büyükşehir Belediyesi, İSMEK Hayat Boyu Öğrenme Merkezi*, April 4, 2006. https://www.ismek.ist/tr/haber_detay.aspx?RegID=162&c. Site inactive on July 20, 2023.

Türem, Z. Umut. 2016. "Engineering Competition and Competitive Subjectivities: 'Self' and Political Economy in Neoliberal Turkey." In *The Making of Neoliberal Turkey*, edited by Cenk Özbay, Maral Erol, Z. Umut Türem, and Ayşecan Terzioğlu, 33–52. New York: Routledge.

Uğur, Etga. 2004. "Intellectual Roots of 'Turkish Islam' and Approaches to the 'Turkish Model.'" *Journal of Muslim Minority Affairs* 24, no. 2: 328–45.

"Vakıf Geleneği, Kardeşliğimizin En Kuvvetli Bağını Oluşturuyor." 2015. *Türkiye Cumhuriyeti Cumhurbaşkanlığı*, June 28, 2015. https://www.tccb.gov.tr/haberler/410/32806/vakif-gelenegi-kardesligimizin-en-kuvvetli-bagini-olusturuyor.html.

Van Doorn-Harder, Pieternella. 2006. *Women Shaping Islam: Indonesian Women Reading the Quran*. Champaign: Univ. of Illinois Press.

Vassallo, Stephen. 2020. *Neoliberal Selfhood*. Cambridge: Cambridge Univ. Press.

Venkatachalam, Meera. 2019. "Turkey in Africa: Voyeurism, Neo-Ottomanism and Islamic Humanitarianism." ASC Working Paper 145. Leiden: African Studies Centre.

Verdouw, Julia Joanne. 2017. "The Subject Who Thinks Economically? Comparative Money Subjectivities in Neoliberal Context." *Journal of Sociology* 53, no. 3: 523–40.

Vestergaard, Anne. 2010. "Identity and Appeal in the Humanitarian Brand." In *Media, Organizations and Identity*, edited by Lilie Chouliaraki and Mette Morsing, 168–84. London: Palgrave Macmillan.

Vicini, Fabio. 2020. "'Worship Is Not Everything': Volunteering and Muslim Life in Modern Turkey." In *Muslim Subjectivities in Global Modernity: Islamic Traditions and the Construction of Modern Muslim Identities*, edited by Dietrich Jung and Kristine Sinclair, 97–120. Leiden: Brill.

Villadsen, Kaspar. 2011. "Neo-Philanthropy." *Social Work and Society* 9, no. 2: 1–3.

Wacquant, Loïc. 2012. "Three Steps to a Historical Anthropology of Actually Existing Neoliberalism." *Social Anthropology* 20, no. 1: 66–79.

Walters, William. 2004. "Some Critical Notes on 'Governance.'" *Studies in Political Economy* 73, no. 1: 27–46. https://doi.org/10.1080/19187033.2004.11675150.

Walton, Jeremy. 2010. "Practices of Neo-Ottomanism: Making Space and Place Virtuous in Istanbul." In *Orienting Istanbul: Cultural Capital of Europe*, edited by Deniz Göktürk, Levent Soysal, and İpek Türeli, 88–104. London: Routledge.

Walton, Jeremy. 2017. *Muslim Civil Society and the Politics of Religious Freedom in Turkey*. New York: Oxford Univ. Press.

Ware, Alan. 2011. "The Big Society and Conservative Politics: Back to the Future or Forward to the Past?" *Political Quarterly* 82, no. s1: 82–97. https://doi.org/10.1111/j.1467-923X.2011.02335.x.

Wedeen, Lisa. 2002. "Conceptualizing Culture: Possibilities for Political Science." *American Political Science Review* 96, no. 4: 713–28. https://doi.org/10.1017/S0003055402000400.

White, Jenny. 1997. "Pragmatists or Ideologues? Turkey's Welfare Party in Power." *Current History* 96, no. 606: 25–30.

White, Jenny. 2002. *Islamist Mobilization in Turkey: A Study in Vernacular Politics*. Seattle: Univ. of Washington Press.

White, Jenny. 2012a. "Islamist Social Networks and Social Welfare Services in Turkey." In *Islamist Politics in the Middle East: Movements and Change*, edited by Samer S. Shehata, 59–68. London and New York: Routledge.

White, Jenny. 2012b. *Muslim Nationalism and the New Turks*. Princeton, NJ: Princeton Univ. Press.

Wilkinson, Michael. 2016. "The Prosperity Gospel and the Globalization of American Capitalism." In *Religious Activism in the Global Economy: Promoting, Reforming, or Resisting Neoliberal Globalization?* edited by Sabine Dreher and Peter J. Smith, 57–73. London and New York: Rowman and Littlefield.

Willner, Lauren. 2019. "Organizational Legitimacy and Managerialism within Social Justice Nonprofit Organizations: An Interest Divergence Analysis." *Administrative Theory and Praxis* 41, no. 3: 225–44.

Woods, Ngaire. 2000. "The Challenge of Good Governance for the IMF and the World Bank Themselves." *World Development* 28, no. 5: 823–41. https://doi.org/10.1016/S0305-750X(99)00156-4.

Yabancı, Bilge. 2016. "Populism as the Problem Child of Democracy: The AKP's Enduring Appeal and the Use of Meso-Level Actors." *Southeast European and Black Sea Studies* 16, no. 4: 591–617. https://doi.org/10.1080/14683857.2016.1242204.

Yağcı, Cahide Hayrünnisa. 2010. "'EDİM Hayır Market' Proje Birincisi Oldu!" *TimeTurk*, April 12, 2010. https://www.timeturk.com/tr/2010/04/12/edim-hayir-market-proje-birincisi-oldu.html.

Yang, Jie. 2014. *The Political Economy of Affect and Emotion in East Asia*. London and New York: Routledge.

Yanık, Lerna. 2016. "Bringing the Empire Back in: The Gradual Discovery of the Ottoman Empire in Turkish Foreign Policy." *Die Welt des Islams* 56, no. 3–4: 466–88. https://doi.org/10.1163/15700607-05634p09.

Yanow, Dvora, and Peregrime Schwartz-Shea, eds. 2006. *Interpretation and Method: Empirical Research Methods and the Interpretive Turn*. Armonk, NY: Sharpe.

Yaran, Rahmi. 2016. "Allah'ın ve Peygamber'in Emri, Toplumsal Huzurun Anahtarı: İnfak, Sadaka, Zekat." *Din ve Hayat* 29: 4–7.

Yarar, Betül. 2021. "Disciplining Pious Female Bodies/Sexualities in the Authoritarian Times of Turkey: An Analysis of Public Moral Discourses on the 'Süslümans.'" In *The Politics of the Female Body in Contemporary Turkey: Reproduction, Maternity, Sexuality*, edited by Hilal Alkan, Ayşe Dayı, and Betül Yarar, 233–55. London: I. B. Tauris.

Yavuz, M. Hakan. 1997. "Political Islam and the Welfare (*Refah*) Party in Turkey." *Comparative Politics* 30, no. 1: 63–82. https://doi.org/10.2307/422193.

Yavuz, M. Hakan. 2016. "Social and Intellectual Origins of Neo-Ottomanism: Searching for a Post-National Vision." *Die Welt Des Islams* 56, no. 3–4: 438–65. http://dx.doi.org/10.1163/15700607-05634p08.

Yavuz, M. Hakan. 2020. *Nostalgia for the Empire: The Politics of Neo-Ottomanism*. Oxford: Oxford Univ. Press.

Yavuz, M. Hakan, and Nihat Ali Özcan. 2015. "Turkish Democracy and the Kurdish Question." *Middle East Policy* 22, no. 4: 73–87.

Yeğen, Mesut. 1996. "The Turkish State Discourse and the Exclusion of Kurdish Identity." *Middle Eastern Studies* 32, no. 2: 216–29. https://doi.org/10 .1080/00263209608701112.

"Yeni İlçe Vakıflarından Sancaktepe Görevinin Başında: 'Halkın Vakfa Ulaşmasında Hiçbir Sıkıntı Yaşamadık.'" 2009. *Dayanışma Dergisi* 5: 55–62.

Yenigün, Halil Ibrahim. 2017. "The New Antinomies of the Islamic Movement in Post-Gezi Turkey: Islamism vs. Muslimism." *Turkish Studies* 18, no. 2: 229–50. https://doi.org/10.1080/14683849.2016.1262768.

Yeşil, Bilge. 2023. "Mediating Muslim Victimhood: An Analysis of Religion and Populism in International Communication." *International Journal of Communication* 17: 2904–2924.

Yetişkul, Emine, and Şule Demirel. 2018. "Assembling Gentrification in Istanbul: The Cihangir Neighbourhood of Beyoğlu." *Urban Studies* 55, no. 15: 3336–52.

Yıldırım, Aziz. 2010. "Türkiye'de Yoksullukla Mücadele ve Sosyal Yardımlaşma ve Dayanışma Genel Müdürlüğü." *Yardım ve Dayanışma* 1, no. 1: 9–17.

Yıldırım, Ceren Ark. 2018. "Cash Assistance by Smart Card: From Multiple Functions to Multiple Legitimacies of a Municipal Social Policy Instrument." *Turkish Studies* 19, no. 4 (August): 593–611. https://doi.org/10.1080/14683849 .2018.1454836.

Yıldız, Ahmet. 2012. "Ecdadımızın İnce Bir Sosyal Yardım Şekli Sadaka Taşları." *Tefekkür Dergisi* 42: 12–18.

Yıldız, Ayselin, and Elif Uzgören. 2016. "Limits to Temporary Protection: Non-Camp Syrian Refugees in Izmir, Turkey." *Southeast European and Black Sea Studies* 16, no. 2: 195–211. https://doi.org/10.1080/14683857.2016.1165492.

Yılmaz, Hale. 2013. *Becoming Turkish: Nationalist Reforms and Cultural Negotiations in Early Republican Turkey 1923-1945.* Syracuse, NY: Syracuse Univ. Press.

Yılmaz, İhsan. 2005. "State, Law, Civil Society and Islam in Contemporary Turkey." *The Muslim World* 95, no. 3: 385–411.

"Yoksul Ailelere 3 Bin Paket Gıda Yardımı Dağıtıldı." 2011. haberler.com, August 23, 2011. https://www.haberler.com/yoksul-ailelere-3-bin-paket-gida -yardimi-dagitildi-2948782-haberi/.

Yörük, Erdem. 2012. "Welfare Provision as Political Containment: The Politics of Social Assistance and the Kurdish Conflict in Turkey." *Politics and Society* 40, no. 4: 517–47.

Yükseker, Deniz. 2009. "Neoliberal Restructuring and Social Exclusion in Turkey." In *Turkey and the Global Economy: Neoliberal Restructuring and*

Integration in the Post-Crisis Era, edited by Ziya Öniş and Fikret Şenses, 262–80. London and New York: Routledge.

Zarzycka, Marta. 2016. "Save the Child: Photographed Faces and Affective Transactions in NGO Child Sponsoring Programs." *European Journal of Women's Studies* 23, no. 1: 28–42. https://doi.org/10.1177/1350506814568362.

Zencirci, Gizem. 2014. "Civil Society's History: New Constructions of Ottoman Heritage by the Justice and Development Party in Turkey." *European Journal of Turkish Studies* 19. https://doi.org/10.4000/ejts.5076.

Zencirci, Gizem. 2015a. "From Property to Civil Society: The Historical Transformation of Vakıfs in Turkey (1923–2013)." *International Journal of Middle East Studies* 47, no. 3: 533–54. https://doi.org/10.1017/S0020743815000537.

Zencirci, Gizem. 2015b. "Illusory Debates: How the 'Sadaka Culture' Discourse Masked the Rise of Social Assistance in Turkey." *Asian Journal of Social Science* 43, no. 1–2: 125–50.

Zencirci, Gizem. 2020. "Markets of Islam: Performative Charity and the Muslim Middle Classes in Turkey." *Journal of Cultural Economy* 13, no. 5: 610–25. https://doi.org/10.1080/17530350.2020.1741426.

Zencirci, Gizem. 2021. "A Just Economy? Unifying and Dividing the Islamic Intellectual Field in Neoliberal Turkey." *Journal of the American Academy of Religion* 89, no. 3: 840–62.

Zencirci, Gizem, and Catherine Herrold. 2022. "Project-Think and the Fragmentation and Defragmentation of Civil Society in Egypt, Palestine, and Turkey." *Nonprofit and Voluntary Sector Quarterly* 51, no. 3: 545–65.

Zevkliler, Aydın. 1995. "Türkiye'de Vakıflar." In *Cumhuriyet Dönemi Türkiye Ansiklopedisi* 15, 1438–46. Istanbul: İletişim Yayınları.

Zhang, Chenchen. 2020. "Governing (through) Trustworthiness: Technologies of Power and Subjectification in China's Social Credit System." *Critical Asian Studies* 52, no. 4: 565–88. https://doi.org/10.1080/14672715.2020.1822194.

Zihnioğlu, Özge. 2013. "The 'Civil Society' Policy of the European Union for Promoting Democracy in Turkey: Golden Goose or Dead Duck?" *Southeast European and Black Sea Studies* 13, no. 3: 381–400.

Zihnioğlu, Özge. 2018. "Islamic Civil Society in Turkey." In *The Mobilization of Conservative Civil Society*, edited by Richard Youngs, 39–43. Washington, DC: Carnegie Endowment for International Peace.

Žižek, Slavoj. 2006. "Nobody Has to Be Vile." *London Review of Books* 28, no. 7 (April). https://www.lrb.co.uk/the-paper/v28/n07/slavoj-zizek/nobody-has-to-be-vile.

Index

Photos, figures, and tables are indicated by italicized page numbers.

Menderes, Adnan, 44, 44n2
mental health, faith and, 175–76
Mert (volunteer), 182, 191–96
MHP. *See* Nationalist Action Party
middle-class Muslims, 9
Middle East Technical University, Social
  Sciences Conference at, 217
Miller, Peter, 214
Ministry of Evkaf (*Evkaf-i Hümayun
  Nezareti*), 39, 41
Ministry of Social Affairs, 57
Mitchell, Timothy, 15, 26
Mittermaier, Amira, 16–17
"model Muslim democracy," 11
modernity, capitalist, 175
month of fasting (*Ramadan*) (*Ramazan*),
  231
moral panic, 176
moral-religious concerns, technical
  terms reformulating, 133
Motherland Party (*Anavatan Partisi*)
  (ANAP), 46–47
Muehlebach, Andrea, 12, 13, 24
muhafazakar. See conservative
Muhammad (prophet), 25, 146, 167
muhtaç. See the needy; truly deserving
  poor
municipal governments, 55–56, *74*,
  111–12
Municipal Law No. 5393, 56
Muratbaşa, Antalya, 115
Murray Li, Tania, 15
MÜSİAD. *See* Association of Independent Industrialists and Businessmen
Muslim believers, global community of
  (*ummah*) (*ümmet*), 231
Muslim calendar, ninth month of the
  (*Ramazan*) (*Ramadan*), 231
Muslims. *See specific topics*
the Muslim Social. *See specific topics*

Müstakil Sanayici ve İşadamları Derneği.
  See Association of Independent
  Industrialists and Businessmen
mütevelli heyeti. See board of trustees

nationalism, Muslim, 14n9
nationalism, Turkish, 191–93
Nationalist Action Party (MHP), 189
Navaro-Yashin, Yael, 26
necropolitics, AKP reinforcing, 223
the needy (*muhtaç*), 231
neo-Foucauldian governmentality,
  19–20
neoliberal governmentality, 7
neoliberal governments, solidarity
  coopted by, 219
neoliberal humanitarianism, 137
neoliberalism, 5, 6n3, 218; AKP and,
  11n7; alternative to, 24; as assemblage, 21–25; assemblage theory
  overextending, 21–22; capitalism
  differentiated from, 8n4; civilizational revival framing, 63; communitarianism and, 51; good governance
  and, 63–65; Islamic charity and, 8;
  limits of, 23–24; public emotions and,
  16n11; religion influenced by, 207–8;
  social, 3, 214; the Social and, 11–14;
  in Turkey, 19–21; welfare programs
  accompanying, 12. *See* Islamic
  neoliberalism
neoliberalism-plus, 12
neoliberalism reinforced, Ottoman-
  Islamic heritage reinforcing, 62
neoliberal piety, 9
neoliberal subjectivities, 19–20, 172,
  172n3
neoliberal volunteerism, social responsibility transferred through, 173

Gizem Zencirci, PhD (University
of Massachusetts, Amherst 2013) studies
the cultural politics of neoliberalism in
Turkey. Zencirci is an associate professor
of political science at Providence College.
Her work has been published in journals
such as the *International Journal of Middle East Studies*, *Journal of the American
Academy of Religion*, and the *Journal of
Cultural Economy*. *The Muslim Social* is
her first monograph.

www.ingramcontent.com/pod-product-compliance
Lightning Source LLC
Chambersburg PA
CBHW020458270326
41926CB00008B/661